ROY WONDER

ROY BENTLEY CHELSEA CHAMPION

ROY WONDER

ROY BENTLEY CHELSEA CHAMPION

ROY BENTLEY WITH JIM DRURY

TEMPUS

First published 2005

Tempus Publishing Limited
The Mill, Brimscombe Port,
Stroud, Gloucestershire, GL5 2QG
www.tempus-publishing.com

British Library Cataloguing in Publication Data.
A catalogue record for this book is available from the British Library.

ISBN 0 7524 3707 0

Typesetting and origination by Tempus Publishing Limited
Printed in Great Britain

Contents

	Acknowledgements	6
	Foreword by Tony Banks	7
1	Champions!	9
2	The Roy Wonder	15
3	A Nation at War	31
4	Geordie Roy	51
5	Blue is the Colour	67
6	On Strike	83
7	Drake's Fleet Sets Sail	93
8	The Road to the Title	111
9	The Bitter End	137
10	England Expects	149
11	Changing Places	173
12	Management, Maxwell and Making Ends Meet	195
13	Champions Again	213

Acknowledgements

Vi Bentley, Ken Drury, Helen Bredin, Robert Dudley, Peter Daniel, Jay Chilton, Sarah Campbell, Judy Ireland, Eve Drury, Tanyss Horsley, Harv Nelson, Terence Bredin, Cathy Hearn, Hugh Cornwell, Jamie Hodder, Glenn Tilbrook, Bill Drury, Mike Banks, Tony Lockwood, Mick Gallagher, Lee Harris, Elizabeth Bredin, Chris Difford and Holly Bennion.

Foreword
by Tony Banks

It's very difficult to explain to anyone who doesn't understand the significance of football how a grown man can feel a sense of excitement tinged with disbelief about being in the company of one of his footballing heroes. At the time of writing I've cracked sixty and been around a bit myself, but still can't quite believe that I can now call Roy Bentley, one of the gods of Chelsea, my friend.

Every time I meet up with Roy or any of Chelsea's 1954/55 Championship team, the memories flood back. Okay, so they might all be in their seventies now, but for fans of my generation they are still the 'special ones'.

Roy and Jim's book is significant in terms of the way it tells the story of a great event in Chelsea's history fifty years ago. But it also serves to remind us of our club's great origins and traditions.

No-one can truly understand the present unless they have some knowledge of the past. That is why history is so important in every sphere of life, including football.

To appreciate Chelsea today requires knowledge of how Chelsea and football used to be. I consider myself privileged to have witnessed many of the events discussed in the pages that follow. Don't get me wrong I wouldn't want to go back to standing on rain-swept terraces at the Bridge, but Roy and Jim have enabled me, through this book, to recapture an integral part of my much younger days. For today's fans the book will help them to take pride in the history of our great club and the story of Roy Bentley, one of Chelsea and England's greatest players.

ONE

Champions!

Dressed in a tracksuit, with a towel wrapped around my neck, I sat alongside my teammates in the home dressing room at Stamford Bridge. Each of us was in perfect silence, listening intently to the tinny voice emitting from a small transistor. Our team, Chelsea, had just won its final home match of the season, 3-0 against bottom-placed Sheffield Wednesday, but we were in no mood yet to celebrate. When we had sprinted into the dressing room a quarter of an hour earlier, we had been informed that the latest score from Cardiff was one-apiece, and that if things stayed that way we would have won the League.

'Come on, they must have bloody finished by now,' said a loud Cockney voice in the corner.

'Shhh,' said another. 'We don't want to miss it.'

Tension was high. Our entire season was at stake. After what seemed like an age, but was actually only fifteen minutes, the plummy English voice finally ended our agonising wait.

'It's full time at Ninian Park. The match has finished Cardiff City 1, Portsmouth 1. That means Chelsea are League Champions.'

By the time the man at the BBC had uttered the words 'Portsmouth 1...' we had stopped listening, a great collective yelp going around the dressing room. Grown men began hugging excitedly, while my less tactile teammates restricted themselves to manly handshakes, albeit with huge grins etched on to their faces. I sat down again and tried to take in what we had achieved. As

I gathered my thoughts, one of the backroom staff ran into the room and breathlessly addressed the team. 'The crowd wants to see the champions,' he gasped before turning to me. 'Roy, can you bring the team up to the directors' box?' I shouted to the others to follow me and we made our way to the stand.

As the team arrived in the directors' box, any feelings of weariness from the effects of eight months of football disappeared at the sight of 40,000 Chelsea fans standing on the Stamford Bridge turf, chanting for us. The hairs on the back of my neck stood up as I looked out on a teeming mass of smiling faces. At that moment I knew I had reached the pinnacle of a professional footballer's career. Only winning the World Cup could possibly compare with this.

A microphone had been wired up in the directors' box and I was informed that, along with our manager Ted Drake and chairman Joe Mears, I would be required to say a few words. An emotional Joe spoke briefly, wiping tears from his eyes before telling the crowd, 'You really want to hear from Roy and the boys, and from the one and only Ted Drake.' Ted then walked to the mike, the noise from the crowd dampening his opening words. He was generous in his praise for the players who had helped him fulfil his three-year plan bang on schedule. 'This is the happiest day of my life, and while I want to congratulate all our players, there are the older ones to whom I offer special thanks. Men like Johnny Harris, Roy Bentley, Ken Armstrong and Stan Willemse were old Chelsea stalwarts when I arrived at Stamford Bridge, but from that day to this they have all been most loyal and helpful. People say I have been able to give the lads that will to win, but no-one can do that unless it is already there.'

Ted was being excessively modest in his analysis. But for his appointment three years earlier I was sure that Chelsea would have remained a lower-table side, struggling perennially against relegation. For the first four-and-a-half years of my Chelsea career we had never looked capable of anything other than survival and a decent cup run, and many of the players had seemed happy with that state of affairs. Ted had changed all this.

1955 was Chelsea's golden anniversary year and, despite having had some of the game's best players on our books over the preceding decades, the club had never got within a sniff of winning silverware. Considering the comparative wealth of the club, its advantageous geographical location and its long-standing First Division status, Chelsea had been massive underachievers. We had been the butt of the music hall comics' jokes from the moment the club signed comedian George Robey as an amateur player in 1907, the year the club first entered English football's top tier.

When I had arrived in January 1948 I had brought with me a burning desire to win trophies and make the Chelsea fans proud of their side, but had found myself frustrated by the club's blatant lack of ambition and outdated amateurism. It had only been when Ted arrived, in the summer of 1952, that we were even allowed to see a ball in training and he had revolutionised each and every player's outlook on the game. He had also encouraged our supporters, who had previously been notoriously polite and at times impassive, to become our twelfth man on the field. The fans had indeed played an important role in our success, and it was with that in mind that I took the microphone after Ted had finished his speech.

I waited for the cheers to die down before opening my mouth and addressing our supporters: 'On behalf of the boys, thank you all. There is no need for me to say how pleased we all are to win the championship, but we are pleased too for your sakes, because you have been behind us in other years when we needed your support. From the bottom of our hearts, thank you very much.'

As my speech came to an end, I thought that it was only fair to ask Johnny Harris to say a few words. Johnny had been the rock upon whom I had depended throughout my time as team captain. I had looked up to him from the day I signed from Newcastle United, and he had been my mentor during my seven-and-a-half-year career at Chelsea. Johnny was captain when I arrived, but three years later had stepped aside without complaint when I was handed the captain's armband by our manager at the time, Billy Birrell. Switched to the role of 'club captain', which basically meant Chelsea's captain off the field, Johnny had been the best ambassador the club had probably ever known. More than any other player, Johnny deserved a championship medal. Johnny had also stood alongside me three summers earlier when the pair of us had gone on strike for eight weeks, a period in which our relationship with Chelsea hit rock bottom. Johnny, a deeply religious and humble man, yet one of the hardest players in the game, was not one to hog the limelight and, as he stood before the microphone, he chose to reiterate Ted's comment that this was the best day of his life.

The one thing missing was the trophy itself. Standing alongside my beaming colleagues I was expecting at any moment someone to hand me that beautiful piece of silverware, with blue and white ribbons attached, so I could hold it aloft to our fans. The trophy never appeared that afternoon, which was a great disappointment to us all. I'm sure the supporters would have liked to seen us parade it around the ground, but no arrangements had been made for the trophy to be presented. Maybe Joe and the other board members didn't want to jinx us by having it delivered and then see us beaten. Sadly, we were never to be formally presented with the trophy and only ever saw it for a team photograph taken during the summer. Footballers want to enjoy the glory when they win a trophy and for us never to get our hands on it was thoughtless on the directors' part.

After the game we went into the boardroom for a glass of champagne and a few telegrams of congratulations were read out, including one from second-placed Portsmouth. It was nice of them to think of us in the midst of their own extreme disappointment. We probably only stayed in the boardroom for half an hour before going our separate ways. I went home with my wife Vi and two daughters, Lorraine and Jane. Some of the other players went for a cup of tea at a café and a plate of chips near the ground. That was about as glamorous as it got in 1955.

The next week we had one match left to play, away to the great Manchester United. Their manager, the legendary Matt Busby, recognised our feat and gave us the kind of public platform that our own club had not deemed necessary. Matt was as pleased as punch that Chelsea had won, and laid out a red carpet for us at Old

Trafford. As we ran out onto the carpet their whole team, including Roger Byrne, Tommy Taylor and young Duncan Edwards, were lined up clapping us, while *Conquering Heroes Come Home* was played over the loudspeaker. It was a wonderful gesture, although United proceeded to beat us 2-1.

We had the misfortune to win the title at a time when many of the national newspapers were not being printed because of a national strike. However, those papers that did appear made much of the fact that Chelsea had won the championship with just 52 points, the lowest haul in history. This was grossly unfair. We had been the best side throughout the season, finishing four points ahead of our nearest rivals. I'm sure we would have won our final game at Old Trafford had it been necessary. One chap, the *Sunday People*'s Maurice Smith sniped: 'Well, well, well, that's that. Chelsea are Football League Champions for the first time. But I'm no nearer solving the mystery of the season – how come that a team that can play such penny-plain stuff so often ends up in front?' The press as a whole were pretty dismissive of our success, accusing us of being a dirty side, and ignoring the fact that we had scored an impressive 81 goals in clinching the title.

It may seem hard to believe in 2005, when the current Chelsea side find themselves the darlings of the press, but when the club first won the title, we were sneered at by the critics. Maybe the reporters couldn't accept that the music hall jokes would have to be left on the shelf forever and that they would need to create new clichés if they wanted to knock us off our perch. Our success had been down to hard work, determination and no small element of skill and talent. We had also learnt not to take any notice of what people outside the club thought of us and our siege mentality had done us proud. It didn't matter what the press thought of us.

As a reward for winning the League we each received a £20 bonus, which was less than two weeks' wages, although the amateurs found themselves excluded from this. We were also handed the choice between a suit from Pollicoffs tailors in the East End and a Crombie overcoat. I chose the Crombie, which I thought looked very smart, although crafty old Stan Willemse walked out wearing the coat he had tried on over the top of his suit. He played the innocent and just walked out of the shop, which we all found hilarious. He was the only player to take both. I hope he got some decent wear out of them. To be honest, financial reward was the last thing on my mind. I had achieved the ultimate in domestic football, captaining my team to the League Championship against the odds. No backhander or swanky overcoat could match that.

As I drove home on cloud nine my mind returned to the past thirty-one years, a road that had been long and hard. It had certainly been an interesting journey for me, taking in animal husbandry, broken limbs, war service, industrial action and debilitating illness. My story had begun on the backstreets of Bristol, a place to which I will now return.

TWO

The Roy Wonder

My formative years were spent in a small three-up two-down council house in the Shirehampton district of Bristol. My parents had met a year or so after the end of the First World War, each having been married once before and my mum having borne three children with her first husband.

My father was called Arthur Joy Bentley – his feminine middle name causing him a fair deal of ribbing from workmates over the years. Dad had certainly led an interesting life before meeting my mother, Ada Brewer. It appeared that as a child Dad was adopted into a wealthy family but, full of wanderlust, he had run away from home and joined the Merchant Navy, travelling the world and set-tling in Australia. Dad's return to England was unplanned, a result of enforced circumstance. He had joined up with the Australian army, mainly in order to play rugby, which he had done in Sydney to a very high standard. I remember Dad showing me local newspaper cuttings reporting his trials for the Australian national team.

Little could my father have predicted that he would soon be fighting in the trenches of Europe. As part of the Commonwealth, Australia was expected to help its 'colonial masters' when it became clear that Britain's conflict with Germany was not yielding the expected quick-fire victory.

Upon the cessation of hostilities in 1918 Dad decided to travel the shorter distance to England rather than return Down Under. Impressed by his athleticism and technical ability, he was signed by leading rugby side Bradford Northern. It was an amateur game, so Dad was forced to find other work to earn a crust. Work was not always easy to find up north in the 1920s and Dad soon headed south where he met Ada and quickly fell in love. Any thoughts of returning to his adopted hometown of Sydney were well and truly out of the 'dunny' window.

He was quite a mystery, all in all, my father. To this day there is still much about him that I don't know. Occasionally, when he'd imbibed a dram or two, he would reel off colourful stories about his life in Sydney, some of them no doubt exaggerated, but each one fascinating.

Some years ago my brother Arthur visited Australia with his wife and traced Dad's military history at an army depot. I'll not go into detail, but it appeared Dad's record was none too impressive and Arthur Junior returned from his holiday somewhat disheartened. Yet, to my mind, the important thing to remember was Dad's record as a father and husband, which was absolutely first class. Mum already had three children, Lionel, Bert and Doris, by the time she got together with him. A lot of men would have balked at the idea of bringing up another man's three children, but Dad evidently took to his new role like a duck to water. His three step-children all loved him and, when Dad had kids of his own, Arthur, Dessie, myself and much later Amanda, he insisted that none of the large Bentley/Brewer clan were treated any differently. The phrase 'half-brother' and 'half-sister' were banned in our house. As far as Dad was concerned, we were all equal.

I was the youngest in the family until Amanda came along four-teen years after me. I felt lucky to have so many siblings, despite the cramped conditions that such a large brood engendered. Mum and Dad were strict but always fair when it came to disciplining us. These were the days when parents would think nothing of giving their offspring a whack or two if the situation required. Dad never gave us the strap but occasionally, if one of his sons had really got his goat, he'd make us put boxing gloves on and take him on in the back yard. He was a great boxer, although he would never strike me too hard. As he was prodding my nose with his fists he'd be saying,

'You know you were in the wrong, son. Don't do it again.' Mum didn't approve of this too much and would go potty, especially if he drew blood. She'd come after him and shout. Goodness knows what would happen if a father did that nowadays, but back then it seemed a perfectly good way to keep your children in check. And, as the cliché goes, I don't think it did me any harm.

Dad was a bright man, but had taken little interest in school and ended up working in the docks in charge of a group of loaders. The docks were a hard place to work and you had to be tough to reach his position. Dad told me that the job of 'boss man' went to the man who was the best scrapper and hardest hitter. Men would frequently fight for the position, but Dad never lost a bout. After a while he was promoted to tally clerk and his boxing gloves went into the closet.

Before I was born Dad began coaching a local rugby team, something he continued during my early childhood. From the age of two he would take me down to training sessions and make me stand on the four-foot high 'push ball'. Players would push the ball from both sides and I would have to keep my balance, backpedalling frantically when the players in front of me became too strong for those behind. This was fantastic training and I have always credited it with teaching me the balance that I would need as a professional footballer many years later. He also taught me and my brothers to be tough and not to cry when we had been tackled hard.

Dad was instrumental in my taking pride in staying fit, something which undoubtedly helped me to continue playing until the age of thirty-eight. All of his sons were sporty and Dad was dead keen on us following his lead and becoming high-class amateur rugby players. He was most disappointed to find that Bristol schools preferred to play a game with a round ball.

I was very fond of my elder brothers and sister. Lionel, Mum's firstborn, was a terrific bloke and I really looked up to him. Like Dad, Lionel worked down at the docks and, after his tea, would cycle down to his night shift. Bert was very practical and could make more or less anything he turned his hand to, including his own motorbike, which he built from scratch. He left school at twelve to help support the family but continued his education by taking correspondence courses and studying from home. When Bert joined the Army he was promoted to sergeant after just ninety days and within three months was in Ops.

When the Second World War finished Bert was in Venice and was offered a job as dock master there, which was an incredible opportunity, but one that he turned down due to his wife's reluctance to leave Britain. Doris was also happy to stay in familiar surroundings and snapped up one of the best jobs on offer in Bristol, working in the offices at the W.D. & H.O. Wells cigarette factory. She always had enough money and was a very generous sister.

Despite the jibes he suffered for being known as Arthur Joy, Dad didn't hesitate to pass on the name to his first son, as tradition dictated, which I found most amusing as we grew up. I would enjoy teasing Arthur about his 'queer' name and needed all my speed to avoid his vengeance as he chased me down the road.

Dessie was the quiet one out of us all. Everyone liked him. We were both mad on football and were always out kicking a ball together, although Dessie wasn't that good, truth be told.

Lack of space in our three-bedroom house meant that Arthur, Dessie and I were forced to share a bed. As the youngest I was the one whose comfort was most dispensable. During the winter I was pushed to the outside by the window, bearing the brunt of the chill air. When it was summertime I was pushed into the middle where I would often find myself trapped in stifling heat. Needless to say, I would probably have done the self same thing had I been in their shoes. Our first house had been even less luxurious, a small hut made of galvanised tin, constructed after the First World War. When I was two years old we moved to 39 Meadow Grove, Shirehampton. The local authorities had finally built some decent housing and those of us living in the huts were first in the queue for a home. Our new three-bedroom house felt like a palace in comparison.

Arthur, Dessie and I were not far apart in years and spent most of our spare time together. We lived near a parade of shops and, on a good day, Dad would make us race there together. First back would get a twopence reward. Perhaps that was how I came to be renowned for my pace in my days as a roving centre forward.

We never considered ourselves poor, although in retrospect sharing a bed with two brothers was hardly the life of luxury. Yet this was far from an unusual state of affairs in Britain at this time. At Christmas we would each get a stocking with fruit, oranges or apples, in the heel and toe. We might get two and sixpence as well if we were lucky, but never more than ten shillings. Sometimes we might even get a Cadbury Selection Box, which was a real treat. We'd each have one main present, but one year Mum apologised and told Arthur, Dessie and myself that this year we'd be getting nothing. She said 'It's your dad's fault. He had too much to drink and I wouldn't let him in last night. He slept in the garden in the Brussels sprouts.' All of us were disappointed, but tried not to show it as we ran off to play our daily game of football. After we'd broken a decent sweat, with me imitating my Arsenal heroes Ted Drake and Cliff Bastin, we heard Dad's usual call. 'Arthur! Dessie! Roy. Get home!' We ran to the house and when we reached the living room there was a pair of shiny new football boots for each of us. He'd bought them for five shillings each at Leonard's sports shop in the village. We ran back outside wearing our new footwear in a state of great excitement, not minding at all that Mum and Dad had tricked us. I don't know if the older three children were in on the joke or not. Unfortunately, when we got back from our second kickabout I left my new pride and joy by the fire. Later in the day some tinder fell out of the fire and burned a hole in the toe of one of the boots, which left Dad none too pleased. I had to patch it up with newspaper before I played again, but the boots still felt special to me and I treasured them. Kids today don't know they're born!

I loved school for the first few years, and especially enjoyed playing football in the playground, eventually representing the school. Having practised with my elder brothers I wasn't bad for a little 'un and by the age of eight I was in the school team alongside eleven-year-olds. Those players who had the slightest build and needed protection were positioned at outside right, which is where I ended up for much of the time.

When it came to leaving primary school I'm ashamed to admit that I made little effort to pass the eleven-plus examination, a decision due entirely to my obsession with the beautiful game. Those who passed the scholarship, as it was known, would attend the local grammar school and were not allowed to leave until they were sixteen. They were also debarred from representing their local town at football, a thought that filled me with horror. So it was with great relief that I heard the news in summer 1935 that I would be attending Portway Senior Boys School, leaving me to pursue my love affair with the sport.

As a precocious kid I was convinced I was going to be the next Dixie Dean, that great Everton forward of yore, and education was an unnecessary hindrance to my route to the top. Of course, I now realise that this was the folly of youth, and had I failed to make the grade who knows what would have become of me? But at the time my confidence in my footballing ability was supreme and I was damned if I was going to waste two years sitting in class when I could be making my way as a player.

There were more than forty kids to a class at Portway and the teachers were sticklers for discipline. Six canes were kept in each schoolmaster's cupboard and if you messed about they would have no hesitation in giving you a whack. The first time it happened I told my dad and he advised me that 'If it hurts, don't show it,' so I always tried to disguise the pain on the odd occasion when I would be caned.

I was a talented athlete at school and excelled at long jump, high jump and both short and long-distance running. All the skills needed for those activities stood me in good stead on the football field. By this time football had become my major focus. I had also boxed as a young lad but Dad said to me that I ought to concentrate on one discipline if I was going to be a sportsman, so I took his advice and plumped for football.

I was captain for my whole three years at Portway and thrived on the extra responsibility. Mum and Dad were very supportive and would cycle to my matches on Saturday mornings on a blessed tandem. I also played centre forward for a local team, Shirehampton

Juniors. I still have all the local press cuttings from that time because, as a teenager, they always gave me a great buzz of excitement. One splendid article was entitled 'Roy Bentley's 160 Goals in Amateur Soccer', although I scored 70 goals in a season for Portway School and Bristol Boys, so I reckon there might have been a few more than the 160 recorded.

In one notable game I scored seven times for Portway in a 13–0 win over St Bonaventure's, and that was from centre half! Most of them were headers from corners, if I recall. In fact, during my career, I played in every position on the park except for goalkeeper and I'd have done that as well if I'd been asked. I just loved playing the game. I would even dribble a ball on the way to school with my good friend Roy Mitchell. I would play endlessly in the back yard when I got home from school and would wear a slipper on my right foot to force myself to become accomplished with my weaker left peg.

I was playing for Bristol Boys by the age of eleven, which was a great thrill. We had the chance to play across the country, which was an enormous privilege – especially at a time when travelling to the next town was still a rarity. The fact that we would play at Football League grounds just added to the excitement. We had a terrific trainer, George Crandon, who was a local headmaster. He introduced us to tactics, which were previously alien to me – and indeed for much of my subsequent professional career – and engendered a spirit and sense of self-belief among us.

One year we thought we were going all the way to the finals of the prestigious English Schools Shield. In one of the early regional rounds we'd beaten the much-fancied Weston Boys side 4–0 with yours truly notching all the goals. Yet again the local paper under-estimated my performance, suggesting I'd scored a mere hat-trick, but who was I to be so churlish as to complain, particularly as I'd had the temerity to miss a penalty early in the match?

Having overcome some serious opposition, we met Norwich Boys for a place in the sixth round. After drawing the first game at Bristol City's home ground, Ashton Gate, we travelled to Norwich City's Carrow Road stadium for the replay. Even though I was later to play for two of the biggest clubs in the country and represent my country on a dozen occasions this match remains one of the most memorable of my life.

We were 2-1 down with two minutes to go when I set off on a mazy run before being brought down in the penalty area by the despairing lunge of a Norwich Boys defender. As captain I was expected to take the spot-kick. After the customary one-minute delay while the referee cleared the area and placed the ball on the spot I smashed the penalty past the goalkeeper. As I ran back to the centre circle it struck me that I had not been nervous at all. I think it was at that moment when I realised I had the nerve to play football at the top level.

We lost the second replay 2-1 and didn't make it to the final, but the tie remains deeply etched in my memory, in spite of the disappointment. Today, with so many distractions offered to children, a schoolboy match at Norwich might not sound so grand but, I promise you, for me and my mates it was the highlight of our school career. Indeed, the great Tom Finney still reminisces about his role as a non-playing member of the Preston Boys team that beat West Ham United two years earlier in the 1936 English Schools Shield final. He rates the parade through Preston city centre as one of the highlights of his glittering career.

Unbeknown to me Bristol Rovers had been watching my progress as a schoolboy. They had picked up on match reports from the local press and sent various scouts down to see me play. The standard of play was high and occasionally professionals from either Bristol City or Rovers would be on the touchline as well. I came off the field one week having scored a hat-trick and Ernie Brinton, a City pro who knew my family, was standing on the sidelines. As I walked past he said loudly to the man next to him, 'That lad Bentley has a future in football.' I was chuffed to bits but when I told Dad he said, 'That's great son, but keep it in perspective. Believe in your ability but keep what he said to yourself. You don't want anyone thinking you're a bighead.' I'm grateful now for that advice, even if I may not have been so thrilled to hear it at the time.

When I reached my fourteenth birthday on 17 May 1938 a Rovers representative approached Portway School and asked for permission to speak to my parents, inviting me to join the ground staff at Bristol Rovers, with a view to one day signing professional forms if I made the grade. When my parents asked me whether I wanted to stay on at school or join Bristol Rovers there was only ever going to be one answer. I felt an incredible thrill and it was hard to keep my feet on the ground that day. My dreams felt within easy reach. Soon I was going to be a footballer and have thousands of fans singing my name. My parents tried in vain to remind me of all the pitfalls that lay ahead, not least the fact that maybe one in ten kids who signed schoolboy forms would ever make a career as a professional.

Within days I had walked out of the gates at Portway for the last time to start work for the princely sum of thirty shillings a week as a playing member of the Bristol Rovers ground staff. Their ground, Eastville, which sadly no longer exists, was a fairly basic affair with a dog track around the pitch, leaving a large space between the playing area and the stands. In fact, it was very similar to the old layout at Stamford Bridge before Chelsea's stadium was redesigned in the 1990s.

Despite my parents' attempts to dampen my boyish enthusiasm, my head was still somewhat in the clouds. On my first day I eagerly walked up the steps to Eastville and looked out onto the pitch, dreaming of making my debut and, more immediately, salivating at the prospect of my first proper training session with a professional club. I was quickly to discover that the last thing on the minds of the Bristol Rovers hierarchy was football training.

My role on the ground staff consisted of helping to maintain the pitch, to sweep the terraces clean, and be a general dogsbody. This I would do from the hours of nine in the morning until five in the evening for five days a week. I wouldn't see a football until Saturday, which I found dumbfounding. It wasn't how I had envisaged my life in football and, at the time, I couldn't see how this was preparing me to follow in the footsteps of my hero, the legendary Chelsea and England centre forward Tommy Lawton.

Although my tasks were a good way of instilling discipline and respect at an early age, performing them at the expense of learning how to use a ball seemed a strange way to make me into a top-class footballer. In the event, much of my schooling in the game came in the form of advice from established first-team players like Ronnie Dix and Phil Taylor, who were never short of an encouraging word. In fact, I think it's fair to say that, apart from on match days, I didn't see a football for another fourteen years, when Ted Drake became manager at Chelsea. Looking back, the amateurism of football in those days was incredible. Even while playing for a First Division side we would barely see the manager except on Saturdays, because he spent most of the time sat in his office dealing with administrative problems. It was left to the trainer to look after the team's preparations, in addition to being the man who would run on with the trusty 'magic sponge' when we'd been hacked down by an uncompromising half-back. His training sessions would rely entirely on running and fitness work. Ball work was for wimps.

In the most peculiar of circumstances, animals were to play a significant role in my early days as a footballer. Traditionally, football and animals each have a special place in the hearts of many across our great nation but, in my humble opinion, it should always be a case of 'ne'er the twain shall meet'. You may recall vintage TV footage of dogs invading pitches and chasing dementedly after the ball in the days when pets were smuggled onto terraces by supporters unwilling to leave them home alone. But, generally speaking, football and animals don't mix well.

One morning I arrived at Eastville to find that, at Bristol Rovers, the combination of football and animals was alive and most definitely kicking. When I looked out towards the pitch I was confronted by a sight that questioned my very sanity. In front of me was a horde of zoo animals, including giraffes, penned into the area behind the goal. Rubbing my eyes in disbelief, I walked into the office to see Fred the secretary and find out what the hell was going on. 'Ah, Bent,' he said. 'You're a country man. This week you'll be feeding the animals every morning.'

To say I was bemused is something of an understatement. It turned out that one of the club's directors, Captain Prince Cox, was a circus magnate, and once a year he would bring his animals down to Bristol a few days before they performed and let them graze on the grass patch behind one of the goals. Terrified by the prospect, I walked out clutching two buckets of water for the animals to drink. Nervously I plucked up the courage to approach the smallest animal I could see, which was a baby giraffe. Just before I reached the infant I heard an incredible screeching sound and felt a great whoosh of air from above. The giraffe's protective mother had smelt danger and lunged towards me with her mighty neck. Fortunately my reflexes were good and I moved my body out of the way. Heaven knows what she would have done to me had I not got out of her path. She pushed the baby giraffe away from me and I quickly fled the temporary zoo. Shaking with fear I returned to the office and told Fred and his staff, 'That's the last time I'm going in there.' They were all extremely amused by the sight of this pale-faced fourteen-year-old scared out of his wits. 'You'll be all right,' said the secretary. 'You'll get used to it.' And, to be fair, by the end of the week I had.

Despite this unconventional start to my apprenticeship I was happy at Rovers and banged in a fair few goals for the youth side on the odd occasion when I was allowed to see a ball. The Western League was very competitive and we played around Warminster and the Bristol area. The grounds we played at were pretty rudimentary, with just a rope between the players and the spectators. There were no stands. During one away match I was whacked by a lady with her umbrella. I don't recall what I'd done to upset her.

It was a great thrill to sit in the Eastville dressing rooms when the first-teamers weren't there. I daren't ever talk to the players, but some of them would offer encouragement. Tommy Mills, a Welsh international inside forward, once approached me and gave me a pair of his old boots. What an honour that was, and even though they were two sizes too small I would wear them week in week out. After a game my toenails would be black and I used to make holes in the nails with a chiropodist's tool to let the blood drain. All the pain would drain away with it, but of course it was very bad for my feet and I still get gyp from a couple of my toes.

Unfortunately Rovers were in poor financial straits and were forced to rely on handouts from one of the directors, the world snooker and billiards champion Joe Davis. Joe was a wonderful chap and saved the club from bankruptcy many times, donating money from exhibition matches whenever he could. I met up with Joe again a few years down the line when I was at Chelsea. I would play him at billiards or snooker and he would give me a seven black start to give me a chance, but I could never beat him.

Joe's help wasn't enough to help Rovers stay out of the red and, with the receivers hovering above the club like vultures, the management decided they had to make cuts all round, including the players' wages. My pay was cut by a third, from 30s to £1. When I got home I told my dad who immediately said, 'You can't have that, son. We'll take you somewhere else.' Fortunately, I had received a lot of exposure in the local press by this stage and when the chairman of Bristol City found out I was available he offered me £2 a week to join. This seemed a fantastic amount of money to me back then. One of my brothers was a charge hand at a local mill and was taking home less than £2 10s a week, and here was I, aged fifteen, getting £2. The ground at Ashton Gate was also much nearer to our house, which meant I could get home for my tea a lot earlier.

Although I was glad to be wanted by City, I was disappointed at having to leave Rovers where I had begun to feel settled. I informed the secretary of my father's decision, which he told me he respected, before shaking my hand and showing me out.

But if I was expecting an easier ride at City my illusions were soon shattered, as my animal husbandry skills were to receive another outlet. My main job for City involved looking after the club's horse. First thing in the morning I had to go to the stables and clean them out before giving the nag some water. When he was ready to move, I then had to attach the heavy metal grass roller to his hind and lead him around the pitch, flattening out any lumps and bumps on the turf or, in winter time, the thick mud. Another job involved me fixing the horse to a cart and leading him down the road to the timber yard where we would collect half a dozen sacks of sawdust.

These were the days before lime was used to paint the pitch mark-ings. Sawdust was used to mark out the playing perimeter, centre circle, penalty areas and penalty spot. It wasn't a nice experience to get any in your eye when you played and most players were quite relieved when lime was brought in as a replacement. After picking up the sawdust one morning I whacked the horse on the backside to signal for it to begin the short trot back to Ashton Gate. As I turned the cart the wheels became stuck in the tramlines and I couldn't get them out. This caused a huge kerfuffle as we were positioned by the tram terminus and our mishap caused all the trams in one direction to be delayed as some bystanders and I tried to wrench the wheels out. Can you imagine Wayne Rooney or Joe Cole ever having to do that when they were fifteen? How times change!

I adapted well to life playing for the red half of Bristol, now that all my misconceptions of the 'glamour' of football had been abruptly ended by life on the ground staff. One of the few perks of the job was being able to pocket all the spare change found while sweeping the terraces. Before first-team games a Salvation Army brass band would play on the pitch and a blanket would be taken around the field for spectators to throw money into it. Not all Bristol City fans had such a good aim, fortunately, and I'd be able to snaffle a few spare pennies and buy a pie for my lunch.

I continued to enjoy playing at weekends and represented City's Boys' Federation team, helping them to a league title in 1938/39. Little did I know that summer how my dream of playing for the first team was soon to be realised. Due to a shortage of players I was drafted into the City first team to play a match at Walsall. I was aged fifteen-and-a-half. Although asked to travel up to the Midlands with the team I still couldn't quite believe I would make my debut at such a tender age. When I was told that I was in the side, playing on the wing, there was no time for me to be nervous. It was just a game of football like any other, and it was only at full-time after I'd scored my first goal in professional English football that my achievement sank in.

I retained my place on the wing for the next match, away to Bournemouth, and again scored to justify the manager's faith in me. However, by this stage, all official League football had been cancelled and the opportunity to make a name for myself was to be delayed by seven years. In September 1939, after a long period of diplomatic hostility between Britain and Germany, our Prime Minister Neville Chamberlain had finally bowed to the inevitable. Having supposedly secured 'peace in our time' twelve months earlier, upon his return from summit talks in Munich with German dictator Adolf Hitler, the British premier was forced into action by Germany's provocative invasion of Poland on 1 September 1939. Hitler's refusal to respond to Britain's demands that he withdraw his troops from the Eastern European nation meant that war was unavoidable.

There was no such thing as a television in the 1930s. Radio was the medium of the day, so it was while they were sat huddled around their living room wireless forty-eight hours later that most of the population heard Mr Chamberlain's momentous words to the nation:

I am speaking to you from the Cabinet Room at 10 Downing Street. This morning the British Ambassador in Berlin handed the German Government an official note stating that, unless we heard from them by eleven o'clock that they were prepared at once to withdraw their troops from Poland, a state of war would exist between us. I have to tell you now that no such undertaking has been received, and consequently this country is at war with Germany.

Instinctively, I wanted to join the Army and fight the Nazis, but of course at fifteen years old I was too young. My four brothers all joined up immediately while my father, who was too old to be conscripted, joined the Home Guard, and was responsible for putting out fires around our street.

Within weeks platoons of soldiers had been assembled and were marching down the main road to Bristol. A barrage balloon camp was set up at nearby Home Farm where members of the Royal Air Force were housed in what were known as bell tents. Gas masks were handed out to schoolchildren in lessons and the first air raid sirens were installed and tested to enable rapid evacuation of the population in the event of a German attack from the skies. Anderson shelters, heavy corrugated-iron structures, about eight feet by six, were given out by the authorities and set up in back yards across the land.

The whole situation seemed quite unreal to start with. Normal life continued for some weeks and when the air raid siren alerts went off at night people would often stay in bed. When the all clear sounded, the Bristol engine works would play *Colonel Bogey* over the tannoy in an act of defiance against the German threat.

It wasn't long before Britain found itself under attack, although Bristol remained largely unscathed in the opening months of the war. But by November the Football League and Football Association had correctly decided that, with conscription taking the sport's best players away to foreign fields, there was little point in continuing the official programme, and all competitions were suspended. In the event they were not to restart until 1946. A less-rigidly organised form of competitive football would resume in 1940 in the form of regional mini-leagues and a War Cup, with clubs' youngsters being joined on the field by any professional player across the country who found himself fortunate enough to be on leave from the front.

War never brings many good things to bear but, looking back, the Second World War would provide me with two positive outcomes. Firstly, the humbling experience of serving my country would help to shape the adult I became, but also the rigours of wartime football would give me a terrific apprenticeship in the game.

THREE

A Nation at War

The Football League's reorganisation into regional mini-leagues meant that Bristol City were grouped together with the likes of Plymouth Argyle, Bath City, Southampton and Portsmouth, along with Welsh sides Cardiff City, Swansea Town and Newport County. Bristol Rovers were still suffering financially and dropped out of football for the war's duration. Matches took the form of local derbies, with fierce regional pride adding extra spice to games. Particularly tough were the clashes with the lads from Cardiff, who were needed in the pits to maintain the nation's fuel supplies rather than joining the forces. They were known as 'Bevin Boys', named after the Minister of Labour, Ernest Bevin, who had proposed the arrangement.

City's team, like most of our competitors, was augmented by a smattering of professionals from other clubs who were on leave from fighting the Germans. Clubs were not able to pay for trans-portation to matches, so players would be offered £2 a match to turn out for the most convenient team to where they were staying, combining the match with a trip to see their family.

Often we would find that our team was two or three players short. Just before kick-off the club would send out a member of the non-playing staff holding a blackboard inscribed with a plea for 'any male spectator who has played a decent standard of football' to report to the dressing rooms. As you can imagine, all sorts of folk would stick their hands up and volunteer for the chance to play with professional footballers. It would be left to the club's trainer, in City's case Len Southway, to face the tricky task of deciding who was suitable to play and weeding out those who were exaggerating their sporting prowess. I watched Len being forced to make these snap decisions on occasion and he made very few mistakes, despite his eccentric method of selection. I remember him walking out of the dressing room one Saturday and questioning a line of players.

'What have you done?' he asked the first.

'I played centre forward for Wolverhampton. Everybody thought I would be an international in three years.'

'Sorry son, not good enough. Next.'

'I played left half for the county and am going to join Southampton.'

'Sorry, son. Off you go. What about you, kid?'

'I love my football. Some say I'm good at it. I'll play anywhere.'

'Okay, you'll do for me!'

One player that would sometimes guest for City was former Arsenal and England captain Eddie Hapgood, who was a local hero. Eddie had been brought up in Bristol and his parents lived in the city, so it was natural for him to represent his home-town club when on leave rather than play for the Gunners. If Eddie was home for a few days he would train with us and I picked up many valuable tips from him. It was an enormous privilege for me as a raw sixteen year old to play alongside a great player who was also such a gracious man.

For some games we would have up to four internationals appearing in the red and white, including Ronnie Dix of Tottenham and England, Billy Mitchell of Chelsea and Ireland, and Eddie. It was a wonderful introduction for a young lad like me making his way in the game. I would often be farmed out to outside right for my protection, where I'd be looked after by my more experienced teammates.

Even though the official League campaign had been suspended, I couldn't have been happier at my situation, playing regular first-team football for my local club. My parents were as pleased as punch for me and would attend City home games religiously. Dad's love of rugby had been pushed well and truly into the background and he became one of City's most vocal and passionate supporters.

Dad would joke that since I'd broken into City's first XI he'd never had more friends. Lads down at the docks frequently badgered him for free tickets and Dad used this as another example of the potential dangers of life as a footballer. He told me, 'Son, there are people who speak to me now who didn't want to know me before. Always remember you can never buy friends. Your real friends will stay loyal, whoever you are.' And he was damned right. I was very lucky because the friends I made during my career remained pals for life.

With the majority of first-teamers serving in the forces I had pretty much an unchallenged place in the side from the age of sixteen, although I never took my selection for granted. I knew that going down that route would prevent me from improving as a player.

I have sweet memories of many wartime games. Scoring a goal alongside England centre forward George Tadman in an 8-1 win over Swansea Town is one that comes to mind. Netting two goals in a 6-0 hiding of Aldershot Town, with George also bagging a brace, was another highlight. After that emphatic win my local paper reported: 'Bentley's clever and most promising display was an outstanding feature of the game. With youth on his side – Bentley is not yet seventeen – we ought to hear quite a lot about him.' I was getting a name for myself, which made all the hard work worthwhile. There was also the occasion when I scored the fastest goal of my career, after seventeen seconds of a grudge Football League (South) War Cup match against Bath City. Our right half played the ball to me deep in our half and I ran more than half the length of the field, evading flying tackles before slotting the ball into the net.

War football was hard and there would be tackles flying about that would make your blood curdle. It's doubtful whether many of the players would have stayed on the pitch for more than ten minutes in the modern game. I'm convinced that this was because many of the players had no real feeling for the clubs they were representing, as they were making guest appearances. The fact that there was a war on and everybody's lives were now so difficult meant playing football was a way for players to let off steam and get rid of their frustrations. My Bristol City teammates weren't always the innocent parties in violent matchday exchanges. At the end of a particularly rough game at Swansea one of our guest players, a South African lad who I will refer to as 'Peter', got the rest of his team into some serious bother off the field. Peter had been running his marker ragged and the guy was not best pleased, especially as the crowd was on his back for most of the afternoon. As we ran off the field a Swansea fan kicked Peter through the fence separating spectators from the players. Caught up in the heat of the match, Peter grabbed hold of the guy's leg and twisted it out of shape, leaving him on the floor in agony. After we had all been in the bath and got changed we walked out of the dressing rooms and made our way to a row of taxis outside ready to take us to the station. As we walked down the pathway we could see a crowd of Swansea fans standing outside waiting for Peter. They were rocking one of the taxis and trying to turn it over. We made a run for the remaining taxis and leapt inside just as the first cab was turned on its side. We made it just in time before the mob spotted us. It was a narrow escape.

At one stage I seriously thought about packing the game in and had a long chat with my dad about it. I had witnessed so much dirty play I wasn't sure that playing my beloved sport was the way I wanted to make a living. Broken legs were common in the game, and risking life and limb getting kicked up in the air every five minutes didn't seem an attractive way to earn a crust. Fortunately I was dissuaded by some of the older players who recognised that I had a bit of talent and didn't want me to throw it away. A number of them insisted that pre-war football had been much fairer and of a far better standard, and that it would improve again after the conflict ended.

Billy Mitchell, a star wing half, took it upon himself to be my protector on the field and would become the biggest single influence on my professional career. He would see it as a personal insult if anyone dared to touch me and his help in avoiding the cloggers was vital in persuading me to carry on playing. Billy had 17 caps, which was several years' worth because in those days each country only played three or four internationals a year. He was coming towards the end of his career and was like a father to me during those tough days. As my own father had done many years earlier, Billy emphasised the importance of fitness and discouraged me from smoking. He also had a good technical brain and taught me to simplify my game. Billy was the most likeable bloke you could meet, a real gentleman, and was as gentle as a lamb off the pitch. Yet when he crossed the white line on a Saturday afternoon he was as hard as nails, because he needed to be. I'll never forget Billy taking me aside one day during training and saying, 'You've got a grand future after the war, lad, but you'll have to protect yourself on the pitch.'

He taught me a few tricks to stop the hard men in their tracks but never approved of his teammates taking liberties themselves. He once said to me, 'If ever I catch you going over the top of the ball to deliberately hurt someone I'll have you off the field.' And I have no doubt that he would have done so. He always made it clear that I should never start trouble on the field, but let it be known that there was nothing wrong with me looking after myself when faced with a dirty opponent.

One of the tricks Billy taught me to combat the 'foulers' was to knock my knee into my opponent's leg as we ran for a ball. The player would fall flat on his face and the referee wouldn't have a clue why. Another ploy he taught me was to shape up for a 50-50 tackle as if I was going over the top of the ball to hurt my opponent, but then to pull back at the last moment. If the other bloke went over the top for that challenge I'd say to him, 'You do that next time and I'll go right through you.' That would usually put paid to any more nonsense.

During one game the opposing goalkeeper knocked me spark out by punching me two-fisted in the head instead of catching the ball. Just before I landed on the floor and lost consciousness I was vaguely aware of being kicked by another opponent running past. As I groggily came round half a minute or so later on the goal-line I saw a huge melee in the back of the net. Five or six lads were having a free-for-all and fists were flying in all directions. Billy was in the thick of it, making sure that my attackers regretted their rash actions.

Towards the end of the war we were playing away to Cardiff. Their team contained five or six Bevin Boys, all of whom had kicked chunks out of Billy during wartime games. Before the match I popped into the home team's dressing room to collect a couple of autographs for friends and saw Billy walk in looking stern. He addressed the whole Cardiff team. 'Lads, I've got something to say to you. All through the war you have kicked chunks out of me. The war is over now and I want to be playing next season. So if any of you "come it" with me today I'll have you.' Not all the Bevin Boys heeded Billy's warning and three of them had to be taken off in the first half after riling Billy with crunching over-the-top challenges. One returned to the field with a huge bandage around his head, looking as though he was wearing a turban. Billy had been very clever. He had jumped for headers with these guys and timed his leap so as to make contact with their heads instead of the ball. All the challenges looked like genuine accidents.

Referees back then were incredibly lenient and sendings off were almost unheard of. If you did get dismissed it was a very serious matter and players often received the ultimate punishment of *sine die*, which meant you were banned for life. Sadly, this happened to Billy just after the end of the war. We were playing down at Newport, on the Lovells Athletics ground, and their inside forward Berry Nieuwenhuys was up against Billy. Nieuwenhuys was a terrific footballer, who played for Liverpool before and after the war, and knew all the tricks of the trade. Before the game Billy said to me, 'I'll have my hands full today. This Nieuwenhuys is forever going over the top or nudging you in the back.' As Billy predicted Nieuwenhuys went after him all game and by the last ten minutes of the match Billy had had enough. He ran up behind Nieuwenhuys, tapped him on the shoulder and, as he turned round, Billy butted him. I think he broke his nose. The referee said, 'I've told you twice before', and sent him off. Billy never played professional football again.

It was a terrible shame, and the only comfort to Billy must have been that he was almost at the end of his illustrious career. He didn't deserve to have his playing days end under such a cloud. Billy's sons would often come over to watch Chelsea and when he died I asked for a dedication to him in the Stamford Bridge programme. His boys wrote to me to thank me for saying nice things about their father. It was the least I could do, I told them. Their father had been a great man.

The less regimented format of wartime football occasionally brought farce to on-field proceedings. On Christmas Day 1941 Bristol City were playing away to Southampton. It was a midday kick-off, so we all had to meet at about eight in the morning and travel in four taxis. There were no such things as team buses then. Only one of the drivers knew the way, which made things tricky because all the road signs had been pulled down in order to confuse the Germans if they invaded. We were going across Salisbury Plain when the third taxi got a puncture. The driver who knew the way stayed behind and said he'd catch up with us later. Of course we got terribly lost and didn't get to the ground until about a quarter to one to find the match had kicked off without us half an hour earlier. Only one of the taxis had succeeded in reaching the ground on time, which meant our team had just four recognised players. An official had taken a board round asking for seven men from the crowd and one of those they enlisted was the reserve trainer for Southampton, who was about forty years old and well past his prime. When we arrived the chap on the gate wouldn't let us in, so we jumped over the fence. He called the police but we managed to evade capture and eventually reached the changing rooms. We were told that the match had been due to restart once we arrived but because Southampton were winning 4-0 the home side were no longer interested in that arrangement. We were banished to the stands to watch the remainder of the first half in frustration as our makeshift replacements took a pasting. Just before half-time one of our 'ringers', the ageing Southampton trainer, went down under a heavy challenge and left the field clutching his heart. Substitutes had not been introduced back then, so it appeared we would be forced down to ten men for the entire second period. As we sat in the dressing room at half-time someone came up with the bright idea of replacing the trainer with Ernie Brinton, who looked fairly similar to the man with the sponge, if a little younger. Len Southway, our trainer, said to Ernie, 'You can pretend to be their trainer. Get yourself changed and put some mud on your face. I'll tell the referee you'll be a bit late coming out because you're still having treatment.'

We went back into the stand to watch the second half and sure enough a couple of minutes later Ernie appeared at the side of the pitch, with mud on his face and holding his heart. Ernie realised that the linesman on the near side would have had a good view of the trainer during the first half because he was positioned close to him, so he walked around to the far side of the pitch and ran on from there. After a few minutes play there was a throw-in and Ernie ended up about five yards from the edge of the pitch. The far side linesman immediately realised that we'd pulled a stunt and flagged for the ref's attention. When he heard what had happened the referee ran up to Ernie and shouted at him to get off. The crowd realised what was happening and, being Christmas, many of them had oranges, which they started throwing at Ernie as he trudged off to the dressing rooms. It was hilarious and we all fell about laughing in the stands as we watched Ernie coming under a barrage of fruit, still going through the motions of holding his hand to his heart. After the game we drove straight home to Bristol having not kicked a ball in anger. I got indoors at about seven o'clock and ate my Christmas dinner, which Mum had left in the oven but was by now looking pretty worse for wear.

Other matches during the war were called off because of bomb damage close to stadiums. In the case of Ashton Gate a match was postponed after a doodlebug landed on the field the night before. Although the explosive never actually detonated, by the time the bomb squad had defused it, the match had already been called off.

Although a regular first-team player throughout the war years, I had been released from the ground staff soon after the conflict's start. City's income had been decimated by the war and they could not afford to keep more than one lad on the ground staff during the week. I was forced to look for another job and at first went to W.D. & H.O. Wills, the cigarette factory where my sister worked. I was placed in the section where snuff was made and was alarmed to see fellows coughing and spluttering through their shifts. These men didn't look well at all and were probably taking far too much snuff themselves. The idea that the same fate might befall me frightened the life out of me so as quickly as possible I took another job as a lorry driver's mate. This involved long hours on the road, which made it difficult to get to training on time in the evenings. After a few months I secured a position at Shell Mex, where my job was to fill tankers with petrol. During wartime this was a pretty dangerous occupation because oil and petrol depots were prime targets for the Nazis. I also turned out regularly for the Shell Mex football side, wearing Tommy Mills' cramped old boots with pride.

Home was rather less crowded than it had been before the outbreak of war. My four brothers had all signed up for the Army and been posted out to France and Italy. There were just four of us left at 39 Meadow Grove: Mum, Dad, Amanda and myself. Doris had moved next door with her two children. We also had two very nice air raid huts, as we called them, erected in the garden and both were very comfortable.

Despite my new sense of freedom at having my own room, I missed my brothers terribly and it was always sad whenever they returned to the front after a period of home leave. My brothers would often write to my parents and I still keep at home some of their letters, which I treasure. There were a few families in the street that lost sons, mostly at sea, and whenever news of such a death reached my parents they would naturally worry that bit more about their own lads.

I helped Dad put out some fires caused by incendiary bombs in the surrounding streets, and those who had suffered burnt-out houses would come to him for help in finding new places to live.

Dad took everything in his stride. There were some very heavy raids at Bristol, especially during the daytime, and I remember seeing British Spitfires chasing away bombers that were headed for the Shell Mex depot. Bristol Docks was another favourite target of the Luftwaffe.

On 25 September 1940, shortly before midday, German bombers attacked the Rolls-Royce engine factory, dropping 300–400 bombs on and around the site before coming under fire from British anti-aircraft guns. A gas main took a direct hit and eleven soldiers were killed by one direct hit. Nearly 1,000 houses were either damaged or destroyed by the raid and more than ninety workers died inside the Rolls-Royce works, many of whom were killed by direct hits on the air raid shelters within the works' boundary. Another fifty or so were killed outside the factory, with hundreds of others injured, and the next day there were more explosions in the Filton area of the city as delayed-action bombs exploded. It was a terrifying experience for the people of Bristol and some people requested that their families be evacuated. This was rather ironic considering that Londoners had come in their droves to Bristol early in the war, viewing our city as a relatively safe haven.

As if Bristol had not witnessed enough comings and goings, the momentous bombing of Pearl Harbour by Japan on 7 December 1941 altered the city's population even further. The United States, previously an interested spectator in the conflict, immediately declared war on Japan, whose German allies in turn declared war on the US. Within weeks plane-loads of American troops had arrived in Bristol. Most people in my neighbourhood had never encountered a foreigner before and suddenly there were hundreds of American GIs strolling through the streets, handing out chewing gum to kids and sweeping young ladies off their feet in the dance halls.

At around this time I had started courting Violet Upton, a local girl who I had met a few years earlier while still at school. She came from a family of four girls and four boys and had lived near the Bentleys while I was growing up. Violet, or Vi as she was known, had stayed in Bristol when war broke out, undertaking various jobs in flour mills, laundries and the like.

My eighteenth birthday was soon upon me and, shortly after we started courting, it was time for me to bid my farewell to Vi and to Mum and Dad, and join the forces. I had already signed professional forms with Bristol City some months earlier, after the club had realised I would be free to play for any of their rivals as soon as I joined the forces. Signing my contract should have been a momentous occasion, but with the clock ticking until my departure for war it passed without much brouhaha.

I was keen to fight, especially as all four of my brothers were at the battlefront. All the family expected me to join the Army, as my brothers had done, but I had other ideas. I had a bit of Dad's wanderlust and wanted to see the world, and I felt that serving the Royal Navy would allow me better opportunities to travel. After I had passed my initial cursory test, my first task for the Navy did indeed involve travel, albeit only to the West Country port of Plymouth. The town had suffered a heavy bombing raid and I was sent as part of a group of five sailors to the large Co-op depot that had been hit. Huge tins of condensed milk had exploded, leaving putrefying white liquid spread ankle deep on the ground that needed to be cleaned up. Such was my romantic introduction to life as a seaman.

I turned down the opportunity to be a physical training instructor and opted for a more hands-on role in the Navy. In late 1942 I was posted to the first of a number of destroyers upon which I would spend the rest of the war on convoy duty. This involved escorting convoys of millions of tonnes of imported food and material to Britain. Our role was vital: keep the flow of goods going to help maintain the vast war effort at home. I was a gunner and during the day I would be on patrol in the destroyer's stern, looking out for icebergs and German U-boats. There would be four seamen at any time looking through large binoculars in half-hour rotations. If we spotted something we thought might be a submarine our vessel would chase after it, although on one occasion we ended up chasing a large shoal of fish. The trail of a dolphin is almost identical to that of a torpedo and whenever I came across what I thought was a torpedo I would issue an immediate warning to the crew.

My ship would make about six transatlantic crossings every time we escorted a convoy across the ocean. It wasn't particularly glamorous work, standing at the ship's stern for several hours at a time in bloody awful weather. Whenever I returned to the galley there was a rope along the side of the ship with knots tied on it to allow us to hang on as we climbed across. If I carried a cup of hot cocoa with me I would sometimes reach the stern only to find that my drink had almost turned to ice. Whenever it was my turn to make my way up to the stern I would run along the side to try and keep my drink warm, although this would have been none too clever had I slipped overboard.

When the weather was rough we would lose people over the side. We never turned back for anyone. By the time a vessel of that size reversed direction anyone who had gone overboard would be dead, frozen by the bitter ocean. The Atlantic was such a cruel sea, although those who worked on the Russian convoys probably found the Russian seas even harder.

If we fired on a submarine, pieces of wreckage would come to the surface and we would have to check it to see if they were genuine remnants of a sub or whether the Germans were laying a trap in order to trick us. There would be many days where nobody on lookout would see anything suspicious and I don't think we were ever fired upon. We were positioned at the rear of the convoys while the more modern destroyers were at the front, involved in the action. Most of the actual exchanging of fire happened quite a way in front of us. If you were sunk in the Atlantic during winter it was pretty much the end. If the bombing didn't get you, the icy water would.

I was fortunate that about half the sixty-strong crew of my first ship, HMS *Vanquisher*, were Bristolians. A number of my friends who had joined up at the same time were on board and this made it easier to settle. There was a great sense of discipline among those on the destroyers, with people from all classes mucking in and getting the job done. The camaraderie onboard was very strong, but the conditions in which we lived made this a strict necessity. There would be up to ten of us slung up in hammocks in a room about

eight feet high by twelve feet wide. Arguments between sailors had
to be sorted out quickly for the good of the ship's morale, even if differences were sometimes settled by a punch-up. Anyone who caused
serious problems would be sent ashore in disgrace and punished.

It often struck me that, had I not subsequently made it as a professional footballer, then a Naval career might have been a good option
for me. I had adapted to life on the ship well and found myself promoted to quartermaster, working on the wheel, hoping to become a
coxswain. Although being in the Navy was hard work and certainly
no place for the faint-hearted, I appreciated the opportunity to visit
exotic countries and witness beautiful sights like dolphins leaping
twenty feet in the air, the spraying water they left behind making
the light appear fluorescent. I wouldn't ever have had those opportunities had it not been for the advent of war. The Navy certainly
helped me grow up.

One of the benefits of being in the Navy was that the food was
both of a good standard and plentiful. We were probably better fed
than most of the folks at home. We were also issued a rum ration,
which I didn't often take. One time when I did drink my ration
was the occasion of my nineteenth birthday, when I had a few
drams at lunch. In the afternoon we had an impromptu kickabout
and I ended up in hospital. I ran for a loose ball and, with the
alcohol clouding my judgment, challenged the goalkeeper who, in
his attempt to clear the ball, kicked me hard in my private parts.
I woke up in hospital with the most horrible sight down below. I
was in hospital for about four days before returning to the ship on
light duties.

Two of my fellow sailors were a couple of scallywag Scousers who
fancied themselves to make a bit of extra money by selling their rum
rations on our regular run from Liverpool to Newfoundland. These
lads would water down their booze and sell it to our American
counterparts whenever we came ashore. One day the Yanks realised
they were being conned and decided to teach the pair a lesson
they would never forget. The two Scousers were about to take
some leave in order to get married and the Yanks took them out in
Newfoundland, got them drunk and shaved their heads and their

nether regions. They were bald as coots. I wonder what their poor wives thought when they saw their grooms-to-be standing at the altar with no hair. You had to feel sorry for the lads, even though they had rather asked for their punishment.

Sometimes I would be given a week's leave or a forty-eight-hour pass and would return home to play for Bristol City, but whenever the battle of the Atlantic took a turn for the worse leave would be cancelled. I would write to my dad to let him know whenever I was available for games and he would contact the club but between 1943 and 1946 my appearances were few and far between. On a handful of occasions when we came ashore to Liverpool for a weekend I played for teams situated in the North. I played the odd game for Hartlepools, as they were known then, and also once represented Liverpool, although I unwittingly played under a pseudonym that day because the match programme had printed another lad's name in place of mine.

Two matches for Bristol City stand out from this period, the first of which happened shortly after I had joined the Navy. When we reached the shore at Weymouth one of the physical training instructors, who wanted me to box for the Navy, instructed me to spar with him in the ring on the Saturday. I told him I was due to play for City but he insisted that I spar with him and said I was not allowed to leave the precincts of the port. We got into a fierce argument that turned into a brief bout of fisticuffs. After the scrap broke up I left the port without telling the PT instructor and travelled to Ashton Gate, played for City, and scored a goal for my troubles. The following day I returned to the ship five minutes before our midnight 'all aboard' deadline. There was a note on my bed instructing me to report to one of the officers first thing in the morning. When I arrived the next day to see him it was clear I was in serious trouble.

'You know the rule about the dock precincts, Bentley. You went home at the weekend.'

'No I didn't, sir.'

'Oh yes you did. You played for Bristol City. Your name's in this newspaper. It says you scored a goal.'

He showed me the newspaper. I had been rumbled. Fortunately, I was able to think on my feet and recalled the recent incident at Anfield.

'My name must have been down in the programme, sir. Bristol City thought I was coming home. The fellow who replaced me must have scored and the reporter thought it was me.'

'That's a good one, son, but I don't believe it.'

Although he clearly hadn't bought my story the officer couldn't prove I was lying and wasn't prepared to go to the length of contacting City themselves. I think that maybe he admired my guile, so he let me off with a warning and advised me with a wink to take up boxing. It later transpired that the PT instructor I had fought with had not reported our contretemps, perhaps because a rookie had whacked him. Otherwise I dread to think what would have happened to me.

Another City game that springs to mind involved another trip to Cardiff to face the Bevin Boys. It was a typically hard-fought game and, playing outside right, I had the better of their full-back, a former international who didn't take kindly to being given the runaround by a young whippersnapper like me. After a while he came up to me and said, 'You do that once more, sonny, and I'll break your bloody leg.' Billy Mitchell had once told me, 'If any of these fellows say they will break your leg, they damn well mean it.' For once I ignored the advice of my protector, replying to the defender, 'You'll have to catch me first. You were a bit slow there.'

Needless to say, the next time I tried to go past the full-back he thudded into my leg and knocked me flying. I hobbled on until half-time when the trainer strapped up my ankle with plaster to keep down the swelling. I carried on despite the pain, although I made little impact on the second half and declined the opportunity to take the ball past my marker again. That night Vi and I went to a dance with my leg still strapped up but, when I woke up the next morning, I couldn't get out of bed. I was due back on the ship that night in Liverpool and after a trip to hospital in Bristol I was told I had chipped a bone in my ankle and was not to travel back. I stayed in hospital for two weeks to recuperate, ruing my decision not to listen to Billy.

Despite spending three-and-a-half years in the Royal Navy, I only represented their football team once in an official game, against the Army. However, I managed to get a run of games under my belt in 1943 in Toronto, representing the Canadian Pacific Railway. The US had lent Britain a number of destroyers and minesweepers to complement the Navy's own stock and we were sent to Toronto to collect one from the Royal Canadian Navy, who were also heavily involved in the war. Many of the American ships were welded, as opposed to riveted, and would often suffer buckling underneath, especially during periods of extreme weather. Upon our arrival we were informed that the vessel was still under repair and would not be ready for some days, so we were all packed off to various people's homes.

I stayed with the family of an ex-Scottish international footballer called Joe McPhail in Toronto, who worked for the local railway, Canadian Pacific. As the days of waiting turned into weeks I was sent by the Navy to work as a PT instructor for the elderly and Joe invited me to play for his team at weekends. The standard wasn't that high because Canada was not exactly renowned for its footballing prowess, but I enjoyed playing regularly again and we started attracting decent-sized crowds. In one match I scored nine goals, the biggest haul of my career, and the Canadian Pacific reached the semi-final of the local cup competition before I was called back onboard.

Football wasn't the only sport I tried my hand at in Canada. I dusted off my boxing gloves and won a trophy for my mates on the Liverpool and Western Approaches. The fight was onboard a converted passenger ship on an island just north of Newfoundland but I never saw the trophy because one of my shipmates pinched it. I also played baseball for a while and was offered the chance to return to Toronto to try out professionally after the war was over.

From 1942 onwards Britain had successfully remained ahead in the battle of the Atlantic, although a total of 3,500 Allied ships were sunk in six years of conflict, compared with fewer than

800 German U-boats. After the success of the D-Day landings in Normandy, victory seemed well within the Allies' grasp and it was little surprise when Germany finally surrendered on 7 May 1945. The end to fighting unleashed a huge wave of patriotic celebration across the land and the VE (Victory in Europe) parties the following day saw Britons across the land weeping with joy and drinking toast after toast to British Prime Minister Winston Churchill and our brave boys. Indeed, in Bristol the pubs ran out of beer shortly after 9 p.m.

Despite the end to hostilities I was to remain on duty in the Navy for a further year, albeit with increased home visits. I wasn't happy to be informed that I had to spend another twelve months away from home, although I had little option but to grin and bear it. As with most things in post-war British life, it would take a while for normal service to resume in professional football. I was by no means the only footballer trapped in the forces after the Armistice and with so many players yet to return home the football authorities chose to retain the regional league system for one further season.

Towards the end of my service I was deployed on minesweepers and my appearances for Bristol City remained a rarity during the 1945/46 campaign. In fact, the game I remember most from that season was one in which I wasn't even involved. Russia's top team, Dynamo FC of Moscow, had arranged a series of matches against the best British teams, including two of my boyhood favourites, Arsenal and Chelsea. No team from Russia had ever before played in Britain and few people here knew much about their style of play. Since the 1920s people in Britain were fascinated by life in Communist Russia and football fans were intrigued to see how the Dynamos would fare against the best of our nation's teams.

(It has been reported over the years that I had served the Navy in Russia and played football in Murmansk, making me one of the first British footballers to play in Eastern Europe. Unfortunately this isn't true, the misconception coming from an interview I gave to a national newspaper reporter. I had told him how much I would have enjoyed the opportunity to play in Russia, and through either his journalistic 'spin' or a genuine misunderstanding my phantom appearance went into football fable.)

Arranging the tour had not been simple for the English FA. The Russian authorities were keen not to lose face to Britain and to their surprise the FA found themselves subject to various demands, including the outlawing of shoulder-charging, which was part of the staple diet of English football. The inclusion of substitutes, who were used frequently in Russia, was also demanded, and a Russian referee was required for at least one of the matches.

The Dynamos' first game was against Chelsea on 13 November, six months after Britain and Russia had helped defeat the Nazis, and an incredible 85,000 spectators crammed into Stamford Bridge. I had been given a week's leave and arrived fresh from Plymouth docks with two friends from the Navy, expecting to be able to pay our entrance fee on the door. Both of them had been drinking all day and were having difficulty walking in a straight line.

It turned out that the game was of such high interest in London that the turnstiles couldn't cope with the number of fans. Thousands forced their way over fences and, when it became obvious we wouldn't get in legally, my mates and I joined the queue to vault into the ground. Room on the terraces had run out, so fans squeezed themselves into any space they could find between the touchline and the stand. Hundreds more climbed onto the roof of the main stand, which thankfully was strong enough to hold their collective weight.

To add more spice to the match, Chelsea, a team who had consistently underachieved throughout their forty-year history, had splashed out on some expensive new signings, including West Ham's Len Goulden, John Harris from Wolves and, most surprisingly, Tommy Lawton from Everton, one of the biggest stars in the English game.

I remember seeing the Russian lads running on to the Stamford Bridge pitch holding footballs, which resulted in dumbfounded stares from the stands. English teams would never touch a ball until the referee had blown his first whistle. When the Russian lads proceeded to hand over bunches of flowers to their Chelsea opponents, a deft piece of public relations by the Russian authorities, you could have heard a pin drop.

The match itself was a cracker and even though my mates and I had to crane our necks to see any action we were all highly impressed with the skill displayed by the Russians. In a ding-dong affair my hero Tommy Lawton looked to have settled the match when he put Chelsea into a late 3–2 lead, but a controversial injury-time Dynamo equaliser meant honours were even. The Russian goalscorer had been at least five yards offside when he received the ball. In a TV interview many years later Tommy later claimed that the referee told him after the final whistle he had been obliged to allow the goal in order 'to be diplomatic'. He wasn't best pleased, especially as the decision had cost the new boy his first Chelsea win bonus.

My mates and I had already left the ground by then in order to make the last train back to Plymouth. We climbed over the fence and onto the railway line. I had to try to get two legless sailors across the track safely, which was no mean feat. I helped the first one across, having told our other mate to wait. When I turned back, he was standing on the tracks. If a train had passed he would have been splattered. How I got them home alive I don't know.

Being demobilised in May 1946 was a great relief. I carefully chose the 'demob' clothes from the options provided by the Navy and took the train home to Bristol, feeling happy that the adventure was over. My family was delighted to see me and we spent a few days catching up with each other before my thoughts returned to my footballing future. I was by now desperate to get back to playing and felt a great sense of disappointment that the football season had drawn to a close. I was now aged twenty-two and desperate to make up for lost time. I vowed to knuckle down to training immediately and lose the excess weight I had gained while in the Navy in preparation for the next season, which would start in three months' time.

The Football League had announced that the 1946/47 season would herald the return of national divisional football. All ninety-two teams were to remain in the division in which they had stood when the League programme was scrapped seven years earlier. This meant that Bristol City would resume action in the Third Division (South) in August. I was counting down the days until I could pull on the red and white of City and was delighted when the club announced a pre-season tour of Sweden and Denmark. Little did I know that this Scandinavian jaunt would mark both my final appearance for City and my departure from Bristol forever.

FOUR

Geordie Roy

Having returned to Blighty after four years in the Navy it was ironic that my first post-war game would be on foreign shores. The Bristol City directors had lined up a brief Nordic tour in June, one that was lucrative for the club, although not of course for the players. In keeping with the times the players were ranked bottom of their list of considerations. Bursting to play, I was devastated to find that my name was missing from the team sheet that had been stuck to the hotel notice board.

For the two-match tour City had agreed to adopt the European custom of including substitutes, and I was chosen as the team's twelfth man for our first game. I sat steely-eyed on the bench, determined to prove the manager wrong if I was given the chance. When I was finally brought on, with twenty minutes to play and City a goal down, I quickly made my point, scoring twice in a 2-1 win. After this match-winning performance I felt sure that I would start the second match but, lo and behold, I found myself on the bench again. This time around I was given just ten minutes to impress, but managed to score another goal.

On the coach journey back to Bristol I sat in silence, fuming at the poor way I felt I had been treated and wondering what I had done wrong. It all fell into place the following week when I was called into the club's offices and informed that Newcastle United had made a bid for me. Newcastle had offered City £8,500, more than anyone had previously paid for a Third Division player. I had clearly been left out of the starting XI to reduce the risk of my getting injured and lowering my price tag.

I was aware that various scouts had been sent to watch me play during the war, but hadn't been expecting a transfer so soon, especially not to a club situated so far from my family. It transpired that Bob Hewson, the City manager, had been a former Newcastle player and recommended me to his United counterpart Stan Seymour. I wasn't entirely convinced that leaving Bristol for the North-East would be a good idea. I had just moved back home to my family and, despite having to share a bed with one of my brothers again, I was reluctant to leave the Bentley household.

The bare facts were that City were far from well off financially and more than happy to accept the transfer fee. I was left with little doubt that the board wanted me to sign for Newcastle, but I wanted to discuss things with my dad before agreeing to anything. I walked home with my head spinning and the words of one director ringing in my ears: 'Come on Bent, you can't turn this down. It's your big chance.'

I knew he was right. The chance was too good to turn down and by the time I arrived home I was pretty sure that I would indeed sign for Newcastle, a far bigger club than Bristol City and one that had a fanatical following. My dad told me that at my age, twenty-two, he thought it was the right move for me, but said the final decision had to be mine. By the end of the evening I had agreed to the transfer.

My one gripe was that I was given only one year's benefit as an *ex gratia* payment by Bristol City, which amounted to £150. Players would generally receive £150 for each year they had been on the club's books. I had been a professional for almost five years by then, but was informed by the board that war years did not count. Not for the first, or indeed the last, time a club would have me by the short and curlies.

At around the same time, City's other inside forward, Cyril Williams, was the subject of another big-money move, in his case to West Bromwich Albion. The City fans were not best pleased at losing two of their most promising players but economically the club had little option. It was unfortunate but they would never be able to compete on a level playing field with the big boys.

Having told Vi about my decision to join Newcastle United I asked her to marry me and was delighted when she agreed to be Mrs Bentley. I travelled up to Tyneside in high spirits to meet Stan Seymour and find somewhere for myself and my wife-to-be to live. I admit to feeling slightly deflated when I realised that Newcastle were not in the First Division, as I had assumed, but in the league below. This feeling disappeared the instant I stepped on to the St James's Park pitch. Standing on the pitch and looking across towards the Gallowgate End, I couldn't help but be impressed by the place and dreamt of becoming a favourite of the Geordie faithful.

The club had found me comfortable digs in a house with a lovely couple, Wally and Lil Armitage. Wally was Scottish, while Lil was a true Geordie and they made me feel at home immediately. I was bowled over by the fanaticism and friendliness of local supporters who accepted me as one of their own from the start and went out of their way to welcome me. The first morning I visited the ground for training I hopped on the trolley bus and a chap of about sixty years old stood up and offered me his seat, which I politely declined. Then the conductor went around to collect the ha'penny fares and when he reached me said, 'You're Roy Bentley. You don't need to pay. Have it on me.' I was so embarrassed. The fans were incredibly generous, but I didn't feel it was right to have special treatment, and so from that day onwards I jogged down to the ground.

I had rather hoped that moving to a high-profile Second Division club might mean that I would finally take part in proper training sessions and receive expert coaching. Pretty soon I realised that this was a pipe dream. The training regime at Newcastle was diabolical and I never really got to grips with it. All we did was run, run, run, either around the edge of the pitch or on the surrounding roads to harden our calves. Nobody seemed to be in charge and when we had finished running we were left to our own devices. Training was disrupted by the continued service down the mines of many of the club's star players, like Jackie Milburn and Len Shackleton, the latter signing for us shortly after the start of the season. Although the Second World War had ended, extra coal production was still required by a people struggling to readjust to everyday life. The 'pit' lads would only train on Tuesday and Thursday evenings. The rest of us would joke that our part-time colleagues ran around the pitch at the dead of night wearing their miners' lamps. I went along one night to see how great players like Jackie Milburn trained, but was disappointed to see that, like the rest of us, they simply ran round and round the pitch until they were exhausted.

Newcastle didn't even issue us training kit, instructing us to buy our own using the clothing coupons that the government contin-ued to issue after the war. Having been struck by how cold the air in the North-East was, I visited the local Army & Navy store where I bought a thick white polo-neck sweater like the guys on the submarines wore.

My first appearance at St James's Park came in the annual Probables *v.* Possibles match that preceded every club's first League game. Pre-season friendlies were still few and far between, so these types of match, pitting teammates against each other for a place in the first XI, were fiercely competitive. I was picked for the Probables, alongside new signing Frank Brennan, a strapping fif-teen-stone centre half, one of eight new arrivals. Although this was not an official fixture, it didn't stop 40,000 Newcastle fans turning up to watch, which I found remarkable.

Before the start of the season it was time for one more important fixture: my wedding day. Vi had moved up to the Armitages a few days beforehand and we got married in Newcastle. Vi looked as beautiful as ever and I was the proudest man alive when she said 'I do' at the altar. Then it was off for a honeymoon at the seaside for a few days. We would have liked to have gone away for a whole week but the League season was due to start a week later, so we had to keep it short.

My debut in the black-and-white stripes of the Toon was away to Millwall at The Den, never an easy ground to play at. My teammates ribbed me beforehand about whether I'd have the right mindset to make my debut in such a cauldron, having been softened by a week of marriage. They needn't have worried. I played one of the games of my life and quickly made an impact, slicing open the Lions' defence with a through-ball for 'Wor' Jackie Milburn to rocket home a glorious strike after eight minutes. Millwall equalised before half-time but after the break we dominated and I cracked home two goals in a five-minute spell early in the second half. I was particularly proud of one of my goals, controlling a difficult ball from over my shoulder before shooting past the 'keeper. Albert Stubbins added a fourth to give us a comfortable 4-1 win. Five days later I scored again in a 2-0 win at Nottingham Forest. I was up and running.

The Newcastle team of 1946/47 contained a fine bunch of players and, on the face of it, we looked the best side in the Second Division by a country mile. Blokes like Jackie (Milburn), Tommy Pearson and George Stobart were all fine players, while skipper Joe Harvey was an inspirational leader. The club's new stopper Frank Brennan was fast, good in the air and difficult to get past. In attack we had a formidable front line, nicknamed 'the Bank of England Five'. It was the envy of every club in the land, despite the club's sale of legendary forward Albert Stubbins to Liverpool within a few days of the season starting. At outside left was Tommy Pearson, a Scottish international who was honest as the day was long and always prepared to give advice to the youngsters. Tommy was brilliant at pushing the ball past a player and running around the other side to confuse him. One or two supporters got on his back whenever the trick didn't come off, but he was a very clever player to have alongside you. Tommy had a great football brain and, after he packed up playing, went up to Aberdeen as manager before becoming sports editor of a newspaper.

At centre forward was Charlie Wayman, a very different player to the usual six-feet-tall beefcakes who appeared in that position. Charlie was a small chap and not too special in the air but he had a terrific left foot. One of those still working in the pits, his tiring day job never affected his speed. Charlie had bags of pace, which was undoubtedly his main asset, and he relied on it just like Jimmy Greaves would do at Chelsea and Spurs a few years later.

At outside right was Jackie Milburn, the fastest man in football. Every year Jackie ran in the New Year's race in Scotland, the biggest

100-yard sprint in the country. He was so easy to play alongside. I would hit the ball right down to the corner for Jackie to latch on to and, even if the full-back only had half the distance to reach the ball, Jackie would invariably fly past him and get there first. He was remarkable. The only fault in Jackie's game when I joined the club was his heading ability, which was atrocious. I always felt he would make a better centre forward than a winger if only he could learn that skill. He was a wonderful fellow and we quickly became pals, so I took him into the gym and spent hours teaching him how to head a ball properly. Within a season he would become one of the best centre forwards in the game and teams would need two men to mark him, which freed up his teammates no end. Jackie should probably have received more caps in his career but at that time there was so much strong competition, with the likes of Stan Mortensen, Ronnie Allen, Jack Rowley, Nat Lofthouse and myself vying for a place as England centre forward.

I was Newcastle's inside right, having established what was to become known as my 'roving' game during the final years of the war. I had noticed that most attacks on goal seemed to come from hitting the ball to wingers who would cross the ball into the box for centre forwards to latch onto. I wanted to try something else to increase my chances of scoring.

Under the old 'WM' formation, practised by all teams, every player knew his position, which meant that play was fairly static. For instance, before any given match a right-back knew he would be marking the outside left, the inside right knew he would be tagged by the left half, and the centre forward knew he would be facing the centre half. This did not allow much room for manoeuvre. Sitting in my hammock on board the destroyers I would muse on trying out a different style of play. My eventual plan, simple though it sounds today, was to move around the whole of the attacking half of the pitch rather than stay in the zone occupied by my marker. My opponent would then be forced to decide whether to follow me and leave a space for my teammates to run into, or to leave me unmarked. I would often taunt the left half who had been instructed to tag me, saying 'Come on, follow me,' and many a marker would be undecided as to what to do. Some would hesitate before following me, while others would rigidly stick to their plan, thinking that I could only be dangerous if I was in the penalty box, and regarding me as harmless when standing thirty yards away. This suited me fine.

Having tried out the new tactic for the Canadian Pacific Railway on the afternoon of my nine-goal haul, I was determined to make it work in League football. However, this style of forward play could only work if my teammates were on board. As matchday tactics at Newcastle were left entirely to the players, I was grateful to have accommodating colleagues who allowed me to practise my ploy. The 'roving' style was to become my trademark in the game and, a few years down the line, helped propel me into the national side.

Completing 'the Bank of England Five' was Len Shackleton at inside left. The move from Len's home-town team, Bradford Park Avenue, six weeks into the season was controversial. He had been asking for a transfer for months, to no avail, only to find out by chance one afternoon that he was joining Newcastle. Having been told to report to a local hotel by the Bradford manager he bumped into Sunderland boss Bill Murray in the lobby. Murray told Len he was disappointed at not being able to sign him that day because the fee was too high. 'Shack' was bemused at this conversation, not knowing he was up for sale, and became even more nonplussed when informed that he was being transferred to Newcastle. If he didn't want to move, it was tough luck. At least I'd been given the opportunity, however small, of saying 'no' to Newcastle. Poor old Len had no such luxury.

However frustrated he might have been by the nature of his transfer, Shack didn't let it show when introduced to us in the dressing room before his first game. The match, at home to Newport County on 5 October 1946, would go into history as arguably the greatest debut of all time in British football. Shack tore the County defence to shreds, scoring an incredible six goals in a 13-0 victory. Three of his goals were scored in a spell of just two-and-a-half minutes. Charlie bagged another four, Jackie got two, and I scored one as the St James's Park faithful cheered us off the park, thinking they had seen a team walking its way into the First Division. Little did they know.

Len was another lad who found his spell down the mines extended after the war and, up until to his move to the Magpies, he was working at the Fryston pit near Castleford in Yorkshire. After his transfer to Tyneside he worked as a labourer for Jackie Milburn, who by this stage was a fitter at the Hazelrigg Colliery.

Shack was an incredible talent, with the longest and thinnest feet I have ever seen, which allowed him to manipulate a football like no-one else. He wore rugby boots because his toes were so long, but could still bring a ball under control instantly from any pace and at any height. To be able to flick one of those heavy old-style footballs with so little effort and with such accuracy was truly sublime. Len had long bony fingers as well, about two inches longer than mine, and used them to show us lots of tricks on a billiard table. He could have played any sport he chose to, he was that gifted. Shack could certainly have been a demon spin bowler with those long bony fingers.

He was also one of the game's biggest characters. During a match at Fulham, their wing halves, Jim Taylor and Len Quested, wouldn't leave Shack and I alone and were kicking lumps out of us. In the dressing room at half-time Len asked our trainer for a lace, which I didn't understand, before returning to the field a couple of minutes early. As Questy ran out Shack handed him the lace and said, 'Now tie that round my bleeding neck and see if you can get any closer to me.' On another occasion, against his old team, Bradford Park Avenue, Len stood on the blind side of one of their chaps who was running up to take a penalty and threw a lump of mud in his eye just before he kicked the ball. No-one saw him do it.

In later years I played against Len for Chelsea after his transfer to Sunderland, and he made my teammate Ken Armstrong look a fool. Chelsea had a throw-in and Shack stood with his back to Ken, who had played with him at Bradford. Pointing, Shack cheekily advised Ken to play a 'one-two' against his back and naively his old pal fell for the trick. When Ken threw it full-pelt towards his friend's back, the wiry Shack whirled around like a dervish and ran off with the ball at his feet. Ken could only stand there laughing. That was Shack all over.

Len had a deadly serious side and wasn't prepared to be pushed about by clubs who treated their players like cattle, but he rightly earned the nickname 'The Clown Prince of Football'. When his autobiography of the same name was released in 1957 Len told me it was going to sell by the bucketload. I asked him how he could be so sure. He replied that he had written a very interesting chapter about football directors. When I bought a copy I turned straight to this chapter, entitled 'What the average football director knows about football,' only to find that it was a blank page. Whether the directors at Sunderland laughed at Len's joke is doubtful.

After a strong start to the season Newcastle were sitting pretty at the top of the table by the turn of the year. I had settled into the team and had scored 12 goals by Christmas, including my first professional hat-trick in a 3-2 win at Plymouth. Although promotion was our ultimate aim for the season, we also fancied our chances in the FA Cup, thinking that our enviable forward line gave us a chance against any defence in the land. On 11 January we showed our intention by thrashing Crystal Palace 6-2 at home in the third round. All six goals were scored by forwards, Shack getting two while Charlie, Tommy, myself and reserve forward George Stobart notched one each.

Two weeks later we turned around a half-time deficit at St James's Park to beat Southampton 3-1, Charlie netting a hat-trick. In the fifth round we were drawn at home again, to Leicester City, but fluffed our lines. Shack's tap-in put us into a second-half lead but a header by Dewis meant a replay at Filbert Street. We won the rematch 2-1, with goals by myself and Tommy Pearson, to set up a quarter-final tie at Sheffield United. It was a tough match, played in front of a noisy 60,000 Yorkshire crowd, but we outclassed the Blades and goals from myself and Jackie put us into the last four. We were closing in on a unique Second Division Championship and FA Cup double.

In the promotion places and one match from the final of the most prestigious cup competition in the world, we should have been a happy camp. Instead the team soon found itself racked with self-doubt, and our preparations for the semi-final fast descended into chaos. Stan Seymour had surprisingly stepped down as manager early in March, and the board of directors had taken charge of team affairs themselves instead of appointing a replacement. This was a foolhardy decision, particularly as some of the team were openly at odds with the club, and the fallout resulted in the spectacular capitulation of our season. Both Joe Harvey and Len Shackleton were angry that the club had failed to find them adequate accommodation since their transfers to St James's Park and were fed up with commuting from Yorkshire. The pair were understandably upset and the fact that the men who had angered them were now picking the team merely added fuel to the fire. I've read that both players informed the directors that they would refuse to play for Newcastle once our cup run came to an end, but I don't know whether or not that is true.

What I do recall is the bizarre countdown to our semi-final date with Charlton at Leeds United's Elland Road. For the entire four weeks following our win at Sheffield United we were camped together at a base in Northumberland and were only permitted to leave on match days. A couple of days before the semi-final the directors sent us to a health spa where we were instructed to get into a peat bath. I found it a strange experience, like having a poultice poured over me. When we got out of the bath we were all hosed down with a powerful jet, then laid on to a bed wrapped in a towel and sent to sleep. It felt terrific, but most of us found the experience far too relaxing. By Saturday morning it felt like my legs had turned to jelly.

Matters worsened when the directors made the strange decision to drop leading goalscorer Charlie Wayman from the team in favour of his best pal, George Stobart, who had struggled to settle since his summer transfer from Middlesbrough. The players were all unhappy with this decision and even George himself didn't feel comfortable with the way the situation had been handled. Reports from the time described the situation in the Elland Road dressing room as a near-mutiny, although I wouldn't go quite as far as that. Certainly this was no preparation for our biggest match of the season.

Charlton were fourth from bottom in the First Division and we all felt that on paper we were the better team and should win the tie without too many difficulties. Of course, football isn't played on paper and we found ourselves a goal down early in the match. Shortly after going behind I had an excellent chance to level the scores six yards from goal but shot straight at their giant goalkeeper Sam Bartram. The *News of the World* described the miss the next morning as 'a deplorable lapse and unquestionably marked the turning point.' This may well have been true, although if I hadn't been running around on legs of jelly I might well have done better with my effort. We headed towards the halfway mark two goals down and desperately needing to hear the referee's whistle to allow us to regroup. On the stroke of half-time Charlton captain Don Welsh nipped in to give the Valiants a three-goal lead and put the tie out of reach. A fourth Charlton goal in the second half confirmed the London side's utter supremacy on the day, and ensured a miserable ride home to Tyneside for us that night.

The crushing blow of the semi-final defeat combined with the deep-seated unrest at the club meant our promotion challenge started to fall away. Although we battered Luton Town 7-2 at home the next week our League form was too inconsistent to maintain our promotion challenge. Towards the end of the season I scored my second hat-trick in a Newcastle shirt, as we thrashed Bradford Park Avenue 5-0 at St James's Park. However, we then proceeded to win just one of our remaining five matches.

By the time the League campaign finally crawled to an end on 14 June, amid scorching temperatures, Newcastle had scored an impressive 95 League goals, Charlie Wayman top-scoring with 30, Jackie on 19 and myself netting a respectable 18. Sadly, our defence had leaked 62 goals during the same period. Our matches averaged almost four goals a game, which made us good value to watch a little like Kevin Keegan's self-destructive Newcastle team of the mid-1990s. The result of our generosity in defence was that we ended the season in fifth position, ten points short of the two promotion places. Our supporters were devastated.

Towards the end of the season the directors, to their credit, realised the error of their ways and appointed Luton manager George
Martin as Stan Seymour's belated replacement. They had also
backed down and solved the issue of Joe and Len's housing, but it
was all too little too late.

In the summer George announced his intention to shore up
our leaky defence and bought goalkeeper Jack Fairbrother from
Preston North End. Jack was a fabulous shot-stopper and a shrewd
signing by George. After a good pre-season we embarked on the
1947/48 season with morale high. The campaign began with an
impressive 6-1 home win against Plymouth Argyle with Shack
scoring two and myself, Charlie and Tommy Pearson among the
goals.

Although 'the Bank of England Five' had provided five of those
opening-day goals it became clear that our new boss wanted to
dismantle the quintet. By the end of the season only one of us
would still be on the club's books. First to go was Charlie Wayman,
who signed for Southampton in October for £10,000 although,
to be fair to the boss, Charlie had asked for a transfer. The decision
sent shockwaves through the supporters, but unwittingly paved the
way for George's most inspired decision, moving Jackie Milburn to
centre forward. Wor Jackie scored a hat-trick in his first outing in
that role, a 5-3 win at Bury, and would go on to become the most
famous number nine in the Geordies' history.

In February Len would join Newcastle's arch-rivals Sunderland
for £20,050, breaking the British transfer record. However, a month
before Len had walked out of St James's Park for the last time, I
was also on my way out of the door.

My departure had nothing to do with any feelings of discon-
tent on my part, contrary to a number of stories printed over
the years. In particular, two explanations given for my leaving
Newcastle were, quite frankly, laughable. The first was a claim
that I had been involved in a punch-up with Frank Brennan.
The truth is I wouldn't have been stupid enough to take on big
Frank at a fight and besides, we were good pals who never to my
knowledge quarrelled.

The second claim, repeated in a recent book about Newcastle United's history, was even more strange: that I had complained about the state of the bath at Lil and Wally Armitage's house. Where that story came from I have no idea. Anyone who knew Lil Armitage knew that she kept her house spotless and that you would need a microscope to find anything unclean. In any case, I was never the kind of player to make silly complaints like that.

The fact was that I loved playing in front of 50,000 fanatical Geordies and felt privileged to be in the same team as chaps like Jackie Milburn. At the time I would have loved to have seen out my career in the black-and-white stripes, but I just couldn't cope with the harsh North-East winters. It may sound a little over dramatic, but my health was suffering terribly at the hands of the chill Tyneside wind. When I arrived at the club I was told that one or two former players had been affected by the climate, and that after every training session they would be shattered and unable to perform to their best on a Saturday. I took that advice with a pinch of salt at the time but, after a few months, I realised that the same thing was happening to me. It was completely overpowering. If I played a round of golf with one of my teammates I would barely be able to stand up by the eighteenth hole. I was lethargic and my weight had plummeted from 12st 5lb to 10st 10lb, despite me eating like a Trojan at the Armitages. This had the effect of ruining my 'roving' game, which was all about running everywhere and taking defenders out of the game. If I sprinted for a ball it would take me a couple of minutes to get my breath back, so I found myself conserving my energy on the field.

By December I had only scored three goals, the last of which had been on 3 September against Chesterfield, and I lost my place in the team. The club were sympathetic to my plight and sent me to Scarborough for a fortnight to recuperate, with an order to drink a couple of bottles of Guinness every night to help regain my strength. By this time my first daughter Loraine had been born, so Vi and I took her there and we enjoyed a nice family break. When I returned to Newcastle I was given a run-out in the reserve team against Manchester City. That night I felt much more like my old self and had a reasonable game, but by the time I played for the first team again, in a 0-2 home defeat against Nottingham Forest, I knew that my holiday hadn't solved the problem.

I went to see the club physician, Dr Conway Stewart to ask his opinion. His advice was simple: to move down south. The next day Dr Stewart asked to see the board and recommended that I be placed on the transfer list for the good of my health. The club grudgingly accepted his advice and agreed to listen to offers.

I was fortunate that my dip in form had not prevented a number of clubs from expressing their interest in signing me. Inquiries were received from Arsenal, Chelsea, Liverpool, Luton Town and Cardiff City, but Newcastle's insistence on a player-exchange deal meant that no concrete offers had been made by any of those clubs. I was beginning to despair at the lack of movement, having been on the transfer list for some weeks, and when Big Ben ushered in 1948 my future looked bleak.

Just when I had almost given up hope of rekindling my career else-where, I was dragged away from a game of golf with my Newcastle teammates and informed that Chelsea had made a bid of £11,000. When I arrived home I mulled over the move with Vi. Chelsea were in the lower reaches of the First Division, although they were a club that had never fulfilled their potential. Situated in the West End of London, the Blues had a loyal following and an impressive squad of players, but had won nothing during their forty-three-year history. That evening I was very impressed to receive a personal visit from Chelsea manager Billy Birrell. Billy told me of the club's ambition to build a championship-winning side and his smooth tongue won me over. Mindful of the shenanigans that Joe Harvey and Len Shackleton had gone through at Newcastle, I insisted that Chelsea find my family a house to live, a demand that they agreed to immediately.

The one remaining problem was that, having heard about my illness, Chelsea insisted that I undergo a stringent medical. Having become so weak in recent months I was concerned about the outcome and was relieved to pass with flying colours. With some regrets I said my goodbyes to both the Armitages and my team-mates, and signed on the dotted line for Chelsea. As I walked into Stamford Bridge for the first time on 9 January 1948 I was blissfully unaware of the eight-year rollercoaster ride that awaited me.

FIVE

Blue is the Colour

I was under no illusions as to what was expected of me when I joined Chelsea. I had been brought in to replace legendary centre forward Tommy Lawton, who had sensationally been transferred to Notts County. Chelsea fans were up in arms at the news of Tommy's departure, barely a year after he had joined the club from Everton. Never a man to suffer fools gladly, Tommy had been unhappy at the slapdash way he felt the Stamford Bridge club was run and had asked for another move. After his transfer request had unexpectedly been granted, Tommy stunned the football world by joining Notts County for £20,000, almost double what he had cost Chelsea. Although County were the oldest League club in Britain, they were languishing in the Third Division and, aged twenty-eight, Tommy was in his prime and a fixture in the England side. To put the move into perspective, it would be a little like Michael Owen choosing Chesterfield over Real Madrid when he left Liverpool in 2004.

Having been such an inspiration to me over the previous ten years it would have been a terrific thrill to have played alongside Tommy, perhaps at inside right. Instead, I was given the tricky task of stepping into the shoes of the man who had scored 26 goals in 34 matches for the Blues. Tommy was one of many star players to have appeared in the blue and white of Chelsea during its long history of chronic underachievement. The likes of Vivian Woodward, Hughie Gallagher, Harry Wilding, Vic Woodley, Jack Harrow, Ben Howard Baker and Alec Jackson had all represented the club. At one time in the 1940s the entire five-strong forward line had all been current internationals. Yet Chelsea had never got within a sniff of winning a major trophy, a War Cup final defeat against Charlton Athletic in 1944 being the sum of the club's achievements. Chelsea were, not unfairly, known as something of a joke in footballing circles and found themselves a frequent staple of the music hall comedians' repertoire. One gag of the time went as follows: 'Are you going to see Chelsea today? No, they never came to see me when I was ill.' Not the funniest response of all time, but indicative of the general contempt felt by many towards the Blues. It made many of the lads very annoyed, but I was determined to use it as an extra source of motivation.

I had been aware of the club's reputation when I joined, but had been impressed by Billy Birrell's insistence that their days of being the league's patsies were over, and his desire to build a championship-winning side. The club certainly had some top-class players on its books, including Len Goulden and Tommy Walker, and I was confident that we could confound the pundits.

Although the fee Chelsea paid for me was substantially less than what they had received for Tommy, expectations in west London were high when fans heard that I was to be the great man's replacement. However, having gone through such a difficult spell at Newcastle, I felt very positive when I first pulled on a blue shirt before the home match against Huddersfield Town. A crowd of almost 42,000 had turned out for the game, eight days after my arrival from Newcastle, and I was eager to make a quick impression on the home fans. Early in the match, Huddersfield's Irish international Peter Docherty caught me accidentally in the groin with a crunching tackle and I played the rest of the game in some pain. I was disappointed not to score on my first appearance, although I did set up our first goal by crossing for Bobby Campbell to net shortly before half-time. This was to be about as good as it got for Chelsea and we ended up losing 4-2, but I felt reasonably happy with my own performance.

My groin injury persisted for a few weeks but, unwilling to relinquish my place in the team, I played on unfit and found myself heavily criticised by spectators expecting me to fit into the team immediately. A series of poor results, culminating in a 0–3 reverse at Aston Villa at the end of February, sent Chelsea into the bottom three, just one place off the relegation zone. Changes in personnel were required and Billy Birrell rightly decided that I should be dropped.

I felt pretty miserable about the unimpressive start to my Blues career, particularly after one poor performance at Stamford Bridge when a spectator singled me out as we left the field. Passing within ten yards of the irate fan on way to the tunnel I heard him yell at the top of his voice: 'Get back to Newcastle where you belong, Bentley!' I can still see the man's face today; I was determined to prove him wrong, along with those other fans whom I heard mumbling that I would 'never replace Tommy Lawton'.

I knew that I had not done myself justice and that a spell out of the side was both inevitable and justified. For the time being I would have to train hard and regain the strength that I had lost in the chill North-East air. After a few weeks I found my weight increasing and, by spring, felt almost back to normal, which was a great relief to me.

The team's performances had improved in my absence and, after a fine 3–0 win at home to Charlton, it struck me that I might not play for the first team again that season. But football is nothing if not unpredictable and within a week I was back in the side after a freak injury to Jimmy Bowie. Playing billiards the night before our trip to Arsenal, Jimmy had lost his balance while attempting a long pot and fallen awkwardly on his leg. Having failed to recover by kick-off time on Saturday, an embarrassed Jimmy had to sit out the match and I was given my chance to impress in his absence.

Throughout my career I always liked playing at Highbury, regarding it as somewhat of a lucky ground for me, and my 'comeback' match for Chelsea would be no exception. Feeling well on the way to my physical recovery, I put in my best performance since leaving Bristol City two years earlier. Bobby Campbell gave us a half-time lead and I extended our advantage five minutes into the second period with a firm shot from outside the area. It was my first goal for Chelsea and secured an impressive 2-0 win. The next week I scored my first goal at Stamford Bridge in a 2-2 draw with Manchester City and I was in the team to stay.

Chelsea successfully staved off the threat of relegation, finishing eighteenth out of twenty-two, but it was clear that things needed to improve the following season if the club was to banish its music-hall-joke status. Mindful that many of his best players, including Tommy Walker and Len Goulden, were ageing, Billy wanted to build a younger side. Judging that some fresh competition was necessary for goalkeeper Harry Medhurst, Billy dipped into the transfer market to acquire twenty-two-year-old Peter Pickering from York City, and the youngster soon broke into the side. Right-back Sid Bathgate was also in his early twenties, as were left-winger Jimmy Macaulay and outside right Bobby Campbell.

The team got 1948/49 off to a winning start by beating Middlesbrough 1-0 at home, in front of 57,000 fans, with me scoring the only goal. Our next match was an away trip to Newcastle, who had belied the acrimony behind the scenes and secured promotion from the Second Division the previous May. I was relieved to be given a warm reception by the Geordie fans, although they were none too impressed to see me score one of Chelsea's goals in a 2-2 draw.

Two further draws and two defeats followed before we met Everton at home, a match that would have a profound effect on my Chelsea career. Len Goulden had suggested that I move from outside right to centre forward and we thrashed Everton 6-0, with me scoring twice. A couple of weeks later I notched another brace in a 4-3 home defeat against Stoke and, after another goal in a 1-1 draw at home to Manchester United, the national newspapers started touting my name in connection with a possible England cap. By the end of the season I would be an England international. In the meantime Chelsea were building up a decent head of steam in the League, even if we were not yet in a position to challenge the big guns for a tilt at the title.

A 4-1 home win against Wolves a couple of weeks before Christmas had Billy thinking he may have cracked the club's age-old problem of our flattering to deceive. By this time I felt that I had finally made a full physical recovery and against Wolves used my regained strength to play my old 'roving' game, scoring twice and setting up both Jimmy Bowie's goals.

All too predictably, the advent of the new year saw Chelsea slide down the league table and we finished a disappointing thirteenth, five points clear of relegated sides Sheffield United and Preston. One of the highlights of the second half of the campaign was our 5-3 victory against Preston, an occasion in which I scored my first Chelsea hat-trick, although I have to admit that it was rather fluky. The first goal was originally credited to a teammate who had slid the ball over the line to make sure it went in; the second bounced into my path off Jimmy Macaulay with the defenders swearing I was offside; the third came when I charged the goalkeeper over the goal-line in the closing seconds. Still, they all count.

In January 1949 the FA Cup provided me with an emotional return to Ashton Gate when Chelsea were drawn away to Bristol City in the third round. There was much interest in my home town surrounding my return and I was asked to write a personal message to the people of the city in the *Traveller* newspaper. It was a lovely idea on behalf of the paper and I was more than willing to take the opportunity to thank the local supporters. They had given me so much encouragement during my eight-year stay at City and I had very fond memories of the club. It was also an opportunity for my parents to watch me play. Living so far from London they didn't get to see many of my games.

The atmosphere at Ashton Gate was electric, with 37,000 fans crammed in, that number being swelled by two ultra-loyal Blues supporters, film star Richard (now Lord) Attenborough and his wife Sheila. 'Dickie' was as surprised as the rest of us when our Third Division opponents took an early lead through young Don Clark. With ten minutes to go my dad was also sweating on the result. A number of his friends and colleagues wanted to bet against Dad on the result but, not being a gambler, he had at first refused to take the bait. When one chap raised the stakes by offering very attractive odds on my scoring a goal Dad's resolve buckled and he laid down what was, for him, a fair-sized bet. He was certainly not enjoying the game.

Fortunately, Benny Jones was to save the day. With City fans dreaming of a First Division scalp and the opportunity to put one over on one of their old boys, Benny ran to the byline and pulled back an inch-perfect cross for me to score with a downward header at the far post. Sighs of relief were audible from the visiting west Londoners and also from my relieved father. Benny then put us into a 2-1 lead before I rubbed salt into my old team's wounds with a third goal in the last minute. It had been a triumphant return home.

Before the end of the season I was chosen to represent the Football Combination in an exhibition match against Belgian side Diables Rouge in Brussels, and also played for the Football League against the League of Ireland. Against the Irish I was given the opportunity to partner my old pal Len Shackleton for the first time since we had both left Newcastle. We won the match 5-0, with Shack and I both scoring twice, and after the game we chatted about how both of our careers had moved on. There was definitely a feeling of sadness that we had not been able to play for longer in the same forward line. A week later I made my first appearance for England against Sweden in Stockholm, one of the proudest days of my life, and one that I will discuss at length later.

1949/50 was an exciting season at Stamford Bridge, despite our talented squad's failure to string a consistent run of results together at any time during the season. Another solid but unspectacular League campaign petered out as Chelsea again finished in thirteenth position, well clear of safety but a long way from championship glory. It would be the FA Cup, the world's oldest football competition, which provided the backdrop for that season's uncharacteristically hard-fought tilt at silverware.

For the second successive year the third round saw me lining up against a former team, in this case Newcastle United. Pitted against big Frank Brennan I knew I would have my work cut out and the wily centre half shadowed me all over the pitch. Fortunately, Frank's teammates were not in such good form that afternoon and we found ourselves two-up within twenty-five minutes. Jack Fairbrother, in the Newcastle goal, made a howler for the first score, allowing a tame long-distance shot by Hugh Billington to spin out of his hands and into the net. Ten minutes later Bobby Campbell and I were involved in the build-up to the second goal, again scored by Hugh. A third goal by Bobby late in the game secured an easy victory and had newspapers crowing over our cup chances. One journalist, Brian Chapman, was particularly fulsome in his praise: 'This new, sparkling, spanking Chelsea that dazzled the daylights out of Newcastle could reasonably reach the final.' Chapman went on to give an accurate explanation of why the team had failed so consistently in the League: 'What was the difference in Chelsea against Newcastle? Simply that the said sparkle, instead of vanishing as usual after twenty minutes, went on for most of the ninety.'

The fifth round saw us drawn at home to lowly Chesterfield, a match that an unusually large crowd of 59,000 expected us to win easily. Realising the futility of trying to outplay a team two divisions above them, our guests resorted to spoiling tactics, sitting back and inviting us to attack their packed defence. The winter months had, not for the last time, caused havoc to the Stamford Bridge turf and the sand-covered surface made our brand of attacking football even more difficult. With less than twenty minutes to go there was still no score but we showed true grit to score three goals and run out comfortable winners. If only we could have applied ourselves in that manner in the league. I scored the first two goals and had the chance for a hat-trick but, spotting Hugh (Billington) in a better position, centred for him to shoot into an open goal. We were through to an enticing quarter-final clash at home to Manchester United.

The match, on the first Saturday in March, was a classic cup tie played at a frenetic pace. The state of the Stamford Bridge pitch had improved enough for us to impose our passing game on United and, starting brightly, we had taken a commanding two-goal lead within twenty minutes of play. Bobby Campbell netted the first with a shot that bounced awkwardly in front of United goalkeeper Jack Crompton. The second goal, scored by me, was one of the best of my entire career. A clever back-heel by Billy Gray came towards me, bouncing slightly as I ran on to it. Thirty yards from goal, I curled the ball hard on the volley straight into the corner of the net. Sadly, this was long before television coverage of football, so I could never show the goal to my grandchildren. What a pity. United fought back strongly after their terrible start but players like Reg Williams, Ken Armstrong and Frank Mitchell played out of their skins and we never looked like surrendering our lead. The scoreline stayed at 2-0 until the very end and, as we left the field, we knew we were only ninety minutes from Wembley. In a typically courteous gesture, United manager Matt Busby visited our dressing room after the match, telling us that we had been 'too good' for his team and wishing us luck in our next match. Crowded around the transistor on Monday lunchtime after training had finished, we were excited to hear that the mighty Arsenal would be our semi-final opponents. Having beaten United so convincingly we didn't feel the need to fear anybody.

The match was played two weekends later, on 19 March at Tottenham's White Hart Lane ground. Pumped up by skipper Johnny Harris's team talk we flew out of the traps and, for the second tie in a row, found ourselves two goals ahead after barely a quarter of the match. Firstly a clearance by Frank Mitchell landed at my feet and, having dribbled the ball into the Arsenal half, I chipped goalkeeper George Swindin who for some reason had advanced towards the edge of his goalmouth. The ball struck the underside of the crossbar before crossing the line. Five minutes later our full-back Billy Hughes played a long ball into the area and I out-jumped the defender to score with a header. Mindful of the dangers of sitting back, we continued to attack the Gunners' goal with gusto but, just before the referee blew for half-time, they scored a fluke goal to get back into the match. The conditions on the day were blustery and when Arsenal's Freddie Cox sliced a corner-kick into the penalty area it caught a freak gust of wind and flew inside the near post.

The goal was a body blow and gave Arsenal the belief that their name was on the cup. In the second half Hugh pulled a muscle and was farmed out to the wing as a virtual passenger, but we continued to hold out against a renewed Arsenal onslaught. Reg Williams should have put the result beyond doubt with fifteen minutes to go, but skied an easy chance over the bar. Our punishment came within sixty seconds. As his side were awarded another corner, Arsenal's Denis Compton, the last man to represent England at both football and cricket, motioned for his brother Leslie to run into the box for the set piece. Their skipper Joe Mercer was livid and shouted at Leslie to get back, but the defender ignored this advice and leapt to meet brother Denis's corner with his head. I was marking Leslie and missed the ball completely. As I landed Leslie headed the ball against my shoulder, altering the flight of the ball and deceiving Harry Medhurst. It was 2-2. I had completed an unfortunate hat-trick.

The momentum was by now entirely with the Gunners and when the referee signalled the end of the ninety minutes we felt relieved, although desperately disappointed at having thrown away a two-goal lead. The replay took place four days later, and was played at White Hart Lane again. The match was a more insipid affair and swirling rain combined with a treacherous waterlogged surface made passing extremely difficult. We ran our hearts out but to no avail, Freddie Cox again plunging a dagger into our hearts with the only goal of the game. The dressing room afterwards resembled a morgue. We had come so close to reaching a cup final, but had nothing to show for our efforts. Arsenal went on to win the final 2-0 against Liverpool.

Having enjoyed a good run of form in the closing months of the season, I was chosen as a member of England's ill-fated 1950 World Cup squad. I will reflect on that tournament in the chapter of this book that deals with my England career. At this point I will just say that 29 June 1950, the date of England's infamous 1-0 defeat to the United States, was one of the lowest moments of my career.

Upon returning to Britain in early July I was dismayed when instructed to report for pre-season training almost immediately. I had been playing football continuously for very nearly a whole year, the nine-month domestic campaign being followed by a gruelling pre-World Cup tour of Belgium and Portugal, and then the tournament itself in the stifling heat of Rio de Janeiro. To this day international footballers find themselves driven to the absolute limit of their physical endurance by the demands of all-year-round competition. It is only in recent years that clubs have begun to accommodate the tiredness of their top players by using the 'squad rotation' system, first championed in the UK by Chelsea managers Ruud Gullit and Gianluca Vialli. I see this as a definite change for the better in the English game.

I felt that I had been worked like a dog and was very fortunate that Chelsea understood my predicament. Having seen me struggling during pre-season running, Billy Birrell took me to one side and suggested I have a two-week break. The fortnight's rest did me the power of good, giving my jaded muscles a break and taking my mind away from the sheer relentlessness of the previous season. By the time the 1950/51 season got under way I was raring to go again.

The club's gesture indicated to me a willingness on behalf of the Chelsea hierarchy to show concern for their players' best interests and a realisation that such a policy would reap dividends for the club itself. I would soon find to my cost that this was to be a rare example of sensitivity to the playing staff. As the 1950/51 season dragged on, it became apparent that the club's attitude was becoming even more rooted in their amateurish pre-war days.

Having finished thirteenth for the previous two years I felt that the next step for Chelsea was to move into the top half, maybe even top third, of the table and I thought we had the players on our books to make this a possibility. When we swept aside newly promoted Sheffield Wednesday 4-0 on the first day of the season, it appeared that my confidence was well-placed. Having opened my account for the season with a brace and providing the openings for both the other goals, I felt on top of the world. However, Chelsea's form quickly plummeted and within weeks the team was in freefall. Part of the problem was that Billy Birrell had lost his way. His methods were stuck resolutely in the 1930s and, in similar vein to many managers both before and afterwards, he had failed to recognise that the game was changing around him. Billy was a real gentleman and a good man-manager, but when it came to tactics his game was pretty basic. For instance, I was still waiting, at the age of twenty-six, for my first professional training session with a football, a state of affairs that now appears laughable. I also found myself deeply frustrated at the complacent attitude among many of my teammates, who seemed to accept that Chelsea were indeed a 'joke team' and that nothing could be done to alter that public perception. In training the players seemingly did as they pleased and gravitated into small cliques of three or four, rather than work together as a team. It was as if some of the players felt they had to live up to the club's music-hall reputation. Having made good friends with skipper Johnny Harris, the pair of us attempted to instil a stronger sense of discipline within the team, but without the support of those in charge this was a forlorn task. Some of the lads seemed more interested in the results of their Saturday bets on the greyhounds or the horses than the matches they were playing in. Up at Liverpool one day the ball went out of play and I ran to get it back in order to take a quick throw-in. One of my team-mates reached the ball before me but, instead of taking the throw immediately, turned to the trainer and asked, 'What won the 2.30?' At half-time Johnny and I gave him a rollicking, but our words went in one ear and out the other.

One of the greatest pros at the club during my early years at Stamford Bridge was the legendary inside forward Tommy Walker. He was a pleasure to play alongside and an exemplary fair-minded professional, the Gary Lineker of his day, if you like. I don't think Tommy was ever booked in his career and I don't remember him ever giving a foul away in his career. There was one incident, though, when Tommy's sense of fair play led to a brief fallout between us on the pitch. Challenging an opponent for a fifty-fifty tackle I won the ball with a hard but legal shoulder-charge that left the defender laid out on the floor. Sensing a goal-scoring opportunity, I carried on running and passed the ball to where Tommy should have been, and where he would have had virtually an open goal. I was astonished to find Tommy helping my opponent to his feet. When I shouted at him for not being in a position to score he told me, 'You can't do that with that lad on the floor.' I wasn't too happy about it, but in a way I respected him for what he'd done. His mentality was certainly different from that which I had encountered during wartime football, where many players actively went out with the intention of hurting you. Interestingly, I was reminded of Tommy's actions that day when Paolo di Canio made a similar gesture while playing for West Ham in a match at Goodison Park in 2000. In front of an open goal di Canio caught the ball in his hands and rushed to help Everton's stricken goalkeeper Paul Gerrard who had turned over his leg attempting to make a clearance. The Italian received a Fair Play award from FIFA for his actions, whereas poor old Tommy just got a mouthful of abuse from me!

Towards the end of the 1950/51 season we were resolutely stuck in the bottom two relegation places. With time running out, Billy Birrell decided to make a change of captain. I had deputised for Johnny Harris while he was out of the side injured and, upon his recall to the side, Billy decided to retain me as team skipper while giving Johnny the title of 'club captain'. My good friend Johnny was typically generous when informed of the decision and was the first player to shake me by the hand and congratulate me. I thought he had been a grand captain and admired greatly his calm temperament and man-management skills. I decided that, rather than attempt a completely different style of captaincy to distinguish myself from Johnny, I would instead incorporate much of his leadership style. Johnny was a great help to me throughout my captaincy of Chelsea and taught me how to approach certain players, telling me how some lads needed kid-glove treatment, while others needed a kick up the backside.

To avoid relegation to the Second Division we needed fighters and there was no greater man to be alongside in the trenches than right half Ken Armstrong. Ken was a tower of strength in the middle of the park, running non-stop for ninety minutes, tackling, being available for passes, even when under pressure, and making valuable interceptions. He rarely made a bad pass, although his utter dependability as the side's engine and willingness to do our dirty work meant that Ken never got the recognition he deserved. It was bordering on scandalous that he only made one appearance in England's colours, especially when you see caps handed out willy-nilly nowadays.

With four games remaining things looked bleak for Chelsea. We were marooned in bottom position, four points behind Sheffield Wednesday and six behind Everton. If there was to be any hope whatsoever of survival we would have to win all four matches and hope that other results went our way. Such a feat would be exceptionally difficult and the mentality around the club had been so negative all year that we looked doomed. I can't remember what odds the bookies were giving on us to stay up, but they must have been lengthy.

Just when all seemed lost the players dug deep into their personal reserves and the team uncovered a hidden fighting spirit at the eleventh hour. We won three games in a row, against Liverpool, Wolves and Fulham, to give us a fighting chance. Even at this stage we were still favourites to go down. With one match to play, we and Sheffield Wednesday filled the relegation spots, each with 30 points from 41 games. Wednesday's final opponents of the season were Everton, who were themselves on 32 points. These were the days of two points for a win, so the only chance we had of survival was to win our own game, against Bolton, and hope that Wednesday would defeat Everton. We needed both these results to happen in order for Wednesday and Everton to be relegated instead of us, on the grounds that they each had a worse goal average. To complicate matters, we also needed both ourselves and Wednesday to rack up large winning margins. If Everton lost only narrowly they would stay in the First Division, unless we hit double figures, which was a virtual impossibility. And if Wednesday won by scoring substantially more goals than we managed, then Chelsea could still be for the drop.

Nowadays English football works on the more straightforward basis of 'goal difference', by subtracting the number of goals a team has conceded from the number they have scored. 'Goal average' was more complicated, relying on the number of goals scored being divided by the number conceded. If we conceded a goal against Bolton our average would be badly damaged, perhaps irreparably. It was all rather confusing, but we knew we just had to try and play our normal game and not allow thoughts of the match at Hillsborough to affect us.

The players felt very positive about our chances and were eager to get on with the match against a Bolton team who were eighth in the table and had nothing to play for except pride. However, in an act of gross ineptitude, the Chelsea board of directors announced a five-day tour of Denmark to take place in the week leading up to the crucial game. In the twenty-first century a manager might take his players to a holiday resort, to relax them and take their minds off football. By contrast, we were told that we would have to play a series of strenuous matches against Danish sides instead of putting our feet up and conserving our energies. I was absolutely disgusted by what I saw as a crass gesture by the directors who seemed to have thrown in the towel and accepted that Stamford Bridge would host Second Division football the next season. As captain I made my feelings known, but my pleas for the trip to be postponed by a week or so fell on deaf ears. We returned to Britain unhappy with the way our own club seemed to have written us off, but determined to prove their attitude wrong.

Matchday mornings were always tense affairs, but the hours leading up to kick-off on 5 May, our day of destiny, were even more tetchy. Sometimes players would walk around and gee up their teammates and maybe share a laugh and joke. On this occasion the dressing room was silent, with players sitting stony-faced, focusing on the task ahead. Billy Birrell gave us a team-talk and told us we had a fighting chance, although he didn't sound entirely convinced.

Roared on by a fervent home crowd, we received an early scare when Bolton's outside right Ronnie Codd lobbed our goalkeeper Bill Robertson. It looked for a moment as though he had been beaten, but Bill threw up a hand and somehow clawed the ball from under the crossbar. Having recovered from the fright, we went all-out on the attack and, after eighteen minutes, took the lead when I headed in from a corner. Two minutes later I scored another with my bonce, from a pinpoint Sid Tickeridge free-kick. One of the most famous photographs of my career shows me appearing to stand on my head as I fall to the ground moments after connecting with the ball, which is nestling in the back of the Wednesday net.

Barely another five minutes passed before young Bobby Smith, our fledgling centre forward, cracked home a left-foot piledriver from the edge of the box. As half-time approached, the score from Hillsborough was put up on the pitch-side manual scoreboard. A great roar went around the ground as the interval scoreline of Sheffield Wednesday 3 Everton 0 was displayed. As we sat sucking our half-time oranges we were unaware that, if the scores stayed the same, we would stay up by the skin of our teeth.

Ten minutes into the second half, Bobby ran onto my pass to strike another fine goal, after which there was no further scoring from our match. Towards the end, the full-time score from Sheffield was displayed on the board, showing that Wednesday had won 6-0. There were no cheers at this news, more a collective gasp, with both spectators and players struggling to work out what the combination of the two scores meant. At the final whistle streams of young lads came running on to the pitch in their blazers and caps, shouting excitedly. This was a day when the boys' hours of working out long division with pencil and pad at school came to fruition. They had worked out that Chelsea were safe by the infinitesimal margin of 0.04 of a goal. We hurried back to the dressing room to find a relieved Billy Birrell sitting alongside his own pad and paper, and he confirmed that we had indeed scraped home. I felt a brief tinge of sympathy for Sheffield Wednesday who, having won by six goals, must have expected to avoided relegation, but my overall feelings were of joy and relief.

It had been a great achievement to preserve our First Division status against such overwhelming odds but, after joining in a brief round of celebratory back-slapping my thoughts hardened. A team like ours, containing so much talent, should not have found itself in such a desperate position and I felt that a proper inquest was necessary into our collective failings. If we were to avoid another season of failure root-and-branch reform was needed, but I knew that, under the current regime, evolution instead of revolution was about the best I could hope for.

It soon became clear that even a small change was unlikely to happen at Chelsea and, as the dust settled on the previous season, I became increasingly disillusioned with life at the Bridge. A series of off-field events would follow, rapidly accelerating my feelings of unhappiness and creating a rift between myself and the club. The subsequent row almost ended my Chelsea career, and indeed threatened my whole future in the game.

SIX

On Strike

The negotiation of playing contracts and transfers between clubs has changed dramatically over the last five decades. The past ten years in particular have seen an unprecedented shift in the power balance between football's employers and employees. In the post-Bosman era of football, Premiership players and their agents are the kings and the clubs mere princes when it comes to negotiating agreements. Footballers today can walk out of their club at the end of their contract and join a rival team without the need for any transfer fee, thereby earning themselves lucrative signing-on fees. Frightened by the prospect of losing players for nothing, clubs will often offer increased wages and bonuses to those on their books who still have two or more years left on their existing contracts. Such a scenario was absolutely unthinkable when I was plying my trade, a time when the term 'player power' merely referred to the speed of a footballer's shot.

In the 1950s, the era when I was at my peak, there was a maximum wage in place, at a level barely higher than the national average salary. The game's top players, like Stanley Matthews, Tom Finney and Stan Mortensen, could not expect to earn much more than a postman. There were no extended contracts for players either. Clubs held the whip hand at all times and were never frightened of flexing their muscles. They only ever had to offer players a one-year extension at the end of the season and none of us would ever know for sure whether we would be among those retained or kicked out of the door. If a player was offered terms for the following year but told the club he wanted a transfer, he was given no choice but to stay. The player's club had the right to retain his registration and prevent him from joining another team if they so desired. In return for all this we were expected to be grateful and show unwavering loyalty to our clubs.

On at least one occasion I was offered lucrative deals to sign for South American clubs, who were from outside FIFA, the game's governing body. The most enticing offer was made by Colombian side Bogota who offered me a huge salary, with a house and car thrown in for good measure. I was very tempted, but knew that I would be burning my bridges if I agreed to the move. I only had to look at what had happened to poor Neil Franklin. England's top centre half in the late 1940s, Neil turned down the opportunity to play in the 1950 World Cup, choosing instead to sign for Bogota. His transfer was regarded as scandalous and Neil found himself ostracised by the English FA. I was not prepared to let the same thing happen to me. When Neil's move turned sour he decided to return home, only to find that the FA had suspended him for a further year. When he was eventually allowed to play, Neil found himself in the humble surroundings of Hull City. No First Division club would touch him with a bargepole. It certainly wasn't an easy life being a footballer back then.

In May 1951 I was called in by Billy Birrell and offered another year's contract. Instead of agreeing immediately to re-sign for Chelsea, I sought some assurances about my personal future and the direction in which the manager saw the team moving. I was unhappy with the club's training regime, or lack of it, and also the directors' ongoing lack of ambition and what I regarded as their unprofessional and uncaring attitude.

One example of the latter came towards the end of the 1950/51 season when the board refused to allow me to appear in a benefit match for my former Bristol City trainer Len Southway. I desperately wanted to play in the game as a small gesture of thanks to Len, who had been so good to me in my early years in the game. Due to Chelsea's involvement in a relegation battle at the time I was forbidden from appearing, and accepted the board's decision, fully understanding their reasoning. However, within a week I was told that I must play in a separate benefit match for a bloke who I'd never even heard of. This smacked to me of double standards and I told the manager exactly how angry I was. For once the club saw sense and backed down.

The fact was that this kind of incident was far from rare at Chelsea. For instance, the debacle of the Danish tour arranged in the build-up to our crucial relegation decider came less than a fortnight later. I had just about had enough of such amateurism and decided to use my position as one of the team's best players to try and win some concessions from the club.

I was keen to find out if Billy would be going into the transfer market to strengthen the team. There were players at Chelsea who had quite simply become too comfortable in the team and needed replacing, although I would never have gone behind their backs and pointed out who they were. After much 'umming and ahhing' from Billy it was obvious that no transfers were forthcoming. I had also been made some promises that I felt needed some clarification. At twenty-seven years old I knew that I had a limited period of time playing at the top, maybe six or seven years, and had begun thinking about my long-term future, being the family's breadwinner. By now my daughter Loraine was four, and Vi and myself were thinking of planning another addition to the family, but we were far from well off financially. I wanted to know where I stood with the club.

I had already decided that after I hung up my boots I would like to stay in the game in a coaching capacity. The previous summer both Billy and the Chelsea chairman Joe Mears had promised me a job as a coach at the end of my career, but nothing further had been mentioned. I wanted a solid offer in writing, but the club seemed reluctant to agree to this demand. I was annoyed. If the offer didn't stand then they needed to tell me outright, rather than shilly-shally around. I knew they weren't being straight with me.

Far from providing me with reassurance, my meeting with Billy had just made me feel even more disillusioned at the club, so I asked for a transfer. This was refused point blank, so in an act of defiance

I refused to sign the contract offered to me, saying I would rather go on strike than play for Chelsea. I gambled that this threat would spur the club into meeting at least some of my demands. As I swept out of Billy's office, I half expected to be called back and told that it was all a misunderstanding; that the club would listen to what I had to say. At most I thought the strike would last for a day or so and then blow over. I had badly misjudged the situation.

As I left the ground I bumped into Johnny Harris, who told me that he too had refused to sign. The previous summer Johnny had been promised the assistant manager's job when Billy finally stepped down but, as with my job offer, the club refused to clarify the position in writing. Johnny was disconsolate. He was the last man to ever cause trouble, a chap with blue blood running through his veins, loyal to teammates and manager alike. Discussing what had now become a two-man strike we walked together along the Embankment and looked out at the river Thames, wondering what on earth to do next. The club were clearly unwilling to give in to a single one of our demands, but realised that their actions risked upsetting the supporters. To lose one captain was unfortunate; to lose two looked very careless. They quickly came out fighting and Billy Birrell gave a newspaper interview stating that we had been offered 'everything the club is permitted to offer'. Billy also made reference to the fact that both of us had undertaken part-time jobs in addition to our role on the Chelsea playing staff. Billy told the newspaper, 'We have offered them more than most clubs do because we are willing to permit them to continue with their part-time jobs.'

This felt a little unfair, firstly because our jobs had never infringed on our obligations to the club. Chelsea's training sessions would take place in the morning, and Johnny and I would then go to work elsewhere in the afternoons, when our teammates had all gone home. Secondly, the reason we had taken out a second job was not because we were in any way greedy. It was because we needed the money to have a decent standard of living in London. The Bentley family were hardly living the life of Riley. For starters I couldn't afford to own a car, taking the

Piccadilly Line into Chelsea after walking to the station from our rented accommodation in the far from salubrious surroundings of 8 Park Avenue, Park Royal. I have no wish to denigrate Park Royal at all. I'm merely pointing out that we were not exactly living it up, eating oysters and drinking champagne. Our house, a modest three-bedroom affair, was being leased from the club, who were reluctant to sell it to us. I was anxious to get my foot on to the property ladder, and earning £12 a week was certainly making this difficult. In order to look after Vi, who was a full-time housewife, and my daughter Loraine and to plan financially for the future, I needed another source of income. I therefore took a job selling stationary for a company called J.C. King and spent my afternoons visiting big companies, trying to secure large orders.

There were suggestions in the newspapers that my combined salary was £30 a week, which was way off the mark and I felt put me in a bad light. The bare facts were that, after tax, I was making an average of £12 a week. In the end I was on strike for eight weeks, which put a considerable strain on my family. Some of the Chelsea lads kept my spirits high, phoning to say that Johnny and I were doing the right thing. A few weeks into our industrial action the chairman of the Players' Union also called to offer his support and acknowledge that Johnny and I were helping his members' cause. A year earlier the Players' Union had threatened to stage a national strike to improve players' conditions but had backed off at the last minute. Unfortunately, the union was pretty toothless back then and resorted to cheering us on from the sidelines rather than giving us any kind of financial or legal support. I wondered why I was bothering to pay my dues.

Early in the dispute I had been willing to stay on strike indefinitely, until all my demands were met, but the longer it continued I could see I was getting absolutely nowhere. Chelsea were not prepared to budge an inch and I knew deep down that my action was damaging the family, as well as giving me a bad name in the press. Chelsea's League season began without either Johnny or me, although my fellow militant could not bear to be away from the action and stood on the terraces wearing a cloth cap and glasses so he wouldn't be recognised by fans. We were both itching to play and felt that we were letting our teammates down by refusing to join them on the field.

On Friday 24 August I spoke to Johnny and told him that I wanted to call off the strike. He reluctantly agreed and we both went back, cap in hand, to re-sign our forms for the 1951/52 campaign. I wasn't prepared to completely roll over though and, after signing the contract, I immediately asked for a transfer. Again the club refused my request. I did manage to secure a brief public relations victory, by giving an exclusive statement to newspaper journalist Alan Hoby, which was then reproduced almost word for word in print. The statement included the following extract: 'The clubs have footballers over a barrel. They've got the money, and we're the tools. They can pay us pretty well what they think they'll pay, no matter how good we are, and how useful we are to them. I knew that by refusing to re-sign I could create sufficient interest for people to want to know my reasons... There was a suggestion that I should show loyalty to the club. But I feel that the way I fought to help Chelsea against relegation last season showed the extent of my loyalty.' More than fifty years on, I still feel exactly the same and, despite the strike's abject end, I am glad that I fought my corner. To this day I find it very hard to believe that the situation ever happened.

During our enforced absence Johnny and I had kept fit by running together along the Embankment a few times each week and also by playing rounds of golf. Once our dispute was over we were still a little off the pace, having not played competitively for four months, and both faced a race to regain our match fitness in time for the following week's trip to Portsmouth. We volunteered for extra fitness training and a photograph appeared in a newspaper of us running on our own around an empty Stamford Bridge. It was a striking image, if you'll pardon the pun.

By the next week I was back in the side and, running out at Fratton Park, I realised just what I had been missing. By contrast, poor Johnny had pulled a muscle by overdoing things in training and was forced to watch from the stands, although at least he didn't need to wear his disguise this time around. I quickly got back into the swing of playing football and, despite my failure to secure any compromise from Chelsea, I was glad to be back. Having gone through such a difficult period, I was more determined than ever to do well for Chelsea.

We lost my first match back in the team 1-0 but, after scoring in four consecutive matches, I decided to let bygones be bygones and came off the transfer list at the end of September. However, the club's season would differ little from the previous campaign and we found ourselves facing another struggle to avoid relegation. A 5-0 home win against Middlesbrough was one rare highlight, with Jimmy D'Arcy scoring a hat-trick and myself getting two. Had I not missed a first-half penalty I would have been fighting Jimmy for the match ball in the dressing room.

Thirty-yard goals were far rarer in the 1950s than today, due to the weight of the old-fashioned lace-up ball, but I managed one such effort in what was arguably our best win of the season, a 4-2 triumph over Manchester United. We had trailed the Red Devils 2-0 and our comeback made the rest of the league sit up. Jimmy was having his best season at the club, notching another two goals, with Bobby Smith completing the scoring, to enhance his burgeoning reputation. However, our League form continued to splutter along in first gear.

The FA Cup was quite another story though, and another two goals for me on 2 February helped us to a 4-0 win at home to Tranmere Rovers in the fourth round. Having got so close to Wembley two years earlier, we were desperate to make amends and, drawn away to Leeds United, then of the Second Division, we started to scent a cup run. After drawing 1-1 in the first match, Bobby Smith scoring our goal, it was back to Stamford Bridge for the fifth round replay. The build-up to this match would see one of the most bizarre chapters of my footballing career, the infamous 'Elephant Gang' episode.

The envelope looked innocent enough, with 'Roy Bentley, Chelsea FC, Stamford Bridge, London' the address on the front, accompanied by two stamps bearing the Queen's head. I was used to getting mail from supporters and was always happy to reply with an autographed piece of paper or photograph. Casually tearing open the envelope I was given quite a shock when I read its contents. 'Listen. You better lose in your next cup game or else you will get your big head bashed in. We told Alec Forbes of the Arsenal. Now he will get it for not taking notice. The Elephant Gang.'

Although quite tickled by the jibe about the size of my head, it was a little unsettling for both myself and Alec, whose Arsenal team had beaten Leyton Orient shortly after he had received his letter. It appeared to be the work of a crank but, not wanting to take any chances, I called the police. They sent the letter to the national press and several newspapers reproduced a photograph of it, in case anyone recognised the handwriting of the 'gang member'. The police never caught the culprit, although he never wrote to me again, and we eventually beat Leeds after a second replay.

Our quarter-final tie at Sheffield United saw us get the kind of lucky breaks that are associated with teams who believe that 'their name is on the cup.' Footballers are notoriously superstitious creatures and the fact that we won the game 1-0 with practically our only attack of the match made us feel that 1952 would indeed be our year. My goal in the twenty-eighth minute, a tap-in after good work from Jimmy D'Arcy, was followed by an hour of playing with our backs to the wall. An unbelievable miss by a Sheffield forward a yard from goal in the closing minutes ensured we would meet our nemeses, Arsenal, in the semi-final.

The Chelsea and Arsenal FA Cup rivalry has been legendary in recent years, with the Gunners well in command. Arsenal emerged victorious in the fifth round in 2001, the final itself in 2002, the sixth round in 2003, and the fifth round again in 2004. The situation was similar in 1952, with the teams meeting for the third time in six seasons. The third round of 1947, before my time at Chelsea, had taken two replays to decide, with Arsenal winning 2-0 at the third time of asking. The 1950 season had, of course, seen us lose another replay 1-0 after throwing away a two-goal cushion in the first tie. We hoped that 1952 would be third time lucky for us.

Arsenal were fighting for a League and cup double, while we were engaged in our annual flirtation with relegation. Yet, although very much underdogs, we were ready to seek vengeance on our North

London cousins. A violent snowstorm caused the postponement of the original match at White Hart Lane and the two teams were asked to go back a week later, knowing that the winners would face Newcastle United in the final. My old team had beaten Blackburn Rovers 2-1 in a replay three days earlier and the thought of facing my muckers Jackie Milburn, Frank Brennan and Joe Harvey at Wembley gave the semi-final even more spice.

Freddie Cox, the man who had done for us two years earlier, again popped up with a goal to put the Gunners in front, but a controversial equaliser by young Billy Gray gave us a second bite of the cherry. Bobby Smith had run on to meet a lobbed pass from a teammate but the lightning reflexes of Arsenal 'keeper George Swindin allowed him to reach the ball at the same instant. The pair collided at high speed and, as the pair lay poleaxed on the ground, our winger Jimmy Smith crossed for Billy to head into an unguarded net. The Arsenal protests were lengthy but the referee, who had been in a good position, awarded the goal and we had earned ourselves a reprieve. In the replay Arsenal were far too good for us and Freddie would again be our tormentor, scoring the first two goals as we were brushed aside 3-0.

Defeat in an FA Cup semi-final for the third time in my career was a bitter pill to swallow. We had enjoyed a brief run of form prior to our clashes with Arsenal and had already staved off relegation, so our final League matches saw us with nothing to play for and the season fizzled out with a 1-1 draw at Charlton, leaving us in nineteenth place.

This was to be Billy Birrell's last game in charge. He had been manager at Chelsea for thirteen years but realised that the game was changing rapidly and that a new man with fresh ideas was needed. Despite their intransigence at the start of the campaign, the directors had enough foresight to share Billy's opinion and decided they should appoint a replacement from outside the club. The board wanted a young, energetic manager to blow away the cobwebs and it was after much deliberation that they announced the identity of the new man in the dugout. Within three years their decision would become regarded as arguably the best in the club's history.

SEVEN

Drake's Fleet Sets Sail

When Billy announced his intention to retire the board did not rush to pick a replacement, choosing instead to listen to various opinions from within the game before drawing up a shortlist. Within weeks one name, that of Ted Drake, stood out as their preferred candidate. Ted had been a star forward at Arsenal in the 1930s, once scoring an astonishing seven goals in an afternoon against Aston Villa, and winning League titles and FA Cups with the Gunners. As a boy my support had alternated between Chelsea and Arsenal, and Ted was one of my heroes. I had even had a picture of him pinned to my bedroom wall at Meadow Grove. Sadly Ted had suffered a bad back injury while serving for the Royal Air Force in the Second World War and had been forced to retire prematurely.

Ted missed playing terribly, but decided to focus on the next best thing, being a football manager. In 1947 he had been appointed boss at Reading, of the Third Division (South). With a very small budget and defying low expectations, Ted had led the team to second-place finishes in both 1948/49 and 1951/52. On both occasions restrictive Football League rules, allowing only the champions to be promoted, deprived Ted of the success his efforts deserved.

Having cut his managerial teeth over five years at Elm Park, Ted felt ready to manage at the top level and his name was put forward for higher-profile positions. Yet, despite his evident ambition, when Ted was offered the Stamford Bridge hot seat, he surprised his suitors by asking for time to think things over. Perhaps realising that he would get just one crack at First Division management, Ted wanted to make sure he was aware of exactly what he was letting himself in for at Chelsea.

His first calls were to myself and Johnny Harris, asking us to accompany him for a round of golf. As club captain and team captain, I suppose we were the obvious players for Ted to approach. I imagine that Ted had also been fully aware of our two-man strike the previous summer, and would have wanted to find out how we felt about the club now that the dust had settled. While strolling along the fairways Ted was full of questions, asking us about anything from the ability of individual players to the training systems in place and the relationship between players and the board. John and I were as honest as we could be, but we told Ted that we wouldn't talk about the players behind their backs. We knew that some of our colleagues were past their best, while others were coasting and needed a jolt, but we both felt that these were conclusions that Ted had to draw himself. Ted said he respected us for our loyalty and seemed fairly happy with the answers we had given him. I was quite surprised then to hear that he wanted to meet for another round of golf before reaching his decision. This went on for some days before eventually Ted turned to the pair of us and said, 'That's enough, lads. I am going to sign.'

At his first press conference Ted told reporters he would need three years before he could win any trophies, or 'pots and pans' as he used to call them. Three years would allow him to get the right blend of players, moulding the best of the current team with a crop of new signings. In the event his prediction would be unerringly accurate.

The first day of pre-season training was revolutionary. After giving a speech about his aims for Chelsea and what he expected from his players, Ted stunned us by producing a huge bag stuffed with footballs. He then handed a ball to each player. This was heady stuff back in 1952! There is a terrific photo from that time of Eric Parsons sitting in a pile of about twenty balls, looking like a kid surrounded by his presents at Christmas. Ball work was to be essential to Ted's philosophy. Although we would still do our fair share of running he wanted us to maximise our creative abilities and play a more attack-minded type of game. One of the first things I asked Ted was how he wanted me to play. He said he liked my 'roving' game and did not want me to change my style at all, saying that it helped bring other players into the game and open up defences. I could see that the pair of us were going to get on like a house on fire.

Well before the days of sports psychology Ted was looking at ways of improving players' self-belief and enabling them to reach their potential. Many Chelsea teams of old had consistently blamed bad luck for their defeats and had seemingly accepted that plucky losing was 'just the way things were' at the club. Luck could manifest itself in a number of ways on a football pitch. You could suffer from poor refereeing decisions, find yourself repeatedly hitting the woodwork, or constantly see the ball running in your opponents' favour. Ted told us that we had to accept that there would be times during every season where fortune would go against us; the important thing was to keep battling for every loose ball and eventually help to make the luck run in our favour.

Ted was also concerned at how quiet the crowd at Stamford Bridge was. The greyhound track around the perimeter of the pitch created an unhealthy distance between players and spectators, and the absence of roofs on either terrace behind the goals meant that what little atmosphere was generated would disappear into the clouds rather than resonate around the ground. Ted felt that the Chelsea faithful were too fair-minded in their appreciation of good play. He felt that opposition players enjoyed appearing at the Bridge because attractive football by rival teams would be applauded by the home spectators. Ted wanted the crowd to be partisan and intimidate our opponents, like the fans he had played for in his days at Highbury and those he had come up against on trips to stadiums like Old Trafford and Hampden Park. Ted issued a rallying cry to the home supporters to be our twelfth man on the field and, to their credit, the fans responded immediately. In one match, early in the season, we went a goal down and began playing badly when I noticed a huge swell of support coming from the Shed. This gave the whole team a lift and inspired us to get back into the game, which we did. I know that many supporters believe that the crowd does not make any difference to players, but they are quite wrong. Every player needs a lift and will raise his game if he feels the crowd is behind him, rather than on his back or indifferent. Some players are immune to the noise of the crowd, but they are very much in the minority. One player who seemed able to switch off was my teammate at Fulham, Jimmy Hill. During one match Jimmy was getting abuse from all angles, and I could hear fans shouting, 'Give it to the rabbi, give it to the rabbi' constantly. Jimmy had grown a small beard, known in the Navy as a 'Sir Walter Raleigh', and this was its first appearance. At half-time one of the Fulham lads asked if he had heard the shouts and Jimmy said, 'No, I was concentrating on the game.' He genuinely hadn't heard a thing, but Jimmy was a rare exception. I think most former players would admit to being affected by a crowd's noise. The guys playing today would perhaps choose not to admit publicly that they hear the catcalls during matches for fear of encouraging further stick.

Ted was also unhappy with the club's nickname, the Pensioners, which he felt gave the club too cosy an image, and asked the board to drop the image as the club's badge, replacing it with a lion. The decision was not popular at first, but it was all part of Ted's plan to focus his team's attention on becoming genuine championship contenders.

Another unpopular decision, one that was entirely misconstrued by the media at the time, was his request to move the Chelsea Pensioners from the front row of the stand and position them further back. The pensioners' bright red jackets were a regular feature of home matches, but Ted's motives were genuine. He worried that, because the front section of the stand was uncovered from the elements, the Pensioners would be soaked whenever it rained. He wanted them to sit in greater comfort, but when some of the Pensioners stopped coming because of the arduous walk to the back of the stand, the press got hold of the story, claiming that Ted was deliberately forcing them out.

Ted's first signing, in summer 1952, was my former Newcastle United teammate Johnny McNichol. I was thrilled when I heard that Johnny was joining us and saw this as a positive statement of intent by Ted. While playing alongside me at Newcastle, Johnny had a pretty unusual part-time job, working in a local undertakers, for which he earned almost as much as he did as a professional footballer. He had then, rather surprisingly, moved to Brighton just before the Geordies began their era of FA Cup domination, having been offered maximum wages by the Third Division club. On the South Coast Johnny had become a highly rated inside right and at one stage had been offered the chance to join Manchester City. When that move fell through and Ted appeared with the offer of First Division football at the same salary, Johnny quickly signed on the dotted line. His was to prove a crucial signing, as were those of Ted's next captures, goalkeeper Charlie Thomson from Clyde and amateur Derek Saunders from Walthamstow Park Avenue.

The new season of 1952/53 started well and two big wins in the space of four days in mid-September seemed to set the benchmark for what would be an impressive season. Blackpool were unbeaten and top of the league when they visited the Bridge for a midweek fixture. Stanley Matthews had been on top form early in the campaign but, on this particular night, found himself marked out of the game by left-back Stan Willemse. One newspaper reporter gave a wonderfully poetic description of poor old Stanley's miserable night, spent shackled by our very own Stan the Man and bereft of support from his teammates: 'What did Mr Matthews do in this outpaced, outmanoeuvred Blackpool team? Just as much as pianist Cortot might do without a piano, Reg Dixon without his organ, or Joe Davis without his cue.'

The crowd had responded to Ted's plea for more noise and shouted themselves hoarse as we racked up a two-goal lead within the opening ten minutes. I scored the first goal, charging the Tangerines' goalkeeper into the goal with the ball, an eager linesman spotting that the ball was over the line. Then I set up Billy Gray to double our advantage. In the second half I was the provider again, setting up my old pal Johnny NcNichol to open his account for the Blues. In the final minute Johnny scored again, somehow heading home while lying prostrate on the ground. The newspapers were full of praise for our display, talking up the new Chelsea team spirit they had witnessed, as well as our 'pace, power and skill'.

The following Saturday we pulled off another 4-0 win, this time at home to Aston Villa. Roving effectively in front of the Villa defence I set up Johnny for his third goal in two matches, a first-time volley from the edge of the box. Again we went in at half-time two goals to the good after my mishit shot had fallen kindly to the feet of Bobby Campbell. After the break I scored a quick double myself, with a header and a right-foot shot. At the final whistle we were ecstatic, having controlled two successive matches from start to finish and knocking in eight goals without reply.

However, the changes that Ted had introduced to the team would take some time to reach fruition, and September proved a false dawn for Chelsea. Six consecutive defeats in the run-in to Christmas left us in the familiar position of hovering dangerously above the drop zone. The mini-crisis engendered by this dreadful run prompted Ted to call a team meeting, during which he assured the players he had great faith in our ability and said that our problems were being caused by a lack of confidence.

I was very impressed by Ted's attitude. In previous years Billy Birrell, although by no means a fool, would only see his team once during the week if we were lucky, and then on match days. Ted was far more hands-on and determined that if his team was to be found wanting then it would not be for a lack of dedication on his part. After he had finished his pep talk I stood up and told Ted that the players were 100 per cent behind him and that he could count on our total commitment to the cause.

The proof was in the pudding two weeks later when we faced Derby County in an FA Cup third-round tie at the Baseball Ground. We found ourselves completely outplayed by Derby in the first half and were two goals down by the interval. In the dressing room at half-time the players remained positive and focused, despite the battering we had received in the opening forty-five minutes. We started the second half fighting as if our lives depended upon not losing and after a quarter of an hour I had scored to put us back in the game. Yet within ten minutes the Derby centre forward had scored two more goals, to leave us on the ropes at 4-1 down with just twenty minutes to play. Still we refused to lie down and die and, when one of the Derby centre halves put through his own goal on seventy minutes, we were handed a small lifeline. Ken Armstrong pulled another goal back with a wonderful first-time strike from the edge of the penalty area and, for the final minutes of the game, we laid siege to the Derby goal. Johnny McNichol then popped up to score a similar goal to Ken's, levelling the score at 4-4 and giving us a well-earned replay.

A few nights later we took to the field for the second match, but it was never likely to live up to the excitement of the first tie. The heavy fog that hung over Stamford Bridge made attractive football almost impossible and, after a goalless ninety minutes, the match went into extra time. The game was finally settled by Eric Parsons in the first period of overtime with a smart shot after a scramble in the box.

Our new-found spirit was to be tested again in an epic fourth-round contest with West Bromwich Albion. Until as recently as 1991 FA Cup matches could continue with an indeterminate number of replays and, on this occasion, it took four meetings to settle the match. The first game had ended 1-1 at Stamford Bridge after the Baggies had taken the lead, while the return match at The Hawthorns ended goalless. A second replay was held on neutral territory, Villa Park, although this seemed much more like home advantage for our opponents. Again we fell behind, only to snatch another draw.

The third replay would be at Highbury, giving us the advantage this time around. Interestingly, with the match being played at a neutral venue, Chelsea wore red, the same colour as the Arsenal side who usually graced this north London turf. Johnny Harris had to miss the fourth instalment of the contest, suffering from tonsillitis, and Ted was also forced to give eighteen-year-old schoolboy Miles Spector his third game in five days on the left wing. The omens were not good.

It was young Miles, sadly never to fulfil his immense promise, who forced a breakthrough, playing Eric Parsons through on goal before 'Rabbit' was upended by the West Brom 'keeper. Nowadays the offending stopper would have been given a straight red card, but sendings off were still a rarity in English football and Norman Heath dusted himself down to save the penalty, acrobatically tipping Ken Armstrong's effort around the left post.

Seven minutes into the second half we took the lead for the first time in 382 minutes of play between the two sides. Belying the effects of playing seven matches in sixteen days, Eric chased a misplaced long ball by Sid Tickeridge and kept it in play before crossing for me to shoot into an open goal. Seven minutes later, young Miles created a goal for Eric. A header by me and a hooked shot by Bobby Campbell completed the scoring. After more than six hours of battle in which the two teams were as close as a Remington shave, we had somehow ended up winning by four clear goals. Perhaps the tiredness of our opponents' legs had got the better of them.

Chelsea were certainly feeling weary and, having avoided the prospect of a fourth replay, which unbelievably would have taken place the following day, there was to be little respite from the fixture list. Just three days later we travelled back to the Midlands, for the fourth time in three rounds, to face Birmingham City. The City lads were understandably fresher than us and it was little surprise that we found ourselves on the wrong end of a 4-0 drubbing. Our cup dream was over for another year.

In between our third replay with West Bromwich Albion and our pasting at the hands of Birmingham City Ted had somehow found the time to strengthen the team, signing eighteen-year-old left-winger Frank Blunstone from Crewe Alexandra for £8,500. Frank was a super lad and as brave a professional as any I had encountered. To illustrate this, Frank's Chelsea debut, against Tottenham Hotspur, was played amid a personal tragedy that would have floored lesser men than this precocious teenager. A few days before the match Frank was pulled aside in training and told to report to Ted's office. Here he was sat down with a cup of tea and given the appalling news that his brother John had been killed in a motorcycle accident that morning. Frank returned straight home for the funeral and, just hours after helping to bury his brother, was telephoned by Ted and informed that he had been selected for the weekend's match. Ted told Frank that he should feel under no obligation to return to London, but the youngster decided to play, believing that was what John would have wanted. After being consoled by his teammates before kick-off, Frank put in a terrific performance that he capped with a goal. Ted had set out to sign men of great character. In this instance he had signed a boy with the heart the size of three men.

Over the second half of the season our League form had stuttered dangerously and our increased team spirit and self-belief had failed to materialise into results on the pitch. In the midst of our 1955 championship success many people have forgotten that Chelsea were very nearly relegated in Ted's first year in charge. Although the team had been revolutionised tactically and given a real sense of destiny by Ted, our learning curve had conversely taken a sharp backward turn. With a single match to play we filled one of the relegation spots, needing to beat Manchester City at home in order to survive and send our visitors down by one point. A sterling performance saw us run out 3-1 winners and players and management alike breathed a huge sigh of relief at the final whistle. Ted knew that his entire three-year plan had been at risk had we been demoted and was determined that, from this moment onwards, our eyes would only be glancing at the top half of the league table whenever we opened our Sunday paper.

Over the previous two years or so I had been lucky enough to be asked to take part in a variety of activities that were completely new to me. In addition to my part-time salesman jobs, firstly with J.C. King and later the electrical firm Halsey's Electrical Co. Ltd, I was approached by an advertising company to endorse various products. In the post-war boom advertisers were waking up to the benefits that a famous face could provide for a company. Several England players of the time were chosen for various ad campaigns, although few products were as glamorous as those that the players today would be involved in. There were no video games or mobile phones in 1950. My most famous advertising campaign was for

Coleman's English mustard. Their newspaper campaign featured me sporting a toothy grin and wearing a suit, alongside a plate of traditional English fare and the slogan 'That's where I like it. In the middle', referring to my penchant for headed goals. I also did a number of advertisements for the Milk Board. It was very flattering to be asked to take part in commercials and the extra money was a bonus. I was still earning the maximum wage of £12 a week and every little extra helped, especially as my second daughter, Jane, had recently been born.

Although happy to trade on my fame as a footballer to sell mustard and milk, one thing I wasn't prepared to do was to live off it to help my sales jobs. I know my bosses would have preferred me to shout from the rooftops about being a footballer whenever I was negotiating a deal. Indeed, they insisted I handed out printed cards with my name writ large whenever I arrived at new premises. I, on the other hand, preferred to use any skill I may have acquired as a salesman to seal a deal, even if it meant losing out on the odd commission. On one occasion I visited a company in the Tottenham area of north London with the aim of securing a large order for wax paper. As I waited in reception I heard the guy who I had come to see telling his colleague that I should 'bugger off'. Having been informed rather more politely that my meeting had been cancelled I left my calling card. I walked up the flight of stairs feeling pretty miffed at my wasted journey, only to hear a panting voice, saying 'Roy Bentley? If I'd known it was you, I'd have given you a big order. Come in.' I was annoyed by this chap's change of heart and told him I wasn't interested in dealing with him anymore. Perhaps I wasn't hard-nosed enough in business, but I didn't want to be a successful salesman just because I was a well-known sportsman.

Another fantastic opportunity came my way in the summer of 1952 when I was asked to play a minor role in the British movie *Cosh Boy*, which starred Joan Collins, no less, alongside James Kenney. Stamford Bridge was a notorious hangout for celebrity football fans and, in addition to fanatical Blues fan Dickie Attenborough, numerous directors and producers would attend home matches. Once, I received a message in the dressing room that a chap called Oliver was asking for me, wanting a ticket. I was puzzled because I didn't know anyone called Oliver. When I walked outside I saw Laurence Olivier, a great Chelsea fan, standing there. That was pretty typical of those days. It was through these connections that the brief opportunity to be a movie star came my way.

The storyline of *Cosh Boy* revolved around a sixteen-year-old juvenile delinquent, played by Kenney, with Joan Collins cast as his girlfriend who starts out an innocent schoolgirl before falling under her boyfriend's bad influence, getting pregnant, and throwing herself into the Thames. Sid James, the star of the *Carry On* films and Tony Hancock's sidekick, had a leading role as a policeman, while one young actor, just starting out in the business, would later become known as one of the greatest soap opera villains in TV history. Johnny Briggs played the character of Slim, but it would be another twenty years before he would reach nationwide fame as *Coronation Street*'s Mike Baldwin.

I played the part of a football coach at a boys' club, a comparatively minor role, and found the whole experience fascinating, enjoying being in the company of actors and film-makers. It was a completely different world from the one I was used to and I relished every minute of shooting. Everyone was so friendly, even the stars, and people were very supportive of me, an imposter who had never acted before in his life. I spoke to Joan Collins a few times and found her rather nice. She was only nineteen years old, but a very pleasant and mature young lady. A photograph appeared in one of the daily newspapers of Joan getting my autograph, I assume for a Chelsea fan, and it tickled me years later when she became one of the biggest showbiz stars in the world. Another photograph that appeared in the press was rather less welcome, showing me having make-up applied by a woman before the start of one of my scenes. You can imagine how well that went down with my Chelsea teammates.

Although a pretty tame affair by today's standards, *Cosh Boy* was one of the earliest films to receive an 'X' certificate and was ahead of its time, giving an even-handed view of the lives of teenage tearaways rather than just condemning them outright. When it was released I felt a slight sense of disappointment when I realised how many of my scenes had ended up on the cutting-room floor. I think I appeared in about three minutes of the film, but then again I was under no illusion that I would ever rival Cary Grant or Jimmy Stewart at the box office. I thought that director Lewis Gilbert did a pretty good job with the film and he must have been saddened when many local authorities banned it from their cinemas. Just before its release the case of Derek Bentley, no relation to me, was causing shockwaves across the nation. The nineteen-year old Bentley and sixteen-year-old Christopher Craig were caught robbing a warehouse and, as they were being arrested, Craig shot a policeman dead. Although Bentley was being held by another policeman at the time he was found guilty of the murder and hanged because Craig was underage and could not be executed. Bentley was eventually given a posthumous pardon almost fifty years later. The publicity surrounding the murder created an almighty stir and led to people accusing *Cosh Boy* of glamorising violence, a charge that I felt was most unfair.

Despite my many brushes with celebrity I was never seduced by fame, and this was largely because of my humble upbringing. My mum and dad had never been interested in where people came from or how much money they had, and I was just the same. It was a great pleasure to be introduced to so many well-known people from the area of sports, entertainment, politics or royalty, but I never felt that those people were necessarily any better than the tea boy at Chelsea or my postman.

One of those whom I had the pleasure to meet was screen siren Ava Gardner, whom I was photographed with at an annual sportsmen's dinner at the height of her fame. I was also introduced to the Duke of Edinburgh on the pitch at Wembley. My brush with royalty came as England were preparing for a Home Nations match against Wales, although being introduced to dignitaries shortly before playing a match was a bit of a waste of time. I was always so focused on the match about to begin that even if I had been introduced to Adolf Hitler I probably wouldn't have batted an eyelid.

The closest I came to meeting the Queen was my regular invitation to the Christmas staff party at Buckingham Palace that I received through Chelsea club secretary Mrs Metcalfe, whose friend Percy Benham had worked in the royal household since he was a boy, starting out serving on the royal yacht. Percy became a great friend of mine and I always looked forward to the Christmas party, which the royals attended. I remember one year seeing Shirley Bassey perform, which was a great thrill.

At the start of pre-season training in July 1953 Ted introduced us to two new backroom staff who would have a major influence on the final two years of the manager's three-year plan. Our new trainer was Jack Oxberry, who had worked with Ted at Reading, while Albert Tennant was appointed as a coach. Although Ted had given each team member their own football for training the previous summer, I think he had felt it unwise to impose all the other changes he wanted in one fell swoop.

After planting his initial seeds during that first summer Ted had waited patiently for a year before appointing his assistants and imposing his revolutionary new training regime. Many times I have been asked what was the main improvement that Ted made to Chelsea. I have always given the same reply – our fitness. The first change that the new trio, along with our other coach Dickie Foss, introduced was an additional training session in the afternoon, although this made things a little difficult for me, with my part-time salesman duties. Much of the early pre-season exercises still involved running, which was essential to build up the players' basic fitness levels. Even nowadays most clubs will spend their first few weeks of pre-season running mile after mile. After we had reached an acceptable level of fitness, Ted then gave us a ball to dribble on our route, which had the dual effect of making running less monotonous and giving us better ball control. It is interesting to note that the current Chelsea boss, Jose Mourinho, makes his players work with a ball during every element of his training sessions.

As the countdown to the season began, Albert introduced us to log work, which at first seemed bizarre. Log work involved throwing a 125lb piece of timber in the air and catching it, before

swinging it from side to side. This exercise strengthened muscles
in both the arms and legs and, after a while, I felt so strong that I
believed I could put my fist through a brick wall. Five-a-side games
of head tennis over a net were also a popular feature of training
and improved some of my colleagues' ability in the air no end. In
August we would also indulge in 'potted sports', which involved
a strenuous exercise circuit using bamboo loops and hoops hanging from the crossbars, and a selection of barrels, boxes and ropes.
Every player, right down to the junior teams, would be expected
to join a team of five, and the group that won the most points was
crowned champions. As well as helping our fitness levels, it also
helped create a strong camaraderie among the entire playing staff,
something that Ted rightly saw as crucial to a team's success. Ted
hated the formation of cliques within a squad of players. Nor did
he like individual talents who would play for themselves rather
than the team. He wanted us to become a close family and often
arranged trips away to strengthen the bonds between his players.
When he felt we needed a break Ted would sometimes take us
to Brighton for a whole week, where we would play golf in the
afternoons after training.

Ted also scrutinised players' backgrounds and wouldn't sign
anyone if he had any doubts about their character. He preferred to
sign married players, because they had more responsibilities than
some of the youngsters. Living in London was a major distraction
to young players, especially to those who had come from a small-
town upbringing. Some would undoubtedly be blinded by the
bright lights of the city and a few went a little off the rails, although
nothing like to the extent of some footballers today. When he took
up his post, Ted quickly found out which players were taking too
much interest in unhealthy off-field activities and warned them to
sort out their act or else he would kick them out of the club. He
stood for no nonsense from his players and led a disciplined ship.

There may have been one or two exceptions, but almost all the
players really liked Ted and desperately wanted to win matches for
him. Although footballers never go out of their way to lose if they
don't like a manager, respecting one's boss has always made a big

difference on a football field. You can have the best eleven players in the world on your team but, if you put a manager in charge that they don't respect and who fails to engender team spirit, your club will never win anything. Players felt genuinely affectionate towards Ted and believed that he had their best interests at heart. The medical attention we had received was much more professional and I know Eric Parsons felt the treatment he received for his ongoing knee problems improved dramatically after Ted's arrival.

Our first game of the 1953/54 campaign showed off the benefits of our intensive summer training programme. Trailing 3-1 at home to Portsmouth we looked dead and buried but, as the second half wore on, Pompey legs tired whereas we looked fresh as daisies. When we got back to 3-2 Portsmouth were hanging on for the final whistle, unable to maintain their levels of fitness, and two late goals gave us a 4-3 opening-day win. Jim Lewis, another amateur signed by Ted, scored a hat-trick that day, despite missing an early spot-kick.

Ted was beaming after the match, slapping me on the back and telling the lads how their increased fitness would help them to hit back in games as our opponents tired. Later in the season, away to Middlesbrough, we found ourselves trailing 3-1 with little more than five minutes remaining, but two goals from Eric gave us a draw against the odds. This habit of coming back from the dead, which had started during our FA Cup run the previous season, was now being transferred to the League, and helped us into the top half of the table.

An early exit from the FA Cup concentrated the minds on ensuring a top-half finish. Our cup conquerors were West Bromwich Albion, with whom we had endured an epic tussle the previous winter. This time around it would take just one match to separate us, the Baggies defeating us 1-0 and exacting revenge for their own exit from the previous competition. West Brom would go on to win the cup, beating Preston 3-2 in a nail-biting final.

Within weeks of being knocked out of the cup we had stunned the football world by beating that same West Brom team, who were top of the table, 5-0 at the Bridge. One reporter, John Camkin, labelled our performance 'the finest I have seen this season', as we racked up an astonishing four-goal lead in the first thirty-four minutes. Derek Saunders scored the opening goal after eight minutes before Johnny McNichol, Les Stubbs and Jim Lewis completed the first-half scoring. I added a fifth goal in the closing stages to round off a remarkable win. The Baggies were still three points clear at the final whistle with eight matches to play, but the pasting they received helped knock them off their stride and their lead began to slip away. By the end of the campaign they had been knocked into second place, four points behind their bitter Black Country rivals Wolverhampton Wanderers.

A couple of weeks before our 5-0 win we had also beaten Wolves at Stamford Bridge, which marked our thirteenth consecutive match unbeaten. The scoring started as early as the first minute when I outpaced a defender and lobbed the goalkeeper, who had rushed ill-advisedly off his line. Eric scored soon afterwards, before Bill Shorthouse reduced the deficit before the break. Wolves' England forward Jimmy Mullen was all over the field during the second period, but our defence held firm and Stubbsy scored a breakaway goal. Wolves came back again through Dennis Wilshaw before I wrapped things up with a late header.

At this point the players' confidence was sky high and we knew we were building a strong team. A week later we travelled to Sunderland, a team marooned in the bottom half of the table. The famous 'Roker Roar' meant that a trip to Wearside was never an easy prospect, but we battered them from start to finish, the 2-1 scoreline not reflecting the extent of our supremacy. The match saw another reunion between myself and Len Shackleton, although the Clown Prince was not at his best that day. Despite an atypically lacklustre showing, Len still managed a trick or two to keep the home crowd's spirits high. I can't imagine how much an entertainer like Shack would be worth in today's transfer market.

This fine Chelsea performance came in the middle of a remarkable run that saw us remain undefeated for twenty-one matches. Game twenty-one saw us play Bolton, who still retained a slim mathematical chance of winning the title. We took the lead after thirteen minutes with a nicely worked goal. Left-back Stan Willemse released me in the middle of the park and I floated a cross just inside the box for Eric to strike home with a glorious volley.

Our second goal was just as neat. The ever-dependable Ken Armstrong hit a long pass upfield that I headed on to Jim Lewis at outside left. I ran into the box to receive a return pass and, when Jim's perfectly weighted centre arrived, I hammered it into the net. The match finished 2-0 although, as Danny Blanchflower would once say so memorably, 'they were lucky to get nil', we were so much the better side. *Sunday People* scribe Bob Morley was astute in his post-match analysis, writing, 'If Chelsea can maintain this form next season they will win everything.'

At this point we found ourselves in the unprecedented heights of fifth place. However, all good things come to an end and we lost our final four games to finish eighth, thirteen points behind the champions. Although we had ended the season on a disappointing note, it was clear that Chelsea were finally heading in the right direction after years of underachievement.

EIGHT

The Road to the Title

As the players began preparations for our Golden Jubilee season there was a growing sense of destiny rippling through the club. Ted's blend of young and old, fearsome and fancy, had begun to mature over the second half of the previous season. Our astounding twenty-one-game unbeaten run had imbued us with enormous self-belief and, when we reported for pre-season training, I was convinced that we had a genuine chance of taking the title. Indeed, in my programme notes for the first home game of the season, against Burnley on 23 August 1954, I predicted that we would be among the championship front-runners. Not that many people outside west London would have agreed with me.

Our pre-season preparations had involved a trip to Canada and the United States. Neither were footballing nations of repute, despite the USA's World Cup humiliation of England four years earlier, and our early games were fairly gentle affairs. At the tour's climax we travelled to Toronto to play three matches against Scottish giants Glasgow Rangers. After a fiercely contested 1-0 defeat, we beat the Scots 4-1 the second time around, before a goalless draw brought our tour to an end. What was evident on that trip, which involved a wonderful visit to see Niagara Falls, was the real sense of camaraderie and friendship of our team. I have always believed that success in football can only come if players realise that a team is only as good as the sum of its parts. That had by no means been evident in my early years at Chelsea, and I'm convinced that the sense of teamwork in the title-winning side was largely down to the meticulous efforts of our manager.

Ted's philosophy was that nobody, be it player, manager or director, was bigger than the club itself, and he insisted that the youngest junior team player and tea lady were equally as important as the team's stars. He also insisted on 100 per cent effort on the field at all times, and despised the thought of players who felt they didn't need to justify their place in the team almost as much as he hated losing. Chelsea had always been known as an attractive team to watch and Ted continued the club's tradition of playing attacking football, but he wanted us to be hard to beat as well. That magic formula would take him three years to brew.

As Chelsea captain, Ted used me as his mouthpiece on the field. We would spend hours after games talking over what had happened during the match and he always valued my opinion. One of his favourite sayings was, 'Is it a black sky or is it a lovely blue?' referring to how I thought our prospects were that week. Ted encouraged me to be his envoy, acting as a middle man between him and the players. If any of my teammates had a problem they knew they could talk to me and that I would then go to Ted and speak to him discreetly. I always refused to speak about players behind their backs and if I was unhappy with a player I would always tell him to his face before I passed on my gripes to Ted.

Ted and I had similar views on the game and how it should be played, and he often said to me that because I was out on the field I had a completely different view from him and saw things happening that he wouldn't necessarily notice. My 'roving' game meant that I moved around the pitch more than any other player, as I sought the ball deep, opening up defences by dragging centre halves out of position. By running all over the park I could relay Ted's message to my teammates and try to keep their morale and concentration levels high.

I relished the captaincy and always regarded it as an honour, never a burden. I had been a captain all the way through my school years and knew there were various types of personalities in every dressing room, and that each player reacted differently to criticism.

Some players needed a gentle word and would go to pieces if you swore at them, whereas others needed more heavy-handed treatment. If I said to someone like Stan Willemse, 'Look here, you're not having a good game. You need to cut out the lazy passes', he probably wouldn't take any notice. But if I went up to him and said, 'Pull your bloody socks up, Stan' he would listen, whereas I could never say that to Ronnie Greenwood.

There were two captains whose methods I had studied closely, and I tried to incorporate the best of each into my own style. First was Manchester United skipper Johnny Carey, who was an excellent motivator who managed to organise his teammates throughout a ninety-minute match, while never losing sight of his own positional role in the team. I also learned a great deal from Johnny Harris. Taking over the captaincy from someone who had held the job for seven years and, moreover, was still in the team could have been a disaster. Yet there was never any sign of jealousy on Johnny's part when I was given the armband and the result was that, in effect, we had not one captain, but two, both of whom had the respect of their colleagues. Johnny was the first player I met when I arrived at Chelsea and he helped me to settle in immediately. Johnny's father had once been manager of Swansea Town and his brother Neil played for Queens Park Rangers, so football was very much in the Harris blood. He was the most loyal and trustworthy person you could meet and, in fact, at one time I hoped he would become one of the family. My sister, who was not married at the time, had moved to London to get a job, and the pair got on like a house on fire, but nothing more came of their friendship. Johnny never really had any interest in women. He was only interested in football and God, being a dedicated Christian who would carry a Bible around with him. We all used to joke with him and ask when he was going to start taking the Bible onto the field. You would never guess Johnny was such a spiritual person if you saw him on the field, mind. He was such a hard man, although, to be fair, he would only dish it out if an opponent was taking liberties. He'd warn them not to keep going in late and if they continued then more fool them. Johnny would have them winded on the ground before they had the chance to say 'Jack Robinson'. He was pretty effective with his elbows and could time a challenge perfectly so it would look as if he was going for the ball when in fact he had deliberately knocked the man over.

I remember one game at Manchester United, when they were sharing Maine Road with Manchester City, after Old Trafford had been bombed. Johnny was having a real ding-dong with dear old Jack Rowley, the legendary England centre forward, and the pair of them ended up on the floor. In the heat of the moment Jack threw some mud, covered with lime pitch markings, into Johnny's eyes. I think Jack immediately realised he had gone too far, especially when Johnny got to his feet, wiped the mud from his sore eyes, and said, 'You will regret the day you did that.' And by heavens he did. The next time United got a corner Johnny and I both went in hard on Jack and left him on the ground gasping for breath. After Jack had got his wind back, Johnny didn't give him any peace for the rest of the game.

Tactics were still in their relative infancy in the 1950s. Everyone played the WM formation, the front five of outside right, inside right, centre forward, inside left, and outside left, forming the 'W' shape. The 'M' was made up of the defence: left-back, left half, centre half, right half, and right-back. Ted wasn't a man to get too deeply involved in tactics and he liked things to be simple. One of his favourite tactics was for our wingers to come back and receive the ball, play it short, and then race up the line rather than just staying out on the wing waiting for a pass. Ted used to hammer Eric Parsons and Frankie Blunstone in training, so they would be fit enough to cope with all the running he had in mind for them. One week he said before a game, 'Well done last Saturday, Eric. You were coming back for the ball and you used it well. What I want you to do now is to come back just a little bit deeper.' Eric, who was a bit of a Cockney, turned around and said, 'Cor blimey, guv, why don't you tie a roller round my middle and I'll roll the pitch at the same time?' Ted laughed his head off, but that tactic worked well for us.

He also told Frankie and Eric to hit the ball hard and low across the face of the goal while myself or one of the inside forwards ran in for the cross. He said that if the ball went in the danger zone between goalkeeper and defenders it would create uncertainty and we'd score a lot of tap-ins, as well as a fair number of own goals. I've noticed that Arsene Wenger has his Arsenal side doing the same thing today.

One of Ted's bugbears was goalkeepers throwing the ball out. He thought it was lazy and encouraged mistakes, because it was more difficult to judge a throw than a kick. Our championship squad had two great goalkeepers, Charlie Thomson and Bill Robertson, but both knew that if either of them was guilty of throwing a ball to a teammate they might find themselves out of the side the next week, even if they'd kept a clean sheet.

Ted had been criticised over his first two seasons in charge for signing players from outside the top two divisions, but it was all part of his ploy to mould a team rather than a collection of individuals. He knew that players from the lower divisions had a lot to prove and would be desperate to succeed, and he scoured those leagues looking for players whom he felt had the ability necessary to make the step up. One of his most important signings was Johnny McNichol, transferred from Brighton & Hove Albion of the Third Division (South), although Johnny was hardly a risk, having started out at Newcastle United.

Stan Wicks had played centre half under Ted at Reading and the boss knew his game inside out. Relatively unknown in the game, Stan had the strength of an ox and was 6ft 4in tall, so he was good in the air and as tough as old boots. Critics have often cited his signing as the final piece in the championship-winning jigsaw. He was brought in by Ted in November to replace Ron Greenwood, who was a better footballer, but not as commanding. Stan became one of the best centre halves around and could easily have played for England, but sadly never got a chance. I was good friends with Stan from day one and kept in touch with him for many years after we had both left Chelsea, until his tragic death from cancer in 1983.

Ted also signed a number of players from non-League teams, including Derek Saunders, Jim Lewis and Seamus O'Connell. All three were great talents who had little inclination to be professional footballers because they could earn more money in other professions. They had been perfectly happy plying their trade outside the League before Ted's scouts had spotted them, and indeed young Seamus would leave the game a year after our title win, seeing greater financial opportunities elsewhere. Seamus made a big impact on the championship-winning side and his role is largely forgotten in the history books, unfairly in my view. Despite playing just 10 League matches during the campaign he scored 7 goals, a tally bettered by only three of his teammates: myself, Eric Parsons and Johnny McNichol.

Seamus was a bit of an enigma who had only arrived at the start of the season. He was the son of a wealthy Irish cattle owner and would work for his dad during the week up in Carlisle. Being an amateur he never trained with us and we'd only ever see him on match days when he'd travel down on the train with his boots hanging round his neck. Seamus was a terrific little player but he earned more money breeding bulls with his dad and, at the end of the following season, the O'Connell family upped sticks and moved to Spain where Seamus and his father bred bulls for use in bullfighting. It was a waste of a talent in many ways because Seamus was easily good enough to make it as a professional, and with a bit of nurturing he could have become an international. But he wasn't interested in a full-time football career and was more than happy with his lot. Whenever the championship side gets together we always talk fondly of Seamus and I've tried to get in touch on numerous occasions, but have never managed to reach him. Perhaps he'll drop me a line if he, or anybody who knows him, reads this book.

Although we only ever saw our amateur colleagues on the pitch, they were all crucial members of the side. Their amateur status meant that they were often underestimated by our opponents, who couldn't believe a non-professional would be fit to lick a pro's boots. This worked in our favour on a number of occasions.

Jim Lewis was a travelling salesman and another important cog in the machine. He played for much of the first half of the season on the left wing while Frankie Blunstone was injured, scoring 6 goals in 17 appearances. Funnily enough, he played the same position as young Seamus and, by the end of the season, had fallen below the cattle farmer in the pecking order, although he was always on hand when needed.

Derek Saunders was one of only two members of our squad to play every game of the championship season and was one of Ted's first signings after starring in Walthamstow Avenue's route to the amateur cup final. After a while Derek signed professional forms for Chelsea, but never forgot his amateur roots. Playing at left half, Derek would never shirk a tackle, but was also a good passer of the ball.

The other members of our title-winning side also merit individual mention. Sharing duties in goal were Bill Robertson and Charlie Thomson, both decent 'keepers who made enough appearances to each get a championship medal. Bill was one of the most nervous players I've ever known, but only before kick-off. He couldn't keep still before matches and legend has it that on his Chelsea debut the club trainer had to pour a couple of measures of whisky down his throat so he could get out of the dressing room. He had originally broken into the side at the tail end of the 1950/51 season in which we stayed up by the skin of our teeth, largely due to Bill's goalkeeping exploits. Out of the two 'keepers, Bill was a little more confident when coming for crosses and his extra weight helped him to be stronger in the air.

'Chick' Thomson was arguably the more agile of the two and, although he only made 16 appearances in 1954/55, as opposed to Bill's 26, he was in goal for the crucial run-in. Ted found it tough to choose between them and the pair of them fought it out for the green jersey in much the same way as Peter Shilton and Ray Clemence did under Ron Greenwood's England stewardship in the late 1970s.

Johnny Harris began the season as our regular right-back but, by the final quarter of the season, had lost his place to the young legs of Peter Sillett. Peter had been signed by Ted in May 1953 from Southampton, where he had forged a reputation as a top-class penalty taker. Peter would score many crucial penalties in the final weeks of the campaign, including one vital spot-kick in our penultimate home match. Yet there was much more to his game than taking penalties. Considering his 14-stone bulk, Peter was deceptively quick and, at 6ft 2ins tall, was rarely beaten in the air. He also had a huge, but at the same time, accurate kick on him. When the team's pretty passing football wasn't working Peter would often launch a seventy-yard ball so accurately in my direction that I would barely have to move to reach it.

On the other flank was Stan Willemse, a naturally left-footed player, who gave great balance to the team and was a fearsome tackler. Not the most graceful of ball-players, Stan did the simple things well and was rarely beaten for pace. He had been at the club since 1949 and had quickly become part of the furniture at Stamford Bridge, without ever taking his place for granted.

Ted's desire to ally an attacking forward-line with three fearsome defenders who would frighten the life out of the opposition meant that poor Ron Greenwood's days were numbered. Ron was a beautifully cultured player who was not afraid to bring the ball out from the back. He believed that defenders could play football the same as anyone else, rather than just bash it down the line. He was proved right as the years went by but, by this stage of his career, he was not a young man and was losing pace. If you wanted to be a 'footballing' centre half you had to be quick in case you lost the ball and had to win it back. Ron was a very sensitive man and would take it to heart if a teammate had a go at him, but he was a great friend to me. He lived near me and we would take the train together in the morning from Ealing. During our daily journey Ron would talk non-stop about football. He was one of the game's great thinkers, a great admirer of the Hungarians, and he foresaw exactly how the game of football would develop in this country. It was no surprise to me that he was such a successful manager at West Ham and then England. I'm sure that his love of ball-playing centre halves must have had an enormous impact on his skipper at Upton Park, the late Bobby Moore. Ron was heartbroken when Ted replaced him with Stan Wicks and signed for Fulham not long afterwards. He left Chelsea under a bit of a cloud, which was sad, because he had done a lot for the team. I'm sure Ron could have played for another First Division club had he not been so hasty. The one silver lining for Ron was that he played half of the League games, which meant he was entitled to a championship medal.

Another Chelsea stalwart was Ken Armstrong, our ever reliable right half, and a player who always seemed to choose the best option on the pitch. If a teammate slipped up, Ken would be there to cover. If a teammate needed to get rid of the ball, Ken was available for a pass, even if he had a man on him. He was outstanding throughout the season, missing just three games, and earning his one and only England cap against Scotland in April.

Eric Parsons and Frankie Blunstone were two of the hardest-working wingers around. Eric played out of his skin that year, but never really got a look-in for England because he was unfortunate enough to be plying his trade at the same time as Tom Finney and Stanley Matthews. Young Frankie was another great signing by Ted, who snatched him from under the noses of his old team Arsenal in March 1953. Ted paid £8,500 for him, which was a lot of money for an eighteen-year-old, but Frankie more than repaid the fee over the years. He was an incredibly fit lad who, because he was only nineteen, had to complete his national service during our title-winning season. Even though he was injured at the start of the season and missed nineteen League games, Frankie played around 100 matches over the year because the Army had him playing twice a week. How he had any stamina left to go on parade I'll never know.

I had already played alongside inside forward Johnny McNichol at Newcastle and was delighted when Ted brought him into the forward line. The pair of us had an almost telepathic understanding and Johnny supplied me with top-quality passes week in, week out. He was also our second-highest League scorer, notching 14 priceless goals. As centre forward, I was the only player to beat that total, scoring 21 times in 41 appearances. One of the proudest achievements of my career is the fact that I finished top scorer for seven consecutive seasons at Stamford Bridge, although such a record failed to save me from a pretty ignominious exit the moment I was deemed surplus to requirements.

Les Stubbs completed the first-choice forward line, an unselfish player who was a good foil for me. Playing at inside left, Les would run all day, making lots of intelligent runs both on and off the ball and being a useful decoy for his teammates. Young Bobby Smith had made a name for himself in the previous couple of seasons up front but for one reason or another he didn't get on at all well with Ted and only played 4 times that season. I liked both of them immensely and it was sad that they couldn't get over their differences because Bobby was a gifted player. He eventually left the club for Tottenham, where his game went from strength to strength, and he became a prized member of the famous Spurs double-winning side.

The season began on 21 August 1954 with a battling 1-1 draw away to Leicester City. Welsh international outside right Mel Griffiths gave the home side the lead after just ten minutes but we hit back in the second half when I headed in a cross after some misunderstanding in the defence. Although an unconvincing result, our scrapping performance showed our battling qualities, as was acknowledged by the next day's headline in the *News of the World*: 'This Chelsea Certainly Can Fight'.

Two days later, on August Bank Holiday Monday, we took on Burnley in front of a relatively modest 30,239 Stamford Bridge crowd, Eric scoring the only goal of the game. The following Saturday the attendance had swelled by more than 20,000 for the visit of Bolton Wanderers, then one of the biggest 'box office' draws in the English League. For the second time in eight days our indefatigable team spirit was in evidence, after we had slipped to a two-goal deficit with less than twenty minutes on the clock. Les Stubbs twice hit the crossbar as we piled on the pressure and, on the stroke of half-time, I pulled a goal back, heading home a Jim Lewis cross. Scoring a goal just before the break is well known to have a huge psychological effect on opponents, and this match would be no exception to the rule. Jim equalised in the second half before a Bolton player put through his own goal to give us a 3-2 win, our second home victory out of two.

August drew to a close with our return match against Burnley and I scored my third goal of the season to secure a 1-1 draw. A disappointing performance at home to Cardiff City ended with the same scoreline, Jim Lewis snatching a point with a late goal. Despite drawing three of our opening five matches, our start had equalled our longest unbeaten opening to a season, which had last been achieved in 1922, and we felt quite happy with our beginning.

Game six saw us take our first stumble, losing 1-0 at home to Preston, although we turned them over 2-1 in the return at Deepdale nine days later. Sandwiched between those games was a 1-1 draw at Manchester City, with both goals scored inside a minute midway through the second half. City's Roy Paul drilled home a superb free-kick to give City the lead but, from the kick-off, we went straight up the other end and levelled with one of the strangest goals of the season. Running onto a cross, my first shot was saved by that Trojan warrior, the German international goalkeeper Bert Trautmann. The ball rebounded kindly to me and I struck it a second time. On this occasion it hit the referee, but when the ball came back to my feet again I made no mistake with my third effort.

A disappointing 2-0 home defeat to Everton, our second consecutive loss at Stamford Bridge, was a worry, but goals by Les Stubbs and Jim Lewis gave us a 2-1 win at Sheffield United the following Monday and restored our spirits. Five days later, 25 September saw me return to St James's Park to face my old team, Newcastle United. I always received a warm reception from the Geordie faithful, who appreciated my efforts in my eighteen-month career on Tyneside, even though I always seemed to get on the scoresheet against them.

Since their promotion five years earlier Newcastle had consolidated their position in the First Division, regularly finishing in the top half of the table and winning the FA Cup in both 1951 and 1952. Ted knew that they were also a tough side and told Johnny Harris to 'take care' of their young forward Bobby Mitchell. Johnny put in a couple of hard tackles early on and little was seen of young Bobby as we ran out 3-1 winners. I kept up my scoring record against my ex-teammates, grabbing two goals, while our other Newcastle old boy Johnny McNichol got the other.

By the end of September we were nicely positioned in fourth place, having played just over a quarter of our forty-two games, and Ted was quietly pleased with our progress. However, the month of October would see the wheels start to fall off our championship challenge, with the team collecting just one point from five games. The first Saturday of the month saw the visit of top-of-the-table West Bromwich Albion, and a whopping 67,440 turned out to see whether we had the nerve to beat them for the second successive season.

Before kick-off Eric Parsons told me he had read in the newspaper that I had scored 99 goals for Chelsea, a fact that had somehow passed me by. In the opening ten minutes I had the ball in the back of the net and turned back to the centre circle feeling a sense of pride at notching up my 100th goal in a blue shirt. However, the referee had other ideas, disallowing the goal for offside when, in fact, West Brom captain Len Millard had played me on by yards. There was no point in grumbling and a few minutes later I did complete the ton, tapping into an empty net after one of Eric's trademark low, hard crosses had evaded the 'keeper. Goals by Jim Lewis and Eric gave us a 3-1 lead with ten minutes remaining but, for once, the 'comeback kings' were recipients of our own medicine, two late goals, the equaliser from Len Millard himself, depriving us of a win. We found out that evening that, had we won, we would have gone top of the league because other results had gone our way. This made the pill even more bitter to swallow.

Still reeling from this draw, which felt rather more like a defeat, we lost our next game away to Huddersfield 1-0, seven days before taking part in one of the finest matches ever played at Stamford Bridge, against the mighty Manchester United. Matt Busby's lads were one of the best teams in the land, containing the likes of Tommy Taylor and Dennis Viollet. It was Dennis who opened the scoring early in the game before Seamus O'Connell equalised on his debut. Jim Lewis scored his fifth goal of the season to give us the lead for the only time in the match, before goals by Taylor and Viollet gave United a 3-2 half-time lead. In the second forty-five minutes the goal feast continued with gay abandon, United's deadly duo Taylor and Viollet scoring another goal each to put United seemingly out of sight at 5-2. Ken Armstrong pulled one back to give us some hope but United's Jackie Blanchflower then scored a sixth United goal. In a game full of defensive mistakes on both sides it was the United back-line who crumbled next, with Seamus grabbing a couple of goals to complete an unlikely debut hat-trick. By the end of the game we had the visiting defence at sixes and sevens but, when the whistle blew, United had won an astonishing match 6-5. I still believe that given another ten minutes we would have won that match because we were running them absolutely ragged, but we just ran out of time.

Our trip to Blackpool the following Saturday was a far less illuminating affair and we travelled back to London after a single-goal defeat. A 2-1 loss at home to Charlton a week later meant that we had now lost four League games in a row, slipping from fourth place to twelfth in the space of a month. A few journalists began trotting out their trusty music hall references, accusing Chelsea of once again flattering to deceive. However, the prophets of doom had underestimated the fighting spirit that Ted Drake had instilled in his players and two goals from Johnny McNichol and one from Les Stubbs earned us a battling 3-3 draw at Sunderland, who were themselves entertaining hopes of a first-ever championship. The match also marked the first appearance of Stan Wicks in a Chelsea shirt.

Although the team had slipped up in October my personal form had impressed the England selectors and I earned a recall to the national side after two years in the international wilderness. Playing in a Home Nations match was always a great honour and I celebrated my return to the England forward line with a hat-trick in our 3-2 win over Wales at Wembley. It was a marvellous feeling scoring three for my country at the home of football, although not quite as historic as when Geoff Hurst managed the feat twelve years later.

Three days later Chelsea played at home to Tottenham and, as I ran out on to the pitch, I heard a huge roar from the crowd. I couldn't work out what was happening and assumed that there must be a presentation of some sort out on the pitch. When the game started I realised that every time I touched the ball the crowd were cheering and eventually it dawned on me that it was because I had scored a hat-trick for England. It was one of the most touching moments I experienced on a football pitch. Not for the last time the Stamford Bridge crowd helped to lift my game and, after Jim Lewis had scored yet again, I bagged the second in a 2-1 win, our first victory in seven weeks. Even a missed penalty by Johnny Harris failed to dampen our spirits.

We had hardly been displaying championship form but the signing of big Stan Wicks had added some well-needed strength and muscle to the backline and we went through November unbeaten. An unconvincing 1-1 draw at struggling Sheffield Wednesday hardly heralded a return to form, but the 4-1 pasting we handed out to championship contenders Portsmouth certainly did. Frankie Blunstone scored his first goal of the season and I made it 2-0, managing to flick a boot at the ball as I fell over. It was hardly my most spectacular goal ever, but a crucial one nonetheless. Pompey got a goal back before the break and it was a tense second period before Johnny McNichol restored our two-goal cushion with a quarter of an hour left. Mindful of the way we had let West Brom off the hook eight weeks earlier, we continued to attack and Les Stubbs wrapped up the win with an incredible shot that rocketed past the 'keeper from forty yards.

Although the end of the month had only seen us rise by one league position we felt that we had regained our momentum and that a good run of form was just around the corner. It was an ideal time to visit Wolves, who were the reigning champions and sitting pretty in top spot. The match was a bit of a grudge fixture for Ted. He had once been good mates with his opposite number at Molineux, Stan Cullis, whom he had played alongside for England. However, the two had had an argument on the touchline the previous season while we were being thrashed 8-1 at Molineux, and their friendship was permanently damaged.

Played in thick mud, 4 December would go down as one of our most crucial days of the season, a game when we showed

that our never-say-die spirit could help us hit back against even
the best sides around. Johnny McNichol's sixteenth-minute opener
was cancelled out almost immediately by Wolves' Peter Broadbent,
before I put us back in the lead. Roy Swinbourne levelled things
up with a quarter of an hour remaining and what had been a firm
but fair contest appeared to be heading for a draw. With barely five
minutes left on the clock an incident occurred that changed the
course of the match and maybe even our season.

Having made a run into the penalty area, Roy Swinbourne
had fallen over in the mud and, despite the fact that there was no
Chelsea man near, had won himself a penalty. We were absolutely
incensed that the ref could have given such an appalling decision
and vented our collective spleen at the officials. As always, the referee's decision was final and Johnny Hancocks stepped up to give
Wolves the lead from the spot. With a sense of injustice abounding,
Les Stubbs scored one of the goals of his life, receiving the ball
straight from kick-off and running at full pelt towards the goal,
swatting defenders aside like flies before letting rip with a shot that
would have taken the 'keeper's arm off had he got near it. With
time running out I scored my seventh goal in five games, bustling
past Billy Wright for pace before burying the ball into the net to
give us a 4-3 win. Gaining those two points on Wolves would be
crucial by the end of the season.

A week later we battered Aston Villa 4-0 at the Bridge, with me
getting on the scoresheet again. Two goals by Johnny McNichol
and one by Eric Parsons completed the scoring. A few days later
came a hotly contested 'friendly' match against leading Hungarian
side Red Banner. The visitors contained many members of the
Hungary team that had slaughtered England 6-3 at Wembley twelve
months earlier, including the sublimely talented Nandor Hidegkuti,
and the entire English nation wanted us to get revenge. We managed a respectable 2-2 draw, although had Johnny Harris converted
either of two penalties we might have won.

Johnny had by now missed his last three penalties and asked to
be relieved from his spot-kick duties. I was asked by Ted to take
over and, lo and behold, in the next match, at home to Leicester,

Chelsea's penalty jinx continued, with my mishit effort being saved, although it didn't prevent us from winning the match 3-1. Eric Parsons and Johnny McNichol got a goal apiece, our other goal being a bizarre own goal. Johnny had struck the underside of the crossbar with a powerful shot and, as it bounced in the air, two Leicester defenders struck the ball at exactly the same time, diverting it into the net. The goal went down in the official records as a 'shared own goal'. I can't remember seeing another goal like it.

Four wins on the bounce meant that our confidence was sky-high for our Christmas Day trip to Highbury, one of my favourite away grounds. The mean Arsenal defence were not handing out any festive gifts though, and a solitary goal by former Blues striker Tommy Lawton, my old hero, gave the home side the points. In the return match two days later I missed another penalty, and it was left to Seamus to rescue a late point. Although the holiday period had been a bit of a damp squib for Chelsea, we ended 1954 in fifth place and feeling in good shape, ready to make a New Year surge for top spot.

It was vital that our two disappointing results against Arsenal didn't spark off another bad run, and Ted was more than happy to see us whack Bolton 5-2 up at their place on the first day of 1955. In previous seasons I had been involved in quite a few battles with their defender Malcolm Barrass, but on a recent England trip his teammate Nat Lofthouse had let slip that Malcolm hated playing against me. I used this psychology on him before the game kicked off and he didn't get near me all afternoon, and I scored two goals. Seamus also nabbed a goal, our scoring being completed by an own goal and, at long last, a successful penalty. Five consecutive misses from the spot had seen Johnny Harris and I removed from duty and it was left to young Peter Sillett to take the responsibility. Peter put away the penalty with consummate ease and retained the job until the end of the season. His cool head from twelve yards was to come in very useful as the season wore on.

Just as the players thought we had regained our consistency we inexplicably fell to a 2-0 home defeat to Manchester City, a loss that led to some strong words in the dressing room. Everyone at the club knew that Chelsea had the best squad of players the club had ever assembled and that, with none of our opponents able to maintain a sustainable lead at the top of the table, this was our best chance to win the title. The fact was that Manchester City had out-thought us with their famous 'Revie Plan', which involved their midfielder and future England manager Don Revie being given the ball at any opportunity and spraying passes across the pitch for his teammates.

A 1-1 draw at Everton hardly helped as we slipped to sixth place, and we knew that a home win against Newcastle was imperative. Again it was the Geordie old boys, Johnny McNichol and myself, who did the damage, with me scoring a hat-trick, although inexplicably I remember little about that particular game, except for the fact that we were coasting at 4-0 up with ten minutes to go, but somehow conceded three goals and nearly threw away a point. Had we done so we may well never have recovered our self-belief in time to challenge the league leaders. By this time Wolves had regained top spot from Sunderland, but we were not too many points behind.

Having beaten Walsall in the third round of the FA Cup, I travelled down memory lane in the next round, visiting my first club Bristol Rovers. Although I failed to score, it was nice to go back and see my family and friends in my home town again. Our cup run ended three weeks later at Notts County on a frozen pitch that would certainly have been deemed unplayable in this day and age. Defeat concentrated our minds solely on the League and a 4-1 pasting of mid-table Huddersfield saw us end February in third place and perfectly placed to make a bid for the crown.

It would be the third month of 1955 that saw us take a stranglehold on the title. Yet the month began inauspiciously at Villa Park when goals from Johnny McNichol and Eric Parsons failed to prevent a 3-2 defeat to a decent Aston Villa side. Disappointed at a loss that left us in third position, some way off leaders and title favourites Wolves, we sat in the claret-and-blue dressing rooms and vowed to remain unbeaten from that day until the end of the season.

Our next match, the following Wednesday, saw us travel three miles along the road from Villa Park to The Hawthorns, home of West Bromwich Albion. Many would cite this match as the turning point in our season, one in which the 'never-say-die' attitude and indestructible team spirit engendered by Ted Drake saw us overcome a dreadful first-half performance that could have spelled the end of our challenge.

The playing surface was covered in snow and the ground was rock hard, making conditions almost unplayable. Nowadays a game would never be allowed to start in such conditions, but these were the days before undersoil heating and groundsheets to keep the snow at bay. There was little option, if clubs wanted to complete their fixtures by the end of April, but to play. Midway through the second half we trailed 2-0 despite bossing the match yet, mindful of our pledge to remain unbeaten until May, we dug into the very depths of our reserves and won the match. Derek Saunders reduced the deficit in the sixty-sixth minute and, when Peter Sillett equalised soon afterwards with a free-kick, there was only going to be one winner. Our persistence was rewarded when we were awarded an unconventional penalty in the game. Les Stubbs had followed through on their 'keeper on a couple of occasions after the man between the posts had already caught the ball. Eventually the 'keeper lost his rag with Les and kicked him in full view of the referee. It was an absolutely ridiculous thing for him to do and there could be no complaints from the home side when we were awarded the spot kick. Our new penalty taker Peter Sillett held his nerve and gave us a 3-2 lead before I added one in the final minute to give us an unlikely victory. It was a hugely significant result.

Ironically, it was after our previous visit to the Hawthorns during the 1953/54 season when Ted (Drake) told us we were on the verge of becoming a side that could genuinely challenge for honours. I'll never forget that moment because we'd just been played off the park by Albion, beaten 5-2, and our heads were on the floor in the dressing room. As Ted walked in we steeled ourselves for the mother of all rollickings, but he smiled and said, 'Well played, lads. We're getting there. That's just how I want you to play.'

1. *Left:* Roy sharing a room with Bristol City teammate Cyril Williams on a pre-season tour of Denmark in August 1946, days before transferring to Newcastle. (Family photo)

2. *Below:* Returning to Newcastle. From left to right: Frank Brennan (obscured), Bob Stokoe, Ronnie Simpson (wearing cap), Roy, Bobby Smith, unknown Newcastle number six. (Provincial Press Agency)

3. *Above:* A bigger squad than Mourinho's all-stars. A mighty Chelsea squad pose for a team group photo ahead of the 1948/49 season.

4. *Left:* Fulham's Jim Taylor challenges Roy for the ball, *c.* 1949.

5. Roy, John Harris and Bobby Campbell looking muddy after a Stamford Bridge training session, *c.* 1950.

6. An appreciative Chelsea fan pats two-goal Roy on the back as he leaves the field after the 1950 FA Cup semi-final. The Arsenal players are Joe Mercer, Les Compton and Wally Barnes. (PA - Reuter)

7. England captain Billy Wright introduces Secretary of State for Scotland Hector McNeil to the England team before their epic 1-0 win at Hampden on 16 April 1950. Goalscorer Roy is third from the right. (PA - Reuter)

8. *Above:* A Hampden crowd of almost 200,000 are stunned by Roy's goal, which deprived Scotland of a place in the 1950 World Cup finals. (PA – Reuter)

9. *Left:* Roy shoots for goal, *c.* 1950. (*Daily Mirror*)

10. Training at Stamford Bridge. From left to right: Jimmy Smith, Jimmy D'Arcy, Bobby Smith, Roy, Billy Gray, *c.* 1952. (Central Press Photos Ltd)

11. Roy shakes hands with his former England teammate Wilf Mannion as Chelsea host Middlesbrough on 16 February 1952. (A. Ronald Traube)

12. Roy opens the scoring with a header away to Chester City in an FA Cup tie on 16 January 1952. (Kemsley Newspapers)

13. *Above left:* Roy running out ahead of Chelsea's FA Cup tie replay with Leeds United on 29 February 1952. (PA – Reuter)

14. *Above right:* A besuited John Harris and Roy leave Stamford Bridge after settling their differences with Chelsea in September 1952. (PA – Reuter)

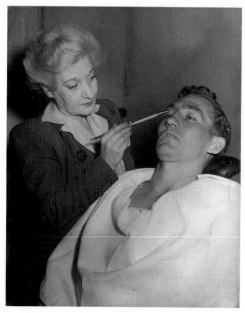

15. Starring on the silver screen. Roy has his make-up applied for his cameo appearance in the controversial 1952 film *Cosh Boy*. (PA – Reuter)

16. *Right:* Roy showing off his shooting technique, *c.* 1953. (Barratts)

17. *Below:* Roy and wife Vi pose with famous hotel magnate Charles Forte (right). (Matthews News and Photo Agency)

18. *Above:* Roy heads for goal against Portsmouth on 30 August 1952. (PA – Reuter)

19. *Left:* Roy demonstrates his shooting technique, *c.* 1953.

20. *Above:* Grounded. Roy on his backside as he attempts to pass to teammate Frank Blunstone (wide right) against Leicester City on the opening day of the 1954/55 season. (Provincial Press Agency)

21. *Right:* Roy poses in Chelsea strip for the annual club pen picture, *c.* 1954. (Provincial Press Agency)

22. Roy goes for goal against Cardiff City on 4 September 1954. (A. Ronald Traube)

23. Roy has a headed goal disallowed away to Burnley early in the 1954/55 League Championship-winning campaign. (Provincial Press Agency, Southport)

24. Roy nets a vital goal against Tottenham to secure a narrow 2-1 win over Tottenham on 13 November 1954, en route to the title. (Sport & General)

25. Roy sees his shot saved by West Bromwich Albion goalkeeper Jim Sanders during a 3-3 draw on 2 October 1954. (Sport & General)

26. *Above left:* Referee Alf Bond tosses the coin watched by Roy and Red Banner captain Hidegkuti before their friendly match on 15 December 1954. (Planet News Ltd)

27. *Above right:* Leading from the front. Roy brings out his teammates on the day Chelsea were to clinch their 1954/55 title with a victory over Sheffield Wednesday.

28. *Above left:* Chelsea manager Ted Drake shakes the hand of captain Roy moments after his team had clinched the title.

29. *Above right:* Screen siren Ava Gardner meets Roy at the sportsmen's dinner at the Savoy Hotel, 11 January 1955.

30. Roy relaxes in his Ealing home with wife Vi and eldest daughter Loraine, *c.* 1955. (Family photo)

31. Roy signs an autograph for an eager fan.

32. Roy and the Chelsea championship-winning team are greeted by the Earl of Cadogan before the 1955 Charity Shield match against Newcastle United. (A. Ronald Traube)

33. Fulham chairman and comedian Tommy Trinder welcomes Roy to Craven Cottage, September 1956. (*Daily Herald*)

34. Jimmy Hill, Roy,
Johnny Haynes and
Bedford Jezzard
enthralled Fulham fans
in the late 1950s.
(PA - Reuter)

35. Pointing the way.
Swansea manager
Roy gives some tips
to British Lions coach
Carwyn James in the
build up to the 1972
Lions victory over the
All Blacks.

36. Roy stands in front
of a frozen pitch at
Aldershot where he
spent eighteen months
as club secretary.

37. *Above left:* True Blues. Some of the boys of 1955 line up with Chelsea's most famous two political fans. From left to right: Eric Parsons, Lord (Tony) Banks, Stan Willemse, former Prime Minister John Major, Roy, Peter Sillett and Johnny McNichol. (Family photo)

38. *Above right:* Roy and his wife of almost sixty years, Vi. (Family photo)

39. Roy shows writer Jim Drury his collection of England caps while working on the book.

40. *Above left:* Roy talks with his fans in Texas over a pint, April 2005. (Family photo)

41. *Above right:* Roy poses with the England shirt he wore when his goal helped England beat West Germany in 1954.

42. The boys of '55 with Lord Banks, one of their biggest fans. (Family photo)

Ted had been delighted that we had finally begun to understand and implement his tactics, which involved attacking relentlessly and making our wingers drop deep to collect the ball inside our own half before bringing it forward in space. Although we had been well beaten, Ted evidently felt we had stuck to our task admirably. Sure enough, the next week we beat Liverpool at home and within weeks began our twenty-one-game unbeaten run. This was longer, incidentally, than any run we would make while winning the title, the best we achieved being ten matches without loss.

After our victory in the Black Country snow we were at home to Blackpool the following Saturday. Blackpool were struggling to survive in the First Division, even though they had Stanley Matthews on the wing, and we were disappointed to draw 0-0 in a hard-fought game. We still felt that we were about to make our break for the title though, especially when we discovered that the point gained had moved us up into second place, the highest position we had held all season.

The following weekend we travelled to local rivals Charlton Athletic at The Valley for a London derby in front of a crowd of 41,155. In goal for the home side was their flame-haired icon Sam Bartram, so often the scourge of the Blues. In the 1944 War Cup final it was Bartram's saves that had helped hand Charlton the famous trophy in their 3-1 win over Chelsea, a result that still stuck in the craw of our fans, who had come tantalisingly close to their first piece of major silverware. I always enjoyed facing Bartram, who was one of the best stoppers in the land and a perfect gentleman, and one of my favourite photographs from my playing days shows me 'helping' him over the goal line with my knee to score a vital goal in 1952. These were the days, of course, when using your physical strength to bundle a ball over the goal line was standard practice and no eyebrows were raised when the referee awarded that goal. In our March 1955 tussle I failed to get on the scoresheet, but goals from Frank Blunstone and Seamus (O'Connell) gave us a comfortable 2-0 victory.

The following Wednesday we travelled to Wales for an evening fixture against Cardiff City. Although perilously positioned in the drop zone, Cardiff were never an easy team to play, especially on their own patch. Arriving at the ground brought back a lot of memories for me of my wartime performances for Bristol City when the Cardiff XI contained the rock-hard Bevin Boys. As I arrived at Cardiff's Ninian Park ground I recalled with a wry grin the day Billy Mitchell, infuriated by a series of appalling challenges, left three City players on the deck after 'accidental' clashes of heads. Fortunately wartime football was now a distant memory and we won an entertaining game when Seamus notched the only goal.

The win at Cardiff put us top of the table and when club chairman Joe Mears came in to congratulate us after the game I looked him in the eye and said, 'We're there for the rest of the season, Mr Mears. Mark my words.' Some of the newspapers went a bit overboard, claiming it was the first time in our fifty-year history that we'd been top of the table, but I'm reliably informed by club historian Albert Sewell that the Blues had held that spot twice previously, in September 1922 and October 1937. Early season success must have been nice for our predecessors but, with all due respect, topping the table at the end of March was a rather more impressive feat.

We now had eight games remaining to clinch the title, divided equally between home and away fixtures. If we won all eight we would take the trophy, although taking a maximum of sixteen points from those games would be incredibly difficult, if not impossible. We were determined not to slip up when Sunderland visited the Bridge for our final game of the month, on 29 March. Despite our ascension to the league summit the attendance was a surprisingly low 33,205, almost a third below our average gate of 48,350. We received a blow before kick-off with the news that Seamus had been injured the previous weekend playing amateur football for Bishop Auckland. Frankie Blunstone was also unavailable, as he was required by the FA to train for England during that week and was forbidden from representing us. Ted was left with little option but to throw in seventeen-year-old Peter Brabrook for his debut on the left wing.

Peter did us proud and set up our first goal after just eleven minutes when his cross was turned into his own net by a hapless Sunderland defender. Yet again Ted's advice to fire in low centres between the goalkeeper and his defence had paid dividends. Almost immediately, Stan Willemse fired in a second goal and we relaxed. Our opponents pulled one back in the second half and we endured a few nail-biting moments before, to our relief, the referee blew for full time with the score at 2-1.

There were just four days to prepare for the following Saturday's trip to Tottenham Hotspur but Ted decided, for the third time that season, to take us to Broadstairs for a break. These days clubs prefer to take their players to luxury five-star hotels in exotic locations, but in our day a trip to Broadstairs was about as exciting as it got. Not that we were complaining, mind. The advent of inexpensive foreign travel was still some years off and a trip to the seaside was about the limit to most ordinary folks' horizons.

Suitably refreshed by the sea air, we returned for the trip to White Hart Lane in good spirits. Sitting pretty at the top of the league we were now the team everyone wanted to beat and 53,169 crammed into the Lane to see if our London rivals could turn us over. The atmosphere was red hot and I've seen a quote from John McNichol saying that one of the Spurs fans spat at Stan Willemse as we came out of the tunnel. How charming.

Again we were forced to come from behind that day, twice in fact, before we ran out 4-2 winners. Our ability to fight back from a deficit was a hallmark of true champions. Johnny McNichol scored two goals that day, while Stan Wicks netted his only goal of the campaign, and Peter Sillett completed the scoring with another penalty.

We had now reached Easter and there were just three weeks left for us to stay in pole position. Good Friday fell on 8 April and we faced the prospect of two home games in the space of twenty-four hours, against mid-table Sheffield United and second-placed Wolves. It's probably fair to say that, despite Ted's warnings, the Wolves clash was on our minds for much of the first game and it was only an Eric Parsons goal fifteen minutes from time that rescued a solitary point.

An impressive 50,878 people had attended the Bridge for the United match, but the next day an incredible 75,043 squeezed into the ground, our biggest gate of the season. In fact, mounted police outside the ground tried desperately to prevent many thousands of locked-out spectators from storming the stadium. Around 3,000 fans did in fact manage to jump the railings and sat around the greyhound track, taking the attendance to about 78,000. Our fans were acutely aware of the importance of the fixture and knew that a victory would leave us on the brink of unprecedented glory.

We were well on top throughout the first half and would have been a couple of goals to the good but for an inspired display by their man between the sticks. I had a couple of chances, one of which was a difficult diving header that the goalkeeper clawed out. Just before the break, Eric ran down the line and pulled a cross back to about eight yards from goal, but I mishit it and my shot was easily saved. This was no time to be feeling sorry for myself. I had to put any negative thoughts to the back of my mind until the end of the game. Only if we failed to win the match would I dare let my mind wander back to that awful miss.

The second half saw us continue to batter the Wolves goal until we finally got our reward fifteen minutes from time. The fit-again Seamus hit a piledriver towards the top right-hand corner and, with the 'keeper clutching at thin air, it was a goal from the moment it left the young amateur's boot. England captain Billy Wright had other ideas. Desperate to prevent the goal that would extend our narrow points advantage over his team, Billy leapt like a salmon and palmed it over the crossbar. You could never see a more blatant penalty if you watched 100 games but amazingly the referee, J. W. Malcolm, only awarded us a corner.

In usual circumstances we would certainly have registered our disappointment at the decision before accepting that the referee's word was final and carrying on playing the game. Yet these were far from usual circumstances. It was the most important match of our lives and we surrounded Mr Malcolm, imploring him to consult his near-side linesman. Fortunately, Mr Malcolm relented and spoke to his assistant for what seemed like an eternity. As he walked back, the ref gave no indication that he had changed his mind and we started to think that we were to be cheated of our rightful penalty. Just as he reached the penalty area Mr Malcolm casually pointed to the spot and we punched the air in delight.

Again, Peter Sillett was required to fight his nerves and place the ball on the penalty spot. There was no need for us to worry. Peter ran up and whacked the ball hard and low into the bottom right-hand corner to send the crowd wild. For the last quarter of an hour Wolves laid siege to our goal, at one stage hitting the post, but we held on until the final whistle. This was the cue for thousands of delighted Chelsea fans to invade the pitch and celebrate. As we left the field Billy Wright, usually an impeccably fair sportsman, apologised for his rush of blood. There was no need. I would have done the same thing in his position.

There was much back-slapping and cheering in the home dressing room after the match but we knew that, despite taking a huge step towards securing the title, the fat lady had not yet sung. She had just taken a few more steps towards the microphone.

One week later we faced the mighty Portsmouth at their tightly packed Fratton Park ground. Pompey, as they were nicknamed, still had an outside chance of the title and, if they beat us, would be within three points of us. The boys were certainly cursing Seamus O'Connell's amateur status in the run up to match day when we realised that our little Irish dynamo was playing at Wembley in the amateur cup final for Bishop Auckland on the same day. Can you imagine Jose Mourinho losing Damien Duff or Joe Cole for a vital League fixture because of an amateur cup match? It would be unthinkable. Les Stubbs made a welcome return to the starting line-up and twice almost gave us victory. In the first half Les's powerful shot was cleared off the line by a Pompey defender. Worse followed during the second period when Les slotted the ball home and wheeled away to celebrate only to find that the referee had disallowed his effort, after the linesman flagged for offside. To this day I can't understand the lino's decision. Les was miles onside.

Although we were disappointed not to win, a 0-0 draw was a pretty good result in the circumstances and set us up nicely for our final home game of the season seven days later against Sheffield

Wednesday. If we won the match and Portsmouth failed to beat Cardiff in their away fixture we would be crowned champions. If both ourselves and Pompey won our matches, we would have to travel to Old Trafford on the last day of the season needing a point to clinch the title. Wolves could no longer catch us, whatever happened.

On paper our opponents should have been a pushover. Wednesday were rooted to the bottom of the league, having lost sixteen of their twenty previous away fixtures. However, the fact that they had been relegated a few weeks earlier had taken all the pressure off their players and, as so often happens in these circumstances, their gutsy performance belied their league position.

Rumour has it that Ted was unable to sleep the night before our clash on Saturday 23 April and there was certainly some tension among my teammates. Our nerves were eased when Eric Parsons headed us into an early lead but, by half-time, there was still only one goal in it. I don't remember if we knew the half-time score from Ninian Park, because we were so focused on what we had to do ourselves. Not long after the second half started the Wednesday goalkeeper was injured when I struck a hard shot at him from close range. It struck him either in the chest or in the face, although the photographs of the incident make it look as if I'd made contact with my boot. I assure you that this wasn't the case. Anyway, he couldn't continue so Wednesday were forced to put one of their outfield players in goal.

Within a few minutes luck continued to go our way when a shot by Derek Saunders struck one of the Wednesday boys on the arm. It looked like a 'ball to hand' incident where the player couldn't get out of the way, and we didn't even appeal for a penalty, but the referee awarded us a spot-kick and Peter Sillett yet again showed a cool head to put us two up. People always say that luck evens itself out over a season and I think that's probably true. Certainly we had suffered our fair share of ill fortune, including our disallowed goal at Portsmouth a week earlier. With eighty minutes on the clock Eric Parsons scored his second goal of the match, shooting home after a run and cross from Frankie Blunstone. Three goals ahead, all that was left was for us was to play out the final ten minutes and await the news from Wales.

At the final whistle most of the ecstatic 51,421 crowd invaded the pitch and we had to sprint to the tunnel. When we got into the changing rooms we discovered that the Cardiff *v.* Portsmouth game had started late and that we would have to wait another quarter of an hour to discover if we were champions. Ted was listening to the match on a transistor radio and told us the latest score was one each. As we waited for the game to end some of us showered while others paced around the dressing room nervously.

When we heard that the game had finished as a draw it was hugs and back-slapping all round. We had achieved what had for so long seemed an impossible dream, to bring the title to Stamford Bridge for the first time in the club's history.

Having been instructed to take the team up to the directors' box to address the fans, the adrenaline was pumping through my veins, belying the fact that my body had taken an eight-month battering. We had finally smashed the myth of Chelsea as the music hall joke team. No longer were we the butt of comedians' jokes. As I looked out towards 40,000 faces on the pitch my mind wandered back to the day when the Chelsea team had been invited to a gala evening at one of London's theatres. A tubby comedian who knew we were in the audience said to the crowd, 'I hear that Chelsea have signed two Chinese players, We Wun Wunce and How Long Since!' As the audience roared with laughter we were forced to smile through gritted teeth. I was delighted to ram that taunt and those of countless others down our detractors' throats.

We had won the ultimate prize. We were Champions of England.

NINE

The Bitter End

The week after our championship season had ended with a 'dead rubber' defeat at Manchester United, 2-1, the directors took us to Ireland for a few days as a reward. It was a fantastic trip, partly because in 1955 luxury food was still scarce in Britain, whereas in Ireland we could stuff ourselves with as much butter, cream and meat as our stomachs could stand. While on a cultural visit, we were taken to a church where a famous Irishman had been buried. I remember looking around the pews and noticing that I was one of the only players there, so I popped my head outside to find most of the team sitting on a wall playing cards. Footballers have never needed much encouragement to get a card school up and running, wherever they are.

Predictably, the Irish tour did involve some work on our part. Despite having just delivered the title, the board were reluctant to let us put our feet up, and we were required to play a friendly fixture against Irish Champions Shamrock Rovers. That game would have been a good opportunity to have presented us with the League Championship trophy that the players had still not seen, but it remained under lock and key in the Chelsea boardroom. Eventually, one afternoon late in the summer, it was dusted down for a photo session. In the event, we didn't receive our medals until the beginning of the following season when the club laid on a small lunch for the team in the boardroom.

When we returned to pre-season training in July the boys felt confident that we could build upon our success of the previous campaign. Our title win had been achieved by a blend of hard work, determination and no small element of skill and talent. We believed that if the team continued where we left off we had every chance of retaining our title and maybe overcoming our FA Cup semi-final hoodoo to finally reach Wembley. However, we soon discovered that if getting to the top had been difficult, then staying there would be another matter entirely, and the 1955/56 season saw us come back to earth with a nasty bump. It would also precipitate another personal crisis for me, one that would lead to my ruthless exit from Stamford Bridge.

The campaign began with a 3-0 Charity Shield win over FA Cup victors Newcastle United. Although it was nice to play against my old mates again, the Charity Shield rarely produced a great footballing spectacle, with its role as a glorified pre-season friendly. The fact that the match was played at Stamford Bridge, rather than Wembley, took any remaining lustre away from the day.

As so often happens in football, Chelsea's status as title holders acted as a spur to the opposition and our League form stuttered worryingly in the first half of the season. Teams would raise their game in order to try and beat the champions, the way that we had ourselves done two seasons earlier when we had demolished West Bromwich Albion 5-0. By the turn of the year we were in ninth place, seven points behind league leaders Manchester United. To retain the title would be difficult, although not impossible, but our final game of 1955 was indicative of how the team had lost our famed ability to fight for ninety minutes. Three-nil up at Portsmouth, courtesy of a Frankie Blunstone hat-trick, we were coasting and about to see in the new year with a bang. By the end of the game Portsmouth had brought the score back to 4-4 and we were reduced to hanging on for a point. It may sound like a terrible excuse but the simple fact was that the players were tired. The amount of effort that we had all put in over the previous three years had drained the team. I would never blame the fact that training was so hard, because we had all got used to that, but there seemed to be no respite from the fixture list and players found it difficult to stay at their peak for a third consecutive season. Perhaps

Ted should have brought in a couple of new players to shake things up, but he obviously thought, 'If it ain't broke, don't fix it' and left things as they were.

Our struggle to maintain the previous season's form was nothing to do with the players taking it easy or not trying. We were all trying like hell, but many of the players found that their bodies couldn't take any more wear and tear. About halfway through the season players were getting lots of small knocks that were taking longer and longer to recover from properly. I can remember being very sore for a day or two after matches, and sensing that my pace and control had been adversely affected. I was still scoring goals but, along with most of the team, I didn't feel I was performing to the same level I had during the championship season.

The new year started with two League defeats, 1-0 away to Hartlepool and a 3-2 home defeat to Sunderland. The latter saw yet another reunion for me and Len Shackleton, but on this occasion the Clown Prince came out on top, putting in a Man-of-the-Match performance and scoring the second goal. My major contribution was to miss a sitter in the third minute with the score tied at 0-0.

The FA Cup began to look a more likely bet for another medal, but an amazing five-game tussle in the fourth round against Burnley left us even more jaded. After drawing 1-1 at Turf Moor in the first game we were favourites to go through and meet Everton in the fifth round, but remained deadlocked in the replay, drawing a goal apiece. The third encounter was fought at Birmingham City's St Andrews ground, and when Peter Sillett equalised an early Burnley goal, we took command of the tie. However, Jimmy McIlroy scored early in the second half and it looked like our cup dream was over until I grabbed a late leveller. Although by forcing another replay we had shown a glimpse of the fighting quality that had served us so well the previous year, we were merely tiring ourselves even more. After yet another draw, 0-0, we eventually won through at the fifth time of asking, 2-0, just three days before the fifth round tie at Goodison Park. Dragging ourselves up by the bootlaces, we managed to turn in a half-decent performance at Everton, but were beaten by the only goal of the game.

By this stage our League form was in freefall, and we lost our next match 4-0 at London rivals Spurs. The next week, on 3 March, we hosted Manchester United, who were by this stage strong favourites for the title. After the eleven-goal thriller of the previous season, the rematch had a lot to live up to, and we chose the first half to raise our game and play our best football of the new year. We started the game brightly and midway through the first period scored two goals in the space of two minutes. Feeling re-energised by the absence of a midweek game for the first time in two months, I took a pass, beat three men and crossed for Eric to score the opener with a firm header. Almost immediately, Eric returned the favour with one of his trademark low crosses for me to score with a drive from the edge of the box. Just when it looked as though we were rekindling the spirit of '55, United hit us with a four-goal burst, with two from Dennis Viollet, leaving us on the ropes.

The final result of 2-4 left us disappointed, but worse was to follow when we visited Burnley the following Saturday, for the sixth time in eight weeks. The Clarets were psyched up and primed for revenge and we found ourselves on the end of a 5-0 walloping. With exhaustion ravaging the squad, we were grateful for the two-week break that followed, but our brief holiday evidently did us no good. On our return to action, West Bromwich Albion ran rings around us, easily beating us 3-0 at The Hawthorns and sending us into the bottom six.

Tom Finney scored the only goal seven days later as we took on Preston, and yet another unconvincing performance that day led respected journalist Frank Butler to let rip at the team, under the headline, 'What Happened to Champion Chelsea?' He wrote: 'Call it the end of the season feeling, or call it what you like, but it baffles me to know what is wrong with a team that wins the league championship in one season, and in the next struggles near the foot of the table. What has happened to the snap, the enthusiasm and the team spirit?'

Unfortunately, Frank's scathing article failed to rouse our troops and we lost our next match 2-1 at Sheffield United. We had taken just two points from our previous eight games and were perilously close to the relegation spots, sitting fifth from bottom. Having come so far in his first three years Ted now faced the very real possibility of leading a championship-winning team into the Second Division, which would have been a unique 'achievement'.

Our penultimate home match was played against our FA Cup conquerors Everton and we really needed the Stamford Bridge crowd to get behind us in what was by now a crucial relegation fixture. It was clear though that the Blues faithful had finally lost patience with the team and a paltry 13,825 turned up to watch us. The annual Scotland *v.* England fixture was being played at Hampden Park at the same time and may have affected our attendance but, even so, there could be no better testimony to the fall from grace of the heroes of '55. To put it in perspective, our final two matches of the previous season had seen us draw an average gate of 63,000.

In the event, those brave supporters who bothered to turn out were well rewarded for their trouble as we recorded our best result of the season, beating Everton 6-1. I scored what would be my final hat-trick in professional football that day, with my forward partner Les Stubbs grabbing two and Jim Lewis notching another. Having virtually secured our First Division status we ended the season on a relatively high note, drawing our next fixture 1-1 at Newcastle before beating second-placed Blackpool 2-1, with myself scoring two more goals to take my season's total to 14 in the League.

Our final position of sixteenth, just four points from the relegation zone and a massive twenty-one points behind champions Manchester United, was hugely disappointing. Things had changed drastically in the twelve months since Matt Busby had rolled out the Old Trafford red carpet for us. However, I had felt that, towards the end of the season, my own game had returned to normal, and believed that 14 League goals, a quarter of the team's total, was a decent return in a struggling side. I had scored five goals in my final three appearances and, although I had lost my England place, I had been chosen to represent Great Britain in a prestigious friendly against The Rest of Europe. As the players said their weary goodbyes for the summer, I had no reason to think that I would not be reporting to Stamford Bridge for pre-season training two months later. Changes were obviously going to be made at the club; Ted had hinted as much. What I hadn't seen coming was the revelation that my career at Chelsea was almost at an end.

Every summer I would have a slight feeling of trepidation when receiving the letter from the club stating whether or not my services would be retained for another season. Yet, as the club's leading goalscorer for the past seven years and the championship-winning captain from just twelve months earlier, there seemed little for me to worry about. So when I arrived at the ground to visit the club dentist and was told that Ted wanted me to pop into his office, my permanent departure from Stamford Bridge was the very last thing on my mind. Ted's opening words chilled me to the bone: 'I'm sorry Roy, but I have a very unpleasant duty to perform. I want you to know from me what has happened before the official letter arrives. We have decided to place you on the open-to-transfer list.' Although the board would give me a year's contract, they wanted me out of the club and to receive a decent-sized fee to compensate them for their troubles.

I was so shaken that I could hardly speak and I left his room without even asking why I was being kicked out of the club. When I got home I told Vi what had happened and she was, as always, totally supportive and told me that maybe it wouldn't be a bad idea if I moved elsewhere. A new challenge might do me good, after all. Although grateful for her kindness, I couldn't agree with her conclusion. I decided to call Ted and ask why he wanted me out. Ted seemed edgy, merely saying that the team was going 'backwards not forwards'. I agreed with that analysis, but didn't concur that I was one of the primary causes of our travelling in the wrong direction.

After pondering the contents of the letter for twenty-four hours, I made some phone calls to teammates and discovered that I was not the only recipient of bad news. Stan Willemse, Eric Parsons, Bill Robertson and Johnny McNichol had all received a 'Dear John' letter in the post, stating that their club 'regretted to inform them' that they were no longer required. Stan was the only one

not surprised at the news. His best days were behind him and he
had already suggested that he was finding life in the First Division
too tough. It wasn't long before he was snapped up by Leyton
Orient, a couple of divisions down, where he would see out the
rest of his career. The transfer-listing of the rest of us was rather
more controversial. Johnny and Eric had scored 11 and 14 goals
respectively in our championship win, and were both aged in their
early thirties, with plenty of football left in them. Bill was even
younger, just twenty-seven and, as a goalkeeper, had up to ten years
left between the posts.

Bearing in mind the way that our season had collapsed, with
players unable to take the physical strain a year after their championship exertions, it was understandable that Ted would look at ways
of reducing the average age of the side. Another factor to take into
consideration was that the youth set-up bequeathed to the club by
Billy Birrell and Ted had produced an exciting crop of youngsters
waiting in the wings for their chance. Our 1955 League title win
had been accompanied by the reserve team winning the Football
Combination League and the youth side winning the South-East
Counties League. The club undoubtedly had some good young
players on the books. The likes of Les Allen and Jimmy Greaves
were all knocking at the first-team door but, in my opinion, those
talents needed to be introduced to the line-up in a series of gradual
steps. I felt that the best way of securing a smooth transition from
the team of '55 to a new team capable of winning a second title
was not to dismiss all the most experienced players at the same time.
That would simply be to throw the baby out with the bathwater.

For a start Jimmy was still only sixteen, and there was no way
he could be expected to come straight into a First Division side
to replace me. In the event, Jimmy would not make his first-team
debut for a further year, although he quickly justified the hype surrounding him at Stamford Bridge, finishing as the First Division's
top scorer for four years in a row.

It seemed that, in my case, there had definitely been some pressure at boardroom level to force me out. A couple of directors
had not forgiven me for my strike four years earlier and had been

waiting for the right opportunity to get back at me. Ted wouldn't be drawn on this, but I later found out from him that it was the directors who were behind the move.

The fall-out from the club's decision to transfer list me was swift. Within days angry fans had painted 'Fair play to Roy Bentley' in three-foot high letters across the gates to Stamford Bridge. 'Why Bentley?' was also painted on a nearby entrance, while other slogans called on Ted to resign as manager. A petition was raised by supporters calling for the club to change their mind, and I received so many letters from fans telling me how annoyed they were that I was forced to abandon my handwritten replies and send out a stock, typed letter of thanks. Such support from the Chelsea faithful meant a great deal to me and helped me to absorb the shock of what had happened. The kind words of my teammates were also appreciated. The board did not appreciate me, the manager might not value me anymore, but the fans and my teammates liked me, and I consoled myself that it was the people who mattered most to me that didn't want me to leave.

The letter pages of the local newspaper also cheered me. One fan, G.A. Fisher of Conway Street, St Pancras, eloquently expressed how I was now completely in limbo, unwanted by the club but forced to stay on until they had received an offer that would swell the club's coffers. He wrote: 'I was under the mistaken impression that loyalty and service mattered at Chelsea. It must give the other players something to think about and has opened my eyes to what the Players' Union means by a "slave system".'

Suffering because of the bad publicity, the club tried to backtrack and Ted was wheeled out to explain how Chelsea weren't in fact forcing me out at all. 'We haven't circulated clubs. We haven't put Roy on the transfer list. We have retained him. We simply stated that we are open to receive offers for the following players.' This seemed to me a pretty mealy-mouthed explanation. If they wanted me to stay, they wouldn't be asking clubs to bid for my services.

Chelsea received a number of offers for me within days, including one from First Division rivals Portsmouth. West Ham and Fulham, who were both in the Second Division, were interested, while Scunthorpe United were rumoured to want me as player-manager. However, any chance of a move was sabotaged by the board, who announced that they would hold out for a fee in excess of the £11,500 they had paid for me eight years earlier. I was outraged. I had, at most, four years left in the top division, and the idea that someone would pay that kind of money to sign me was absurd.

Fulham made a firm bid of £8,000 that, although below Chelsea's valuation, was regarded by myself and most of the footballing press as more than fair. The prospect of such a move interested me. Although it would mean dropping down a division, I would still be able to live in Park Royal and keep my children in the same schools. Fulham would also pay me the same salary I was earning at Chelsea. Yet the board refused to let the transfer go ahead, fearing that some fans might follow me to Craven Cottage. I found that idea bizarre, but Ted himself admitted in an interview with leading football journalist Peter Lorenzo that the close proximity of the clubs ruled out a transfer. He said: 'Fulham interested in Roy? I bet they are. How far are they from us? No, we'll forget all about that.'

I was dismayed when I read Lorenzo's article. Having been told my services were no longer required, I had no wish to outstay my welcome and sit in Chelsea's reserves, merely making up the numbers. I accepted that my future lay elsewhere and had begun to think positively about a move to fresh pastures. Yet the club's insistence that I couldn't join the most conveniently located team, and their extravagant demand for a high fee, was making this impossible. It was the ultimate nightmare situation. Chelsea wanted me to leave, I wanted to move and clubs wanted me in their team, yet the board was wilfully putting me out of reach of interested parties. I was utterly powerless.

I felt like I was being treated like a piece of meat and, by the time I reported to pre-season training at the end of July, I felt incredibly disillusioned. When asked by journalists how I was feeling I would tell them honestly that I didn't want to be at Chelsea anymore. 'My heart is no longer at Stamford Bridge,' I said in one interview. 'I'd be happier elsewhere.' But what I thought was irrelevant.

Having discussed the situation with Vi, I vowed to train as hard as I could and try to ignore the possibility that I would still be at Stamford Bridge by the opening week of the campaign. Rather surprisingly I found myself included in most of the pre-season friendlies, scoring a few goals and, when the League programme got underway in mid-August, I was astonished to find myself still in the team. A 2-0 defeat at Burnley resulted in yet another public humiliation when I was made the scapegoat and dropped, just one game into the season. As my name continued to dominate the back pages for off-the-field reasons, Chelsea's form continued to suffer. A miserable 1-0 home loss to Preston was followed by a couple of draws at Leeds and Cardiff City, and by early September Chelsea were in the bottom four.

For the home game against Birmingham City on 15 September, Ted decided that drastic action was required and recalled myself, Eric Parsons, Johnny McNichol and Bill Robertson to the side. The 'new, improved Chelsea' had proved to be no better than the team that had completed the previous season and Ted decided it was necessary to bring back some experience to stabilise things. The return of four of the championship-winning team was made public a few days before the match, which may have something to do with the Stamford Bridge attendance almost doubling that day to 40,530.

Ted's ploy was an immediate success and we recorded our first win of the season, although our 1-0 triumph did not reflect our dominance. The Sunday newspapers, finding fresh legs in Roy Bentley's on-off transfer saga, had a field day. Scotty Hall, in the *Sunday Express*, was particularly playful. 'Don't do it, Chelsea, don't sell Roy Bentley. No gently Bentley touch about his return here before a rapturous 40,000 crowd. It was Bentley back with a biff and a bang. And that cheer that took him off at the end. You'd have thought that Roy had won the league championship, the FA Cup, the World Cup, and the St Leger all on his own. "We want Bentley," shouted the fans up to the directors' box at the end of this surprisingly one-sided match that Ted Drake's boys ought to have won by a bucketload of goals... Pardon the repetition, Chelsea, but don't do it. Nobody needs Roy Bentley more than you do.'

When I read the article I was touched at Scotty's sentiment but at the same time embarrassed. I was only one individual in an eleven-man team and I didn't think it was fair on my teammates to have to put up with the press's obsession with me in this very public tug of war. The situation was doing no good for the team and I could sense a softening in the club's attitude. It was becoming obvious that the best thing for all parties was that a resolution be found fast. The club had let the issue drag on for so long that to take me off the transfer list at this late stage would leave them humiliated. They had to get me off their books as quickly as possible.

I felt that my hand was now at its strongest and gave an interview to the national press a couple of days later in which I expressed my desire to be left out of the team for the next match against Sheffield Wednesday. In a public message to Ted I advised that 'it was his decision to bring in the youngsters and I think he should stick to his policy'.

My brinkmanship worked. On the Friday I was called in to Ted's office and when I arrived found him sitting with Frank Osborne, the Fulham manager. They were quite merry and I think had both had had a few drinks by then. Ted told me that the board had accepted Fulham's offer but that he didn't want me to go, claiming that I wouldn't like being at Fulham as much as Chelsea. I was staggered to hear him say this, but I reckon it was Ted's way of telling me that his hand had been forced by the board. He told me I would be a success at Fulham, shook my hand and wished me well.

I walked out of his office relieved that the matter had finally been resolved and also pleased that Ted and I had made friends again. Ted had been a huge influence on my career and I had always looked up to him. Many years later, a month or so before he died, Ted confessed to me that he had never wanted me to leave Chelsea in the first place, and that the board had told him to get rid of me. I'm sure that Ted's belated apology was genuine and I finally realised how hard the situation must have been for him at the time.

The whole incident showed how little leeway a manager had if the board chose to put their foot down. Only a year had passed since Ted had brought the club the first silverware in its history and he was at the peak of his managerial powers. Yet he was still being told by the board who he could and couldn't pick for his team. Somehow I can't see the current Chelsea hierarchy trying the same trick on Jose Mourinho. Nor would they want to, I imagine. In mitigation, the fact was that, back in 1956, most clubs acted in the same fashion. Clubs were ruthless in the way they treated their players and Chelsea were no exception. On the very same day that Chelsea placed five of their title-winning side on the transfer list, four leading British stars were receiving the same treatment from their clubs. Former England international Bobby Langton was told he was no longer wanted by Blackburn Rovers, along with talented teammate Eddie Quigley, while Aston Villa were releasing John Martin and Irish inside left Norman Lockhart. Footballers were regarded as dispensable and loyalty was a one-way street. I was given a stark reminder of this as I popped into the club's boot room, having left Ted's office for the final time. I was due to make my debut for Fulham the next day and needed to pick up my boots to take with me to Craven Cottage. I looked around for about ten minutes, but they were nowhere to be seen. Mystified, I asked one of the staff where my boots had been left, only to be informed that, because the club had paid for them, they were technically the club's property. My boots had already been given away.

As my career in the Second Division beckoned, so my international career came to an end. I had experienced a great many ups and downs during six years flitting in and out of the England side, and it is to this period that I will now turn.

TEN

England Expects

'Dear Roy, I have much pleasure in informing you that you have been selected for the FA party to undertake the tour of Europe.' The telegram was from Sir Stanley Rous, secretary of the FA, and arrived at my house in May 1949 while I was on the golf course at Sudbury. The League season had finished a few days earlier but, while strolling across the fairways, my mind had remained on football. I knew that I was in the frame for a first cap, having finished the League campaign strongly, but realised that form in itself was no guarantee of selection.

At the time the England team was not picked solely by the manager, Walter Winterbottom, but by a selection committee. It was an archaic formula, rather like the one that still exists in Test cricket, and it only changed when Walter was replaced by Alf Ramsey in 1962, after sixteen years in the job. My inclusion in the twenty-three-man squad had been the subject of lengthy media speculation, although similar calls for my selection earlier in the season had fallen on deaf ears. I was taking nothing for granted, even though the party was an unusually large one, including players for both the full England side and a 'B' team.

When I arrived home late that afternoon and saw a telegram on the table bearing an FA postmark I was elated. They wouldn't write to me unless it was good news, but it wasn't until I checked the contents of Sir Stanley's telegram that I could allow myself to celebrate.

The next day I took the train to Northolt in Middlesex where I would meet my new teammates at the RAF airport, before our departure to Stockholm. I was immediately made to feel welcome by the likes of captain Billy Wright and Tom Finney, and quickly settled into the camp. The first match of the tour was to be played in Stockholm itself, pitting the full England side against Sweden. I had no idea whether I would make the team, although I knew that at the very least I would get a run out in the 'B' team, whose first match was against Finland in Helsinki two days later.

On the morning before the Sweden match the team sheet went up in the hotel and my eyes scanned the list nervously for my name. When I saw that I was in the starting XI it was all I could do to stop myself from leaping up and punching the air. Had I been alone I may have done so, but I didn't think it would impress my colleagues too much. I was walking on air, knowing my schoolboy dream of representing my country was thirty-six hours from being realised. I went back to my room buzzing, although feeling incredibly frustrated that I didn't have access to a telephone so I could call the folks back home. It was left to the following morning's newspapers to inform my wife and parents that I was playing.

When I read through the England line-up, written in pencil, I felt thrilled to be in such exalted company. The team was as follows: Ted Ditchburn (Tottenham), Eddie Shimwell (Blackpool), Jack Aston (Manchester United), Billy Wright (Wolves), Neil Franklin (Stoke), Henry Cockburn (Manchester United), Tom Finney (Preston), Stan Mortensen (Blackpool), Roy Bentley (Chelsea), Jack Rowley (Manchester United), Bobby Langton (Preston).

The day before the match I came down with a heavy cold and there was some doubt in the selectors' minds whether I would be fit to play or not. I had no doubts at all that I would be okay and surprised a few of my colleagues by arriving at the final training session wearing two sweaters and a scarf, in my attempt to sweat out the cold. The ploy worked and, twenty-four hours later, on 13 May 1949, I stood for the national anthem, proudly sporting the three lions crest on my left breast. Competition for places among the forward line was fierce, with the likes of Nat Lofthouse, Jimmy Mullen, Wilf Mannion and Stanley Matthews among those left out. Yet the selectors still managed to shoehorn three centre forwards into the England attack instead of one, as was the custom. Under the WM formation one centre forward would usually be accompanied by two inside forwards, and both myself and Jack were a tad bewildered that we would each be playing at inside forward.

We did not practise our new roles in training and, on the night, the tactic failed miserably, with all three forwards getting in each other's way, and rarely looking like scoring. It was left to winger Tom Finney to notch our late consolation goal in a sorry 3–1 defeat. Yet it might have been so different had I taken an early chance to score with my first touch in international football. Chasing a long, bouncing pass from our own half I reached out with a boot and tried to lob the advancing goalkeeper, but connected badly with the ball and it was scrambled away. Sweden went on to score three first-half goals after Billy Wright had lost the toss and they had kicked off with a bright setting sun behind them. Poor Ted Ditchburn said afterwards that he had been completely blinded for two of their goals, which I could well believe. We regrouped at half-time and both Tom and myself hit the post before I set him up to reduce the arrears midway through the second half. At the final whistle I felt a great sense of disappointment and knew that I had not done myself justice on my debut. I was not surprised to discover that I had been dropped from the side to face Norway in Oslo five days later.

As a consolation prize I was selected for the 'B' team to face Holland in Amsterdam the same night, lining up alongside Jack Rowley for the second game in a row. This time around, with one less centre forward to worry about, our partnership clicked, and I scored my first goal in an England shirt, running onto a through ball from Jack before firing home. A young Eric Parsons, then of West Ham, stole the show that night, long before the two of us would forge our successful partnership at Stamford Bridge.

England had beaten the Norwegians 4–1 in the first team's game and, unsurprisingly, the selectors kept faith with the same forward line for the final match of the tour, against France, which was won 3–1. There was no reciprocal fixture for the 'B' side, so I returned home feeling apprehensive about my mixed performances. When

I failed to make the squad for either of the Home International matches that autumn, I feared I may have blown my chance, particularly when England stuffed Northern Ireland 9-2 in the second game at Maine Road. My partner on the European tour, Jack Rowley, scored four goals that night and I couldn't see how I was going to dislodge him from the side.

For weeks afterwards I found myself reflecting on my hitting the post against Sweden and wondering how things might have been had my shot gone a couple of inches inside the woodwork. The history books include a litany of 'one-cap' wonders who have disappeared from the England international scene almost as soon as they arrived. More than fifty years after my debut the Derby County midfielder Seth Johnson almost scored with his first touch for England against Italy, but was never picked again. I know how he must have felt.

My name came back in the frame quite by chance the following January, as England prepared for a 'B' international against Switzerland in Sheffield. On the morning of the match it had been decided that each side would be allowed one substitute, something that had never been tried before in an England fixture. I received a phone call at Stamford Bridge instructing me to get on the next train to Yorkshire. After picking up my boots I rushed to the station, arriving at Hillsborough with two hours to spare. Shortly before half-time my Chelsea teammate Billy Gray limped off injured and I was summoned to the field, where I became the first English international to appear as a substitute. I put in a decent performance as we thrashed the Swiss 5-0.

The FA selectors evidently received a good report about my efforts because, in early April, I received a second letter from Sir Stanley Rous informing me that I had been selected for the full England side to play against Scotland. My Chelsea form had been good during the second half of the 1949/50 season and a two-goal performance in the FA Cup semi-final against Arsenal had probably tipped the balance in my favour.

The importance of the match against the Scots cannot be underestimated. The annual fixture between the 'Auld Enemies' was one of the two biggest events of the football calendar, along with the FA Cup final, and this particular year there was even more at stake than national pride. The game at Hampden Park was the last remaining fixture of the yearly Home Nations Championship. The top two teams in the group, which also included Wales and Northern Ireland, would qualify for the following summer's World Cup tournament in Rio de Janeiro. England and Scotland, neither of whom had appeared before in a World Cup, filled the top two berths in the Home Nations table, having won both their previous matches. Both of us could conceivably qualify for the tournament, no matter what the result. However, the Scottish FA had other ideas and, mystifyingly, had informed the world's governing body FIFA that they would only attend the tournament in Brazil if they won the Home Nations outright. For reasons known only to themselves, the Scottish chiefs had made their players unnecessary hostages to fortune.

It seems unbelievable that a country would deliberately sabotage their participation in a World Cup when countries nowadays would jump at any backdoor entry to a major tournament. The Danish team that won the 1992 European Championships certainly didn't need a second invitation when asked to take Yugoslavia's place at the event.

However shocking it appears now, such a reaction was not entirely surprising in Britain back in 1950. The English FA themselves had consistently snubbed the World Cup since its inception twenty years earlier. In their arrogance, they believed that English football was the best in the world and did not wish to dignify the competition by sending a team. The last tournament had taken place in France in 1938 before the outbreak of the Second World War but, over the ensuing twelve years, the English FA had finally been won over to the idea. I was very excited to be given the chance to stake my claim for a place in Rio and, despite being picked at inside forward, I was determined to take my second chance.

Playing at Hampden Park for the only time in my career was an incredible experience. The Scottish supporters were rabidly anti-English, a point made publicly years later by one of my teammates that day, Alf Ramsey. When the team arrived at Glasgow Airport for the annual Auld Enemy clash Alf, by then the national manager, was greeted by a reporter uttering the words, 'Welcome to Scotland.' Alf's typically deadpan reply was priceless: 'Welcome to Scotland? You must be effing joking.' Alf was right. I have never experienced such hostility from a British crowd as I saw and heard that day, although I found the effect uplifting rather than unsettling and believe that it helped raise my game.

Although by no means the greatest football tactician, Walter Winterbottom had done his homework for the match at Hampden, coming up with the novel idea of switching Stan Mortensen and myself between inside forward and centre forward at varying intervals. According to a match report, Stan and I changed positions every quarter of an hour or so, at a given signal, and the Scots found the tactic virtually unplayable, backing off and giving the England attack lots of extra room. Although we had dominated the first half it finished goalless but, eighteen minutes into the second period, our perseverance with switching paid dividends. Bolton's Bobby Langton raced down the left wing and, ignoring the decoy run of Wilf Mannion, crossed for where Stan should have been positioned. Stan had swapped with me a minute or so earlier, and I appeared from nowhere to reach the ball. With the defence at sixes and sevens I flicked the ball past the despairing lunge of the nearest Scottish defender before letting fly with my right foot. The 'keeper got half a touch on the ball but couldn't stop my shot from nestling in the corner of the net. As 37,000 away fans roared and 100,000 Scots stood in silence, I wheeled away in delight, having scored my first goal for England at the mighty Hampden Park. It was an incredible feeling. Even today I regard this as the favourite goal of my career.

The rest of the match continued at a frenetic pace, with the Scots throwing everything but the kitchen sink at the England goal. In the closing minutes one of the Scottish lads was put through on goal with just goalkeeper Bert Williams to beat, but his shot crashed off the underside of the crossbar to safety. At the end of the game the Scots trudged off disconsolately, knowing that we were on the road to Rio while they would be stuck at home listening to the tournament on the radio. As a national inquest into the home team's defeat continued over the ensuing weeks, the Scottish FA could have only themselves to blame for their silly act of bravado.

Some weeks later I was handing out the prizes at an awards ceremony of a London amateur club when a fuming Scotsman walked over and gave me a piece of his mind. He turned the air blue with a long tirade, accusing me of having ruined Scottish football for the next ten years. They certainly took the game seriously up there. For my own safety, I thought it probably sensible not to point out to the chap that the Scots' failure to qualify was their own damned fault.

I retained my place for the next game against Portugal, the first of a two-match mini-tour of Europe in preparation for the forthcoming World Cup. Playing in Lisbon was a smart move on the FA's part, helping us to acclimatise to the temperatures we would face a month hence. Tom Finney, Wilf Mannion and Stan Mortensen all stayed in the attack, while my old mate Jackie Milburn replaced the unfortunate Bobby Langton, who had done little wrong up at Hampden. Neil Franklin, Man of the Match against Scotland, was by now a football pariah, having chosen to join Bogota in Colombia instead of representing England. Although the rest of the team remained the same, the loss of Neil was a devastating blow to us. Alongside Billy Wright, Neil had played in all twenty-seven of England's games since the war and the pair had built up a tremendous partnership.

When we arrived at the Hotel du Parque in the Portuguese capital, I found myself absolutely stunned by its beauty. I have never stayed anywhere as posh in my life, and it seemed to be something out of Hollywood. Sitting in my plush hotel room I really felt that I had arrived as an international footballer. The matchday preparations were also pretty special. Wanting to impress their English guests, the Portuguese FA had shipped in turf from Cumberland, which they were watering heavily in the build-up to kick-off.

Perhaps our hosts made things too comfortable because, within weeks, my teammates and I would be dreaming of that lush playing surface as we struggled in the dust bowl of Rio. For those two final warm-up matches the FA had issued us with pairs of special lightweight boots that were designed for playing on the hard and dusty pitches we were to encounter in Rio. I have to say that I never got used to them, finding them too pointed and lightweight, and they were far from ideal on the lush playing surface in Lisbon.

As we trotted on to the National Stadium pitch, Stan Mortensen turned to me and said, 'Watch out for the cushions, Roy.' I had no idea what he meant by that comment and just laughed but, as we left the field after a 5-3 win I fully understood his warning. Thousands of leather cushions, provided for those who wished to sit on the stone slab terrace steps, rained down on us from above. The home fans were throwing them at their own players as a way of show-ing their disgust at the defeat, but their aim wasn't always the best, especially among those who had drunk a few beers. Heaven knows what it must have been like the last time England had played in the National Stadium, when we had beaten the Portuguese 10-0.

The match itself had seen a strong England performance, with Tom Finney scoring four, including two penalties, and Stan Mortensen adding a spectacular fifth. Although I hadn't scored myself, I felt happy enough with my performance and was pleased to retain my place for the trip to Brussels four days later. This would be England's final warm-up match for the World Cup, even though the tournament itself was four weeks away. Having grown accustomed to playing in intense heat in Lisbon, it seemed a little strange to play our next match in the milder climes of Belgium, but ours was not to ask why.

When it dawned on me that the selectors had chosen the same starting XI that had played against Portugal I knew that a place in the World Cup team was mine, so long as I didn't mess up. The match was played in the Heysel Stadium, a ground where one of Europe's worst ever football disasters would take place thirty-six years later.

On the night England put in a nervy first-half performance and we found ourselves one down at the interval. Jackie Milburn had turned an ankle early on and was replaced by the Wolves forward Jimmy Mullen, who thus became the first substitute to represent

England in a full international fixture. After the break Jimmy equalised, in the process earning himself his second record of the night as the first England substitute to score a goal. Stan Mortensen and Wilf Mannion then netted to give us a commanding 3-1 lead. Although I'd had a hand in all three of our goals, I knew that one for myself might be necessary to assure my place in the side to face Chile in the tournament opener. I was therefore somewhat relieved to score with practically the last kick of the game to ensure an emphatic 4-1 victory.

In the days leading up to our departure for Rio our squad of twenty-one players trained at Wembley Stadium, which was quite an eerie experience. I had yet to represent England at the 'home of football' and I found playing there in front of four empty stands a rather surreal experience.

The days of fast jet travel were some way off and our journey from London to Rio required stopovers at numerous places, including Paris, Lisbon and Dakar. We were in the air for a total of thirty-one hours and, as we walked down the gangway at the airport in Rio, we were all pining for our beds. However, sleep was the last thing on the minds of our excited hosts. As one of the pre-tournament favourites, we received a rapturous welcome upon our arrival in the Brazilian capital. Shaking off our tiredness, the carnival atmosphere that surrounded our hotel was nice to start with, but when it started disrupting our sleep night after night it became less of a bonus. I found Rio a beautiful city, but was appalled by the poverty I saw all around us. There were labourers and children living in what were no more than holes in the ground. I had no idea that this was what life in Brazil was like before we had arrived and the memory stayed with me forever. Brazil was, in general, not an easy place for us to be based. Most players found acclimatising to the thin Brazilian air very difficult and several of us required oxygen at the end of training sessions. We were also bewildered by the fact that the FA had, in their wisdom, sent one of our best players, Stanley Matthews, on a goodwill tour of Canada shortly before the game. Although they had made special arrangements to fly Stanley to Rio, he never made it in time for the match. It was a ludicrous state of affairs and typical of the blinkered way the FA is usually perceived to have been run at the time.

Our first game was against Chile in the newly finished Maracana Stadium, which held 200,000 fans but for this match contained a mere ten per cent of that number. Our opponents were certainly favoured by the humid conditions, but we ground out a work-manlike performance and won the game 2-0. I was relieved to get through the game, having contracted a minor stomach bug, and was happy with my performance. Jimmy Mullen, who had retained his place in the team at the expense of poor Jackie Milburn, crossed for Stan Mortensen to head in England's first ever World Cup goal in the opening half. Chilean forward George Robledo, who was plying his trade in England for Newcastle United, struck a post after the break before I set up Wilf Mannion to score the all-important second goal.

Unfortunately there were no tactics or game plan at all, and my roving game quite understandably passed my teammates by, who didn't really know how to play to my strengths. As we put on our 'civvies' after showering Walter congratulated us on our perform-ance but said ominously that we could play a lot better. As we found out a week later, we could also play a hell of a lot worse.

Our next game was against the United States, a nation who had little interest in football, and the match was regarded by everybody, including the team, as a foregone conclusion. The Americans were all part-timers, players who were no better than those appearing in the English Third Division. By contrast, we were representing the most famous football nation on Earth. It was surely only a matter of how many goals we would stick past the poor Yankee 'keeper.

The match was played 300 miles inland at Belo Horizonte and the England squad moved bases in advance to a luxurious camp up in the hills. We were glad to leave Rio, which was a beautiful city, but one in which we were finding it increasingly difficult to sleep. I'll never forget the drive up the remote dusty roads to the hills. The setting was idyllic, with miles of natural beauty, and we stayed in beautiful log cabins. The water was fresh from the hills, and we enjoyed ice-cold showers in the morning.

Although the camp itself was fairly primitive we were well-provided for as official guests of a gold mining company, an English-owned firm employing 2,000 British workers. We felt more relaxed than we had ever done in Rio and were looking forward to winning our second match and reaching the next stage of the tournament, although we did not treat the Americans as pushovers. The press stayed at the camp with us, something that is unthinkable now, but the journalists were careful to maintain their professional distance. After the subsequent debacle against the US, the press's independence would come fully into play as they turned against us remorselessly.

Although England had been far from at our best against Chile the selectors refused to recall Stanley Matthews to the side. The FA's chief selector was a fish merchant from Grimsby called Arthur Drewry, and it was his view that a winning side could not be changed that prevailed over that of Walter Winterbottom, who wanted Stanley to play.

In front of a crowd of not much more than 10,000 we performed poorly on an atrocious, narrow pitch, but playing against such feeble opposition we still made all the early running. Tom Finney, Stan Mortensen and Wilf Mannion were all guilty of missing good chances, before an incredible thing happened. After thirty-seven minutes, with their first attack of the match, the Americans took the lead, Larry Gaetjens scoring the goal by deflecting an off-target shot with his head past a wrong-footed Bert Williams. Although we were shocked to go behind, there was no need for panicking at this stage. We still had the best part of an hour left to win by a hatful but, as the game wore on, fear started to creep into our game and our efforts became increasingly desperate. With the Americans camped in their own half, we discovered that fate was very firmly against us. At one stage Stan Mortensen appeared to have equalised when his shot was cleared by a defender a yard or so over the goal line, but neither the referee nor the near-side linesman spotted it, and we remained 1-0 down. I also hit two shots that beat the goalkeeper but struck the woodwork and rebounded to safety. In addition, we had two clear-cut penalty claims turned down, one of which was the most blatant foul I saw in my whole career. The American goalkeeper, a former ice hockey player, rugby-tackled Tom Finney to the ground after Tom took the ball around him. It was a clear penalty. Unbelievably, the referee waved play on.

When the ref blew for full time I felt sick to my stomach. England had suffered their worst defeat ever and as I watched Larry Gaetjens being carried off the field on his colleagues' shoulders I felt embarrassed to have been part of such a momentous loss. Despite our poor performance, we hadn't deserved to lose, shooting at least thirty attempts on goal compared to just two by our conquerors. The referee had certainly done us no favours either. If the match had been played in the age of live television, there might have been an inquiry into the performance of the official. In the event, our feelings of being hard done by were largely ignored.

Sir Stanley Rous came into the dressing room and told us that it would be unsportsmanlike to complain about the referee, instructing us to take the defeat on the chin. I suppose he felt that, whatever we felt privately, we had been beaten by part-timers and there could be no justifiable excuse for such a dreadful result. Sir Stanley immediately banned the team from talking to the press, although the journalists at Bela Horizonte hardly needed the players to confirm what an appalling result we had suffered. The reporters were savage in their criticism, turning on us bitterly and calling us the worst England team ever. Who could blame them? The players certainly didn't, and when we read what they had written it didn't stop us acknowledging them at breakfast.

A measure of just how big a shock our defeat had been was the reaction of my dad. Turning to the 'Stop Press' section of the following day's newspaper he thought there had been a misprint, believing that the score must have been 'USA 1, England 10'. It would take sixteen years for English football to fully erase the shame of that day. Ironically it would be one of my teammates that day, Alf Ramsey, who was the architect of that atonement when he led England to their one and only World Cup triumph, against West Germany in 1966.

Changes to the England forward line were inevitable and unsurprisingly, as one of the less-established members of the team, I was
sacrificed, along with Wilf Mannion and Jimmy Mullen. Replacing
us were Stanley Matthews, Jackie Milburn and Eddie Baily, but such
radical surgery failed to work and England were beaten 1-0 in a
game marred by underhand Spanish tactics.

Having been talked up by the whole of England as World
Champions elect, we had been utterly humiliated. The England
squad had left British shores to a great fanfare and with good
wishes ringing in our ears but, when we returned home to Blighty,
we were in disgrace and all of us would be forever tainted by our
appearance in the match. Little did I know it but, as I stepped on
to the tarmac, I would not be reacquainted with my England colleagues for a further two-and-a-half years.

Getting back into the England team was a hard slog. I only
had to look at the names of some of the other forwards to realise
just how strong the competition for a place in attack was. Stan
Mortensen was one of the best headers of a ball to ever appear
for England, as was Nat Lofthouse, who had begun to emerge
as a serious contender. I have already written about the fantastic
talent belonging to my former Newcastle colleague Jackie Milburn,
whose international career had strong parallels with my own. Wor
Jackie's England record of 10 goals in 13 appearances was very
similar, while both his first and last caps were received within six
months of mine.

Inside right Wilf Mannion was a footballing genius who would
have been even more celebrated in this country had he not played
in the same side as Tom Finney and Stanley Matthews. Wilf was a
small lad who looked like a puff of wind would blow him over at
any moment, but he had the heart of an ox and brilliant awareness, which allowed him to make defenders look silly. He was the
perfect link between defence and attack, roaming around the field
in a similar fashion to myself. Fortunately, we rarely got in each
other's way on the field.

Finney and Matthews were undoubtedly the best players I ever
played with, and were arguably the best two English footballers

ever. The fact that Walter Winterbottom had the luxury of picking them both, on alternate wings, showed just how unfathomable our dismal World Cup exit had been. Both of them were so skilful and, despite the fact that they were at times rivals for the same position, they were great friends. The press liked to make out that the two of them were bitter enemies, but nothing could have been further from the truth. Tom was a permanent fixture in the England side, scoring 30 goals in 76 appearances over a twelve-year period. Stanley's England career lasted an incredible twenty-three years and continued until 1957, when he was forty-three, making him the country's oldest international of all time. He made a total of 54 appearances for England and one wonders just how high that total would have been had it not been for the outbreak of the Second World War two years after his debut.

Jimmy Mullen and Jack Rowley were two other great finishers, the latter being particularly unfortunate to receive only 6 caps considering the fact that he averaged a goal a game for his country. Even more surprisingly, Len Shackleton, one of the stars of my generation, made just 5 appearances for England. Perhaps Len's unique talent was just too troublesome for Walter Winterbottom to harness into his side. Having looked around at the varying fortunes of my contemporaries, I felt reasonably pleased with my total at the time of 6 caps, although I desperately hoped that I would get another outing for my country. In the event I would double my tally of international appearances by the end of my career.

I should also mention how privileged I felt to play alongside captain Billy Wright for each of my appearances for England. Billy was the first Englishman to represent his country 100 times, a supremely talented wing half and later centre half, as clean cut as he was talented. A superb defender, his tackles were invariably timed to perfection, while his passing was the equal of many of those who played in more advanced positions. Billy led by example on the field and was the best captain I ever played for.

Despite my good form in the 1950/51 season my recall to the national side was delayed for eighteen months. At first this was because of my strike at Chelsea in the summer of 1951, which apparently made the selectors shy away from me. After my differences with Chelsea had been settled, I found myself selected in April 1952 for the England squad to face Scotland at Hampden, the scene of my greatest international triumph. It was rather ironic that, having made my peace with Chelsea, my run of form that had got me back into the national side would in itself prevent me from making my comeback appearance.

Scoring the winning goal in Chelsea's FA Cup quarter-final at Sheffield United had helped me get the nod over some of my rivals, but that goal would come back to haunt me. When our semi-final against Arsenal was postponed, the FA inexplicably decided to reschedule the match for 5 April, the same day as England were playing at Hampden. In the event, England won 2–1 in front of a bumper crowd of 133,991 and I was denied the chance of a second appearance in the Scottish cauldron. Not that I begrudged an FA Cup semi-final appearance, mind.

England's next match, on 12 November 1952, was against Wales in the following season's Home Championship, for which I was recalled at inside left. Although I would have liked a try out at centre forward, I was as pleased as punch that my international exile was over. A mere four of my teammates from the infamous defeat in Bela Horizonte remained in the side that day; Billy Wright, Alf Ramsey, Tom Finney and Portsmouth's Jimmy Dickinson. Finney, at right wing, was the only forward among that quartet, and the pair of us were joined in attack by Burnley's Billy Elliott on the left wing, debutant Redfern Froggatt of Sheffield Wednesday at inside right and the mighty Nat Lofthouse of Bolton as centre forward. It was six months since Nat's famous two-goal performance for England in Austria earned him the nickname 'The Lion of Vienna' and I was happy to have the chance to play alongside him.

The conditions were difficult, with driving sleet falling from the sky and ice patches on the grass, but two goals inside the first ten minutes by Tom and Nat settled the home team's nerves. Sunderland's Trevor Ford pulled one back for Wales a few minutes before England's Jack Froggatt was involved in a terrible collision and had to go off for treatment. Jack was a fearless fellow though and, after some lengthy treatment, hobbled back on to the field, five minutes before he restored England's two-goal advantage with a powerful header.

Ten minutes into the second half I achieved a lifelong ambition and scored my first goal at Wembley, burying a twenty-yard snap-shot just inside the corner. An almost identical goal by Wales' Trevor Ford sixty seconds later failed to take the shine off my moment of glory and we wrapped up a 5-2 win when Nat got his second goal of the match.

The selectors chose the same eleven players two weeks later for England's friendly at home to Belgium. I already held happy memories of playing against the Belgians, my goal against them two-and-a-half years earlier ensuring my place in the 1950 World Cup, but I was to be less fortunate this time. Nat Lofthouse notched another pair, as did Billy Elliott, with Redfern Froggatt scoring the other goal. The closest I came to adding to my tally of three international goals was a header that struck the crossbar before falling to Billy to put in the rebound. The match finished 5-0 to England and, although I hadn't scored that day, I felt I had done enough to warrant another run-out for England. Yet, by the time the team reconvened to play Scotland at Wembley five months later, I had lost my place to Manchester City's Ivor Broadis. Ivor's two goals in an entertaining 2-2 draw with the Scots pushed him further above me in the pecking order, and it would be a further nineteen months before I would pull on the famous white jersey again. However, when that day finally arrived, on 10 November 1954, it was well worth the wait.

In the months before my recall the England team had suffered a defeat that was as shocking as the World Cup loss against the USA. I was stood in the stands alongside Ted Drake on that cold night in November 1953 when the unheralded Hungary side visited Wembley for what appeared to be a routine friendly match. Along with the British press, most supporters and quite possibly the play-ers, the pair of us in our ignorance assumed the game would be a walkover for the home side. How wrong we were.

A few titters were raised half an hour or so before kick-off when the Hungarians came out onto the field to warm up. This was completely alien to an English crowd and appeared to us a rather eccentric gesture. People were also pointing fingers at the short, tubby Hungarian number ten strutting around and thoughts abounded of an even bigger victory than had first been assumed. That chap would be lucky to last forty-five minutes, let alone ninety, we all thought.

The identity of that number ten would be known to everyone by the end of the evening. Ferenc Puskas's name still sends a shiver down the spines of those old enough to remember the match and remains synonymous with English footballing humiliation. Puskas's unathletic frame disguised an enormous talent and throughout ninety spellbinding minutes he helped make England look like a team of schoolboys. Puskas orchestrated the Hungarian team like a classical conductor and scored two fantastic goals in the process as the visitors ran out 6-3 winners.

Hungary's tactics were light years ahead of our own, with coach Gusztav Sebes abandoning the rigidity of the WM formation and implementing a revolutionary 4-2-4 system that left our defenders utterly confused as to who they were supposed to be marking. In addition to Puskas's double, forward Nandor Hidegkuti scored a hat-trick as the Hungarians racked up the most goals an England team has ever conceded on their own soil.

The pounding that England's self-esteem took that night would take a long time to overcome. Scotland were the only other country to have beaten England at their spiritual home, winning three times there by then. But the defeat to Hungary was the first time a non-British nation had beaten England at Wembley. The game is often mistakenly referred to as the first game England lost on its own soil to a country outside the UK, but the Republic of Ireland can lay claim to that record, having won at Goodison Park four years earlier. However, this result was far more momentous and forced English football to pull its collective head out of the sand and radically alter its approach to tactics.

Even then, the awful reality did not fully sink in until six months later. The FA had ill-advisedly fixed up a return game in Budapest as

England's final match before that summer's World Cup tournament, in the vain attempt to prove the Wembley result a fluke. The score the second time around was even worse. Slaughtered by seven goals to one in the Hungarian capital, there was little doubt that English football's pomposity had finally been punctured. Radical change was necessary to rescue the game in this country. It is arguable that both Hungarian drubbings were necessary for English football to be shaken out of its arrogant complacency. Some might say that those defeats resulted in the planting of the first seeds of our World Cup success twelve years later.

As a fan of English football, I was bitterly disappointed with both of those crushing defeats although, on a professional level, rather relieved to have taken no part in either game. Having been in the England side beaten by the United States in 1950, I don't think I could have coped with yet another humiliation of that nature. I may well have never played for my country again, however unfair such a scapegoating may have been.

The defeat came too late for changes to be made to England's squad for the 1954 World Cup in Switzerland so I was left at home, while England battled gamely to reach the second stage of the tournament. Defeat against Uruguay in their final group game led to a second successive undistinguished World Cup exit and within four months I was recalled to the side for England's second Home International against Wales.

England had won their opening fixture at Windsor Park, Belfast, beating Northern Ireland 2–0 five weeks earlier, and I was surprised to find myself picking a telegram from the FA off my doormat. I hadn't scored in my last five appearances for Chelsea and, having turned thirty six months earlier, I had rather assumed that my England days might be numbered. However, this unexpected recall was to kick-start my most productive spell in the national side.

When I looked around the Wembley dressing room before kick-off only one of my teammates from my previous England appearance against Belgium was present, the indefatigable captain Billy Wright. Stanley Matthews, out on the right wing, was one of three other faces familiar to me. I was also joined by Len

Shackleton, who I had never before played alongside for England, while my Chelsea colleague, young Frankie Blunstone, made his debut on the left wing.

Half an hour into the match Wales took the lead against the run of play when Sunderland's Trevor Ford sold his marker an audacious dummy, allowing Ivor Allchurch to drive the ball low and hard for John Charles to tap in at the far post. John was one of my favourite players of the time and had flown back to Britain for the game from Turin in Italy. John had recently become one of the first British stars to play club football abroad without making himself persona non grata, his move to the mighty Juventus from Leeds United that summer making him a world star. Had I not been picked that day, I would have gladly paid on the gate just to see the best footballer in Welsh history perform.

Instead, as the opening half drew to a close, I was ruing the 'Gentle Giant's' decision to return for the game. Welsh defenders Ray Daniel and Derek Sullivan had been forced off for treatment, leaving the visitors temporarily down to nine men. In a desperate move, John had switched from centre forward to centre half, almost single-handedly repelling the England attack until the pair's return. John was equally adept at both ends of the field, a point made perfectly by his former Leeds teammate Tom Holley many years later. Tom said: 'Nat Lofthouse was asked who was the best centre half he had played against and without hesitation named John Charles. The same week Billy Wright was asked who was the greatest centre forward he had faced, and he too answered "John Charles".' That says it all.

When the two Welsh lads returned to the fray, Ray Daniel sporting three stitches, it looked as if I had missed my best chance to return to scoring ways for England. Midway through the second half we still trailed 1-0 but, just as I started to worry that my international comeback would be short-lived, everything started to go my way. Stanley Matthews and I exchanged passes before the wing wizard set off on a trademark dribble. He unleashed a perfect diagonal cross that I ran on to and headed home from inside the box. Within ten minutes I had scored a second, giving England the lead. Again my goal was scored with my head from another cross by Stanley after his trickery had taken him to the byline.

Not long afterwards the England defence gave John Charles too much room on the ball and he levelled the scores at 2-2 with a magnificent shot. Time was running out but my confidence was sky-high after scoring two goals and I thought I had the best opportunity I'd ever have to score an international hat-trick. Football has always been so much easier when you play with self-belief. A forward can always find an extra spring in his step, and will seek out the ball and make audacious attempts on goal whenever he is on top of his game, and I was no exception. When Frankie Blunstone capped an impressive debut with a cross that goalkeeper John King fumbled, I was on hand to tap into the empty net and complete my trio.

After the referee had blown for full time I lingered on the Wembley turf, eager to enjoy every last minute of the glory. I felt on top of the world, having achieved something I had rarely dared to dream about. If only that feeling could be bottled, the inventor would make millions. Even had he wanted to, Walter Winterbottom couldn't have dropped a striker who had scored a hat-trick, so I was fortunate to be a shoo-in for the prestigious Wembley friendly against West Germany three weeks later.

It was nine years since the end of the Second World War and feelings still ran high among many who, like me, spent our youth fighting against the Germans. There was much anti-German feeling in the country, although I never held any grudges. I only needed to look at what a terrific ambassador the German goalkeeper Bert Trautmann was for his country to realise that this was futile. Even so, the contest had a lot more spice than the average run-of-the-mill friendly, and it was inevitable that the thoughts of myself, Tom Finney and all the others who had served the British forces during the conflict would turn to our fallen comrades.

The old rivalry between the two nations was increased further by the West German FA's insistence that England wear their change strip of red in deference to the World Champions. The Germans had won the game's top prize the previous summer, having come from two goals down to beat Puskas's Hungary 3-2 in the Swiss capital Berne and they, not unreasonably, wanted to rub our noses in it. The English lads had other ideas.

The atmosphere was white hot when the teams walked out together in front of a capacity crowd on the evening of 1 December. All 100,000 tickets for the match had sold out within a single morning and, roared on by a buoyant England crowd, we took the lead after twenty-eight minutes. Stanley Matthews hit yet another perfect centre for me to score with another header. It was my fourth goal for my country in little over forty-five minutes' play. Incidentally, Stanley had been in the English line-up an incredible nineteen years earlier when Germany had last been the visitors, before the division of the country by the victorious Allies. What an amazing man.

Two minutes into the second half, the West Bromwich Albion inside forward Ronnie Allen snatched a second, before the Germans pulled a goal back. With ten minutes remaining Len Shackleton scored his only goal for England with a cheeky chip to give us a famous 3-1 victory. Although not as celebrated as the win over the West Germans twelve years later, I can assure you that it felt pretty good to have helped us put one over on the old enemy that night. Rarely has so much pride been at stake for an international friendly and the win helped regain a fragment of English football's self-esteem that had been decimated by the debacles against Puskas and co.

As was customary, the England-Scotland fixture marked the close of the Home Nations tournament the following April. Four months had elapsed since our victory against the West Germans and, somewhat harshly, I found myself dropped from the squad to play at Wembley. The match was played the same day as Chelsea were homing on their first League title by winning 4-2 at Tottenham, so I wasn't exactly sat at home pining. My first priorities were with my club, after all. England had already plucked Frankie Blunstone from the Chelsea side, so it was probably for the best that I wasn't selected to face the Scots. However, I wouldn't have been human had I not been slightly disappointed to discover that my replacement, Dennis Wilshaw, hammered in four goals as Scotland were thrashed 7-2.

I needn't have worried though, because three weeks after Chelsea had secured the League title I was selected for England's two-match Southern European tour. Having sweated off the extra pounds I had put on scoffing cream and meat on Chelsea's post-title trip to Ireland, I was picked for the first game against Spain, in Madrid. Dennis Wilshaw, unsurprisingly, had retained his place, and we were joined in attack by Nat Lofthouse, Stanley Matthews and Sheffield Wednesday's Dennis Quixall. The great Duncan Edwards was also in the team.

My Chelsea colleague, the penalty king Peter Sillett, had deservedly won a place on the tour and I tried my best to make him feel at home and prevent his nerves from getting the better of him. Peter was told to share a room with the old pro Stanley Matthews in the hope that some of the winger's wisdom would rub off on the young pretender. The pair didn't get off to the best of starts, though. Unable to relax the night before the game young Peter lit up a cigarette, only to find himself on the end of his room-mate's wrath. Leaping out of bed, Stanley grabbed the cigarette from the shell-shocked full-back's mouth and lobbed it out of the window, along with the rest of the packet. 'If you want to make a career in this game, my lad, you'll give those a miss,' he said. After recovering his poise young Peter reached into his pocket a few minutes later and pulled out a bag of boiled sweets to suck on, again with the intention of easing his nerves. As quick as a flash Stanley was out of his bed again, grabbing the bag and throwing the offending sweets out of the window to join the cigarettes fifty feet below. 'If you want to make a career in this game, my lad, you'll give those a miss,' came the familiar refrain.

When I heard this story I burst out laughing. It was typical of Stanley, who prided himself on his impeccable fitness. I can remember watching in awe as he trained alone with a skipping rope, working alone on his fitness for hour after hour. He was scolding Peter for the new boy's own benefit and certainly didn't mean Peter any harm at all. If I recall correctly, Stanley was one of the first to congratulate the newcomer after his sterling debut that night.

The match was a very bad-tempered affair and Nat Lofthouse played the whole of the second half without a number on his shirt, after one of the Spaniards had ripped it from his back. I managed to score England's goal in the 1-1 draw, having been put through on goal by Nat, and retained my place for the trip to Portugal. Unfortunately, we did not return to either the beautiful Hotel du Parque nor the National Stadium in Lisbon. The match was instead played at the Antas Stadium in Porto. I scored early in the game, my sixth goal in four matches, but sadly our 3-1 defeat marked the end of my international career. Thousands of Portuguese fans left their cushions behind and ran onto the pitch to mob their victorious team at the final whistle. It showed just how big a scalp England was in those days. Fortunately, I didn't realise that my England career was ending on such a low note.

Having scored 9 times in 12 appearances for England I fully expected to stay in the team for the following season's Home Internationals but, up against the likes of Ronnie Allen and Nat Lofthouse, I lost my place and was never to win it back. Although disappointed at the time, half a century later I have no regrets. I feel very fortunate to have played for my country, the ultimate individual honour for a footballer, and I look back on my six-year international career with great affection. My twelve blue suede international caps are, along with my Bristol Schoolboys cap and League Championship medal, among my proudest possessions, safely under lock and key away from my home. They are joined in the safe by a number of my England shirts, including the red jersey that I wore when scoring England's first goal against West Germany in November 1954. That shirt, made of heavy cotton, has retained its bright colour over the past fifty years, and must be worth a few bob now, although I doubt whether I'd ever part with it. I hope that one day I can pass all my mementos down to my two daughters, and eventually to my grandchildren.

Although my international career ended unexpectedly on 22 May 1955, five days after my thirty-first birthday, I actually declined an international recall three years later, after I had moved to Fulham. Having made the successful transition to centre half, certain newspaper journalists were calling for me to be picked in the build-up to the 1958 World Cup. Walter Winterbottom approached me after a game at Craven Cottage and asked me if I fancied playing in England's next friendly. In retrospect, perhaps I should have said yes, but I had read Walter's comments in the newspapers that he wanted to build a youthful side and I told him I was not a long-term bet. I didn't want to be scrabbling around at the age of thirty-five for one last international fling, getting in the way of a younger man and perhaps coming unstuck at the top level. Maybe I shouldn't have been so stubborn. A cap was a cap, after all.

But at the time it felt the right thing to do and I would have hated to have embarrassed myself and ended my international career as a has-been. Had I not represented England since the devastating defeat against the USA in Bela Horizonte I might have been more inclined to play. However, I felt that I had been given a fair crack of the whip and achieved all I could justifiably have hoped for when I first signed professional forms sixteen years earlier. My hat-trick at Wembley and the winning goal at Hampden Park were undoubtedly the major highlights of my England performances. I was also thankful for the opportunity to play in a World Cup and to test myself against the best players in the world during an age when playing against foreign teams was rare. In addition, I was given wonderful opportunities to visit countries like Brazil where I would never otherwise have gone.

Despite a few disappointments along the way, I thoroughly enjoyed playing for my country. Those twelve appearances have provided a host of happy memories to sustain me in my old age. I am very grateful for them.

ELEVEN

Changing Places

Having made my way over to Craven Cottage the morning after my transfer, I was handed a pair of boots on my arrival and introduced to a new set of teammates in the dressing room. My Fulham debut was taking place that afternoon, so there was no time for me to settle in. This may have been for the best, because it completely took my mind away from the fact that I was no longer a First Division player. Instead of lining up for Chelsea in a prestigious fixture against championship-chasing West Bromwich Albion, I would be leading the Fulham attack against the less-than-glamorous Rotherham United.

Despite dropping down to the second tier for the first time in eight-and-a-half years I was determined that the First Division had not seen the last of me. As I looked around the dressing room and saw players of the calibre of Johnny Haynes and Eddie Lowe putting on their boots I knew that I had not joined a bad team. The problem with Fulham was that, like Chelsea had been when I joined in 1948, they were a team of chronic underachievers who had consistently failed to make the most of their undoubted collective talent.

I had watched Fulham from the terraces earlier in the season. I had been at a loose end one afternoon, with my Chelsea teammates playing away from home and, with my transfer looming, Fulham were by now very much in my thoughts. It was two weeks before I joined the club and I looked on very impressed as Fulham put Swansea Town to the sword 7-3.

I ran out at Craven Cottage for my debut to a warm welcome from the supporters. There was a larger-than-average Fulham
crowd on the day, 22 September 1956, although I'm sure it can't
all have been down to my first appearance in a white shirt. The
team's recent mauling of Swansea must have been another reason
why a few thousand extra fans were packing the terraces, although
doubtless Ted Drake wouldn't have agreed.

I was pleased to be again playing football for a manager
who wanted me and for a team in which I would be a valued
member of the side. The alternative was to become a bit-part
squad member making the odd appearance for Chelsea when
someone else was unfit.

Free from the status of club outcast that I held during my final
two appearances in a Chelsea shirt, I soon remembered just how
much I loved playing football. Early in the match my teammate
Jimmy Hill gathered the ball in the midfield and brought it forward before spotting me advancing towards the Rotherham goal.
Jimmy struck a low cross-field pass towards the six-yard box and
I raced in to smash the ball into the net from close-range, giving
us the lead.

Despite my obvious delight at scoring on my Fulham debut I
was unable to celebrate. Not because my heart was still at Chelsea,
I hasten to add. I had merely been unable to stop in my tracks after
striking the ball, and ran smack into the goalpost. I was fortunate
not to knock myself unconscious nor suffer any serious damage,
and was able to continue. Ironically, later in the game, I accidentally
knocked opponent Laurie Morgan spark out with a hard-hit volley
that struck him full in the face.

After our winger Tosh Chamberlain had netted a second I was
heavily involved in our final goal, scored with a quarter of an hour
remaining. The goal was originally credited to me because my shot
had been on its way into the corner when Arthur Stevens applied
the finishing touch, but I was more than happy to give him the
credit.

Having pulled off my shirt in the dressing room, my first thoughts
were for my old teammates at Chelsea. I was genuinely sad to hear

that they had lost 2-1 and bore no ill will to the club or my former colleagues. I would continue to follow their results for the rest of my time in the game, years before we became better reconciled. The chapter of my playing career at Stamford Bridge was in the past and I was more than content to be embarking on a new one just three miles down the road in SW6.

The following Monday I arrived at the Cottage, as the ground was affectionately known, for my first training session with my new teammates. Considering the fact that my career had involved expensive transfers to Newcastle and Chelsea and representing England at the World Cup, I had assumed that my days of encountering animals at football grounds had ended with my apprenticeship at Bristol. Yet I had reckoned without the eccentricities of Fulham trainer Frank Penn and his friend, the player Charlie Mitten, who owned a number of greyhounds that he raced competitively. While enjoying a quick chat with my new colleagues before the start of training, one of the lads piped up with a piece of strange advice.

'If you pick up a knock in a game, Roy, make sure you get down to Frank's room like a shot.'

'Why's that?' I asked in my innocence.

''Cos Frank will be treating one of Charlie's greyhounds in there.'

'Eh?'

'Yeah,' said another voice. 'His greyhounds are always getting pulled muscles. He's probably giving 'em a rub down now.'

I laughed off the advice, taking it as a bit of playful banter. Footballers always try to put one over on the new boy to get a bit of rapport going, and I carried on with my chuckling, assuming that they were playing the fool. It was only when I saw those damned dogs scuttling around the pitch, being watched eagerly by Frank and Charlie, that it dawned on me these guys were deadly serious. I didn't know whether to laugh or cry.

It became obvious over the following weeks that discipline, in general, was rather lacking at Fulham. The club was in a transitional period, with Frank Osborne having recently handed over managerial duties to Dugard Livingstone, while taking on the role of general manager. Frank was a lovely chap, but had been something of a reluctant manager who had been fond of practising his golf swing in his office. He certainly wasn't a tracksuit manager and had delegated most of the week's preparations to his old mate Frank Penn, leaving the players to compete with the greyhounds for attention. It felt like a similar situation to the one I had encountered in January 1948 when I first walked into Stamford Bridge. The two Franks had been connected with the club for more than thirty years and were as thick as thieves. They had both enjoyed impressive playing careers at the club, and Frank Osborne had been the first Fulham player capped for England back in 1922. They were a great double act and everything at the club bore their legacy but, in my early days at Fulham, I felt that things were a little lax. Duggie was an inspired choice to replace Frank Osborne, as laid-back and friendly a bloke as his predecessor but able to install in his talented bunch of players a winning mentality.

Being one of the most experienced players at the club I was looked up to as a sort of father figure to many of the young lads, and was sometimes called upon whenever anyone wanted to go 'into the gym' with one of them. This was our euphemism for sorting out arguments with a boxing match, and I would sometimes step in if I felt the older player was out of line. It makes me laugh when I read reports about the 'novel' strategy of current managers, like Iain Dowie at Crystal Palace, of introducing boxing in training. We were doing it fifty years ago, although on a rather more ad hoc basis. Such an event was quite a rarity though and, looking back, I regard the group of lads at Fulham just as highly as those great friends I'd made over the years at Newcastle and Chelsea. There were also some terrific players.

I would rate Johnny Haynes as one of the best footballers I ever played with. He was as good as Tom Finney, Stanley Matthews or Billy Wright and it's incredible that he played out his whole League career at unfashionable Fulham. Johnny had been at the club for four years when I arrived and I was already well aware of his talent, but it was only when I found myself in the same team that I realised just how good he was. Johnny played for Fulham for eighteen years, making the most appearances in Fulham's history, while earning almost 50 England caps. Nowadays the club would have been lucky to have kept him for three years. He'd have been snapped up by Arsenal, Chelsea or Manchester United for millions and been paid £100,000 a week. Instead he was on the maximum wage of £12 a week, although that did increase to £20 a week soon afterwards, and eventually to £100 a week.

I always felt that Johnny was born twenty years too soon. His vision was incredible and, had he played in the 1970s and 1980s, he would have become a world star on a par with George Best. Johnny's accuracy in kicking the old lace-up 'medicine' balls was exceptional back in the 1950s, so heaven knows how he would have manipulated one of those lightweight balls used today. David Beckham wouldn't have got a look-in when it came to taking free-kicks had Johnny been around. Johnny could weigh up so many options and was like a snooker player, somehow having enough time on the ball to check all of them before delivering a pinpoint pass. Playing alongside him, I tried to learn how to predict Johnny's movements, in the same way that he seemed to know what I would do in a match. Even when Johnny had his back to me, he appeared to be aware of where I was and could instantly spin around and pass to me in one movement. It must have been so frustrating for Johnny to play in the Second Division. His talent cried out for a higher stage but, although he never won a notable trophy in his career, Johnny never complained about his lot. He loved playing football, regardless of the surroundings, and I'm sure his illustrious international career was some consolation for missing out on personal glory.

I once asked Johnny why he hardly ever headed a ball, considering he was so proficient at that skill in training. He told me, 'I was brought up to make goals, not score them.' Johnny regarded his role purely as a playmaker and I think he felt that scoring goals with his head would sully his incredible talent, whereas for me it was my bread and butter. Johnny hated the long-ball game and would pass along the ground whenever he could. Because he was the focal point of the team this made us attractive to watch. It was an absolute privilege to play in the same team as him. Johnny became known as the first £100-a-week footballer, and it was impossible to begrudge the man a penny of it, although he told me at the time that the figure had been exaggerated.

It was ironic that the man who would do more than anybody to provide Johnny with his deserved salary hike, however much the actual figure was, would be our teammate Jimmy Hill. From 1957 until 1961 Jimmy was chairman of the Professional Footballers' Association (PFA), an organisation that took over from the out-dated Players' Union. Coming to national prominence during the protracted saga that led to the famous 'Eastham ruling', Jimmy was at the forefront of the decision to abolish the wage limit imposed on footballers.

Jimmy's calling with destiny began in 1959 when English international George Eastham was barred from leaving Newcastle United and signing for Arsenal. Having ignored umpteen transfer requests, Newcastle informed George that he was their property for as long as they wanted and that they would use the 'retainer' system to prevent him ever signing for another club. This punitive system was a restraint akin to slave labour, and George bravely decided to retire from the game at the age of twenty-nine in protest at Newcastle's stance. It was a stand that I understood fully, having undertaken similar action with my Chelsea team-mate Johnny Harris back in 1951, but this time around George received total backing from the new union, led by Jimmy. If the clubs thought that Jimmy and George, as professional footballers, would be pushovers, they had another think coming. Sticking to his guns and refusing to take the easy way out by returning to Newcastle, George's protest brought a wave of publicity to the players' cause, unlike my own strike eight years before. In 1951 the Players' Union had been about as much use as a chocolate teapot, and it is very much to Jimmy's credit that he offered his full support to George, while at the same time keeping the issue on the back pages throughout his dispute.

George was out of the game for a year in total, which must have been an excruciating experience, but both his and Jimmy's persistence paid off when Newcastle finally realised they could no longer bully him and agreed to his transfer to Arsenal. Neither George nor Jimmy were prepared to leave the matter there, though. Both men knew that the momentum was with them and decided to apply to the High Court in a bid to abolish the entire 'retain and transfer' system. Their resulting victory in 1961 heralded the abolition of the maximum wage ruling and allowed the likes of Johnny Haynes to negotiate a salary rather more akin to their talent than they could previously have dreamed of. I know that Johnny bought Jimmy a drink to thank him.

As one of the first footballers to go on strike to challenge the financial straitjacket imposed by clubs, I was delighted by Jimmy's achievement, although a little rueful that his success had come rather too late in the day for myself. The most I would ever earn was £40 a week in my final season at Queens Park Rangers, but I was proud to have played my small part in abolishing such an unjust practice.

Jimmy remains one of my greatest friends in the game and he hasn't changed from the warm-hearted, generous chap I knew almost half a century ago. I can't recall another player with so much energy, both on and off the pitch. Jimmy took on so much additional responsibility besides his playing duties, but never allowed it to affect his performance. As chairman of the PFA he would travel all over the country throughout the week, working flat-out for his members and frequently having to make late-night stopovers in hotels. Yet he would race out onto the pitch every Saturday and run non-stop for ninety minutes. He was an inspiration to all his teammates.

Although not the most skilful of players, Jimmy made the most of his talents, always making himself available to teammates for a pass. He was a superb decoy for his fellow forwards and was definitely an unsung hero of the side, with a knowledge of football that was second to none. It came as no surprise to me when he went to Coventry City as manager and took them out of the Third Division and up to the First, barely spending a penny in the transfer market.

Jimmy is one of the brightest people I've met in football. He was one of the pioneers of televised football, single-handedly inventing the concept of a panel of pundits for ITV back in 1970, and allowing the channel to challenge the BBC's supremacy. He is also one of the nicest people in the game. Despite all the power and prestige he has held in his various roles as manager, chairman, director and TV star, Jimmy never got carried away with his own importance and remains as down to earth today as he was in 1956.

Another great lad at Fulham was left winger Tosh Chamberlain, one of the game's natural jokers. In one famous incident Tosh sat cross-legged on the pitch after being kicked up in the air by an opposition defender. When one of his teammates ran up to him and asked what he was doing, Tosh said, 'I'm sitting down until that bleeding ref apologises.' That was Tosh, always joking. He was built like a weightlifter and had a ferocious kick on him, something our poor goalkeeper Tony Macedo discovered when Tosh gave him a backpass one day. For some reason Tosh put all his weight behind the pass and broke a couple of Tony's ribs. During another match against Orient he went to take a corner and missed the ball completely, snapping the corner flag in half with his boot. He had one of the best left feet I've ever seen though, and was one of the team's most effective players. He was skilful, although not always the most subtle of players, and was also as hard as nails. This made him a very handy player to have, because we were a team that liked to play the ball around and, in those days, we might have found ourselves kicked off the park had we not had a couple of hard men in the side.

Like Johnny Haynes, wing half-back Eddie Lowe was Fulham through and through, making more than 500 appearances for the club. Eddie was such a consistent player I don't remember him ever having a bad game. Then there was our left-back Jimmy Langley. He was the worst trainer I saw during all my days in the game, yet on a match day Jimmy never stopped moving. He was extraordinary. I worked out after a while that Jimmy was one of those rare players who saved all his energy for matches. Had he worked harder in training then he would have been half the player when Saturday afternoon came around. I found this a useful lesson to learn when I subsequently became a manager and had to attempt to tailor training sessions for players with a variety of physical attributes. Jimmy scored quite a few goals in his time and became a big influence on young George Cohen, who was breaking through into the first team when I arrived. Both players loved to get forward and were each brilliant at overlapping the winger in front of them before sprinting back into their defensive position to avert danger.

George was an incredibly determined youngster when I joined Fulham. I don't think I've ever met a lad who was so dedicated to succeeding. He was so quick as well. We had sprinting competitions and, even though I was no slouch, I'd have to be given a few yards start to get anywhere near him. He was probably faster than one of Charlie Mitten's greyhounds. George was very adaptable and could have played anywhere on the pitch. He was also so willing to learn that I took a particular interest in his game, particularly when I moved into the centre of defence. The pair of us would often stay behind for extra training, and I like to think I played a small part in George becoming the player he was. I was so proud when he played for England in the 1966 World Cup final and I still feel that sense of satisfaction whenever I see the famous photo of George hoisting Bobby Moore into the air.

Not long after I signed for Fulham, Duggie had the idea of moving me to wing half. I was a little apprehensive at first, having played my whole career as either a centre forward or inside forward, but I gave it a go and found that the new position suited my game. I could still 'rove' to my heart's content and enjoyed my deeper role, particularly revelling in supplying Johnny Haynes. Duggie was a funny bloke and used to motivate us with his own eccentric brand of team talks. Once we were in the dressing room before a match at Derby and he told us, 'Get out there and score a quick couple of goals before they realise what a load of rubbish you are.' The players loved him. Duggie was well-respected in the game and had come to Fulham after Newcastle had bizarrely sacked him within weeks of winning the FA Cup.

As any manager will tell you, it takes time to blend a team together and, at the end of his first season at Fulham, we finished a disappointing thirteenth in the Second Division, way below what the team was capable of. Duggie was not finished with us yet. Having worked us hard in pre-season training, the 1957/58 campaign was a different proposition altogether. I'm sure we would have been promoted had it not been for our outstanding FA Cup run that year.

After beating non-League Yeovil 4-0 in the third round of the cup, we were then faced with two difficult London derbies en route to the quarter-finals. First up was a tricky fourth-round trip to Charlton. Despite being down to ten men for twenty minutes when Robin Lawler went off with a gashed head, we were in command for most of the match. I scored the opening goal shortly after half-time, slotting in the rebound after Tosh's thunderous shot had been saved. Having settled into the position of wing half it was rare for me to get among the goals and I enjoyed my brief return to the Sunday newspapers' goal-scoring columns. Arthur Stevens, one of Fulham's elder statesmen, scored the second to clinch the match and set up a tie with West Ham at Upton Park.

The Hammers were rather like us, a team that liked to play football the right way, and the two sides put on an entertaining game that saw five goals. The lead changed hands twice that afternoon before Johnny Haynes grabbed a late winner to secure a 3-2 win. In the quarter-finals we again avoided First Division opposition, being drawn at home to my first club, Bristol Rovers. Before a bumper 40,000-plus crowd we won 3-1 to set up what was an emotional semi-final clash with Manchester United.

The game took place just two months after the dreadful Munich air disaster. Eight United players, including Duncan Edwards, Tommy Taylor and captain Roger Byrne, were among twenty-three people killed when the team's plane crashed on take-off following a European Cup match in Germany. It was the worst disaster ever to strike a British football team and, when it came to our cup semi-final at Villa Park, Matt Busby's United team, known as the Busby Babes, quite understandably had the support of every neutral fan in the country. It was a difficult atmosphere for us to play in, but we knew that our opponents would not want us to let our sympathy get the better of us and allow them to win. We had to put all thoughts of that appalling accident, involving the loss of some of the best footballers of our generation, to the back of our minds and play the game as if it was any other. On a purely professional level, all of us were desperate to make a cup final appearance, none more so than me, who had already been on the receiving end of three FA Cup semi-final defeats.

The match, played in front of 70,000 people, was a quintessential English cup tie played at a frenetic pace, with four goals in the first half. United took an early lead through Bobby Charlton, but goals by Arthur Stevens and Jimmy Hill put us in front. On the stroke of half-time our opponents equalised with another goal by Bobby Charlton, who was then aged twenty and still traumatised by what he had witnessed on the Munich runway. Bobby had emerged from the wreckage with barely a physical injury, and bravely returned to action within weeks, despite the awful mental scars he suffered.

In the second half United bombarded our goal and we had our young goalkeeper Tony Macedo to thank for keeping us in the match with a string of incredible saves. The match ended 2-2, necessitating a replay four days later. Having played in two previous semi-finals for Chelsea against Arsenal that had resulted in replays, I was left with a slight sense of déjà vu. When I heard that the replay would take place at Arsenal's Highbury ground the parallels seemed even stronger, but I desperately hoped that this time I would finally emerge on the winners' side.

For once an FA Cup semi-final replay lived up to the original tie, and was arguably an even better contest, eight goals being scored. With the scores locked at 3-3 and Fulham having had a goal disallowed, a bout of extra time was beckoning. Unfortunately, Tony Macedo, usually such a reliable 'keeper, made two bad errors, one in the final minute, and United ran out 5-3 winners.

Tony was a terrific goalkeeper and was harshly criticised afterwards by the press, who had conveniently forgotten his heroics in the first game at Villa Park and, indeed, his form throughout the season. He didn't deserve to be made the scapegoat and, as a young man who had only broken into the team the year before, Tony's confidence could have been shot to pieces by the excessive criticism. Fortunately, the young lad from Gibraltar was made of stern stuff and went on to guard Fulham's goal for a further twelve seasons.

After the game I felt gutted at having lost a fourth semi-final, realising that the chances of my ever making a FA Cup final appearance at Wembley were fast receding. However, I soon put my disappointment into perspective, remembering that eight United players had recently lost far more than a football match. As anyone who played at Hillsborough, Heysel or Bradford will tell you, it's only a game.

Returning to our League campaign, we were still in the hunt for a place in the First Division but our FA Cup run had left us with a fixture pile-up, which unfortunately contributed to our missing out on promotion. Yet when the season finished there was still a great deal to be happy about. Over the past two years Duggie had created a strong winning mentality in the players, and our record of finishing fifth and almost reaching a cup final in the same season was no small achievement. The players felt that we were on the verge of great success and, while heading off for our summer holidays, we vowed that Duggie would lead us to promotion the next season. However, we had reckoned without the homesickness suffered by Duggie's wife's and, much to our disappointment, our jovial manager turned down a new contract in order to move back up northwards and manage Chesterfield.

The Fulham board of directors chose to keep the subsequent managerial appointment in-house and offered the job to Bedford Jezzard. Known to the players as Beddy, he had scored more than 150 goals for the club before a broken ankle had forced his retirement from the game. Appointed as a coach after hanging up his boots, Beddy found himself in the difficult position of being part of the management team, with responsibility for many of his former teammates, never an easy transition to make. The board were impressed with how easily Beddy had managed the leap from being 'one of the lads' to a respected coach and had no qualms in appointing him as Duggie's replacement. It was a good decision by the board and Beddy wisely kept a great deal of continuity in the team's preparations, acknowledging that the side was on a steep upward curve. He believed that, with a small amount of tinkering, he could mould us into a promotion-winning side. Although our attitude to him changed a little when he became manager, he never asked to be known as 'Boss.' He was always 'Beddy' to us, and created a friendly atmosphere on the training ground, while not being afraid to be ruthless or tough when it was needed.

One of Beddy's first decisions was to move me from wing half to centre half after regular stoppers Joe Stapleton and Derek Lampe both got injured. This was quite a big change at this stage of my career, having played football in the attacking third of the pitch all my life. Suddenly, at the age of thirty-four, I was expected to break up attacks and bring the ball out from the back, which was a rather different proposition to what I had experienced before. I adapted quickly and found that centre half was the easiest position I had ever played. I liked the fact that at the back I was always facing the play until the ball came my way, which was quite unlike the centre forward's role where I played with my back to goal and had to turn once I had received a pass.

I had always been powerful in the air, which was a vital quality for a centre half. I found that my many years of playing as a forward meant that I knew what to expect from my opponents, and I could anticipate much of what a centre forward would do. Billy Wright had made the same move early in his career, while John Charles was equally adept at both ends. Over the years many centre forwards, including Kenny Burns, Dion Dublin, Chris Sutton and Garry Birtles have made the switch successfully, using their striker's instinct to sniff out danger. Alan Shearer, like those I have just mentioned, a terrific header of the ball, could probably play until he was forty if he moved to the back. Not that he would agree, I'm sure.

I relished playing in defence, particularly as I had George Cohen and a young Alan Mullery alongside me, both strong tacklers who allowed me to concentrate on the centre forward I was marking. I knew Alan when he was a youth, before he broke into the side midway through the 1958/59 season, and discovered that he had the same enthusiasm for the game as George. Coming towards the end of my career, I was more than happy to pass on the knowledge I had gained over the years to both lads. I well remembered how helpful the likes of Billy Mitchell and Eddie Hapgood had been to me when I was a youngster.

Both Alan and George were honest players and willing to work hard, a characteristic that is vital to becoming a top-class footballer. If ever I am asked to give advice to youngsters hoping to make the grade I tell them that hard work and dedication are the best habits they can develop. Kids growing up playing football should forget all about the money, the flash cars and the glamour that they may associate with the modern-day footballer. All those things will come in time if they want them. But without hard work, all the talent in the world can come to nothing. I've seen so many great talents throw their careers away, letting it all slip through their fingers before they have realised it.

The 1958/59 season was to become one of the most memorable in Fulham's history, and indeed my own career. Beddy had kept us playing attacking football and, with Johnny Haynes at the peak of his powers, we were too good for most opponents. After a strong showing in the first half of the season, we soon found ourselves battling it out for the two promotion slots with Sheffield Wednesday and Liverpool. After the first game of the new year, a 2-1 home defeat to Swansea Town, we found ourselves in third place behind Liverpool on goal difference. This was long before the Shankly-Paisley era, two decades when the red half of Merseyside would dominate English football. Liverpool were a big team back then alright, but they had been in the Second Division for five years, giving no indication that they would soon become the biggest team in British football.

Our encounter with Liverpool at Craven Cottage in October 1958 bore witness to the slipshod way in which football injuries were regarded. Going up for a ball with Liverpool full-back and future Reds manager Ronnie Moran, the pair of us clashed heads, leaving Ronnie spark out on the ground, and me with a badly gashed eyebrow. Frank Penn trotted out in his tracksuit and, in my groggy, semi-conscious state, I saw that he had opened up his ancient first aid box and was wielding a pair of rusty scissors and a string of catgut. Better known as tennis racquet string, the thick material was being used by Frank to sew up my gaping wound. I still wince when I think of what he did.

Frank was by no means unusual in his role as a trainer. The term 'physiotherapist' was unheard of in 1950s football. Club trainers were, generally speaking, ex-players who helped out with the training and rubbed us down with the 'magic sponge' whenever we took a knock. The idea that a club needed someone with years of medical expertise learned at university to deal with injured footballers would have been puzzling. Frank was employed as much for his status as a mate to the players as anything else. I once tried to engage him in a conversation about football injuries and failed dismally to get a serious answer.

'What was the worst injury you had to deal with, Frank?'

'Once I repaired a bloke's broken leg.'

'How did you do that?'

'It was easy. I got some Elastoplast, wrapped it around his leg as tight as I could, and he stood up and walked away.'

'He walked away with a broken leg?'

'Yes. It was a wooden one.'

I gave up asking him after that exchange.

After three wins in a row in February we visited Anfield for our rematch with Liverpool. We were three points ahead of them in second place and a hard-fought 0-0 draw kept us firmly in the promotion driving seat. Had Liverpool's legendary forward Alan Arnell scored with the last kick of the match, things might have been very different.

The next week we continued our promotion surge by beating Middlesbrough 3-2. Among their scorers that day was a certain Brian Clough. Long before he was a controversial manager, leading Derby County and Nottingham Forest to remarkable triumphs,

Brian was one of the best young centre forwards in the game. I had been marking him all game and had done a pretty good job of keeping him away from Tony Macedo's goal, but someone of Brian's calibre only needed one chance to score, and so it turned out that day. Fortunately, goals by Graham Leggatt, Johnny Haynes and Tony Barton gave us the win that kept us on course for the promised land of the First Division.

On Good Friday we overtook Sheffield Wednesday at the top of the table by thrashing them 6-2 at the Cottage. Although we were now one point clear, Wednesday had a crucial two games in hand, and it wasn't long before they had regained their place at the table's summit. A Second Division Championship medal to go with my First Division gong from four years earlier would have been nice, but the most important thing was to gain promotion. This feat was managed on 25 April when we played Barnsley in our penultimate fixture of the campaign. Goals from Jimmy Hill, Maurice Cook, Graham Leggatt and an own goal gave us a comfortable 4-2 victory and elevated us to the top tier. During their fifty-two-year history Fulham had only spent three years in the First Division and this was a cause for great jubilation.

We wrapped up the season with a 4-0 home win over Rotherham United, with Johnny Haynes netting a hat-trick, although Sheffield Wednesday's 5-0 pasting of relegated Barnsley ended our hopes of winning the title. Nevertheless, I felt a great sense of achievement at helping the team gain promotion, a feat I had never previously experienced in my career, and felt pleased that, in my late thirties, I was to get one last crack at the First Division.

Our first game back in the top flight was certainly a baptism of fire. When the 1959/60 fixture list had been drawn up, an away trip to Blackburn Rovers hadn't looked to be the most difficult of opening games but, after a 4-0 drubbing, we had to take a long, hard look at ourselves. The result could have been even worse had it not been for an inspired display of goalkeeping by Tony Maceno. Having regrouped for two days on the training field, we proceeded to win our first two home matches against Manchester City and Blackpool, sparking off an impressive run of form at

Craven Cottage. City were sent away with their tails between their legs after we spanked them 5-2 and a 1-0 win over Blackpool the following weekend meant that we had a healthy two wins from our first three games. Another two home wins, against championship favourites Wolves and strugglers Luton Town pushed us up into sixth place in mid-September. However, our away form was poor and, when we visited Wolves for the return game a week after we had beaten them at the Cottage, any misplaced hopes of sustaining an unexpected title bid were well and truly quashed. Smarting from their defeat to the new kids on the First Division block, Wolves absolutely battered us, scoring nine goals without reply.

This defeat was hardly ideal preparation for my first game against Chelsea since my departure three years earlier. I was determined to show Ted Drake and the boys that I could still cut it at the top level but, despite a good Fulham performance, we lost the match 3-1. Jimmy Greaves, a player I had watched when he was a boy and who would become a great friend to me, scored a typical poacher's goal that day. Having brushed off the disappointment of that defeat, we hit a purple patch, winning our next five games and scoring sixteen goals in the process. By Christmas we were sixth in the table and repaying the board's faith in Beddy Jezzard.

After we were knocked out of the FA Cup by Leicester in the fourth round, there was one game on the calendar that stood out a mile for me. On Saturday 13 February I was to make an emotional return to Stamford Bridge. In the build-up to the match I hoped the Chelsea fans would give me a decent reception, appreciating the effort I had put in for their team over eight-and-a-half years. Their reaction on the day brought tears to my eyes. As I ran onto the Stamford Bridge turf for the first time since September 1956 the whole crowd cheered me, and I felt ten feet tall. Although Chelsea beat us again, this time by four goals to two, I enjoyed the match tremendously and was honoured to be asked for my autograph by home fans as I left the field. That day was one of the highlights of my Fulham career, something I was reminded of during Chelsea's penultimate home match during their recent Premiership-winning season. Fulham were again the visitors that day and, with Chelsea on the verge of clinching their first title since 1955, the club asked me if I would like to be introduced to the crowd. As I walked out on the pitch I was moved by the reception from both sets of fans. Most of them were too young to have ever seen me play, but the warmth I felt towards me as I walked around waving will stay with me until the day I die.

Fulham finished our first season in the First Division in tenth place, having won three of our final four games. However, our next season was rather more difficult and we ended up in seventeenth position, four points ahead of our relegated rivals. I felt that now was perhaps the time for me to begin winding down my career. Within two weeks of the 1960/61 season ending I celebrated my thirty-seventh birthday and, although I believed I could still cut it at the top level, I wasn't sure for how long. Having enjoyed more than two decades in the public eye the last thing I wanted was to end my playing days as somebody regarded as a has-been by the fans and a liability by my teammates. I felt that the best thing would be to move down a level or two and I talked it over with Beddy Jezzard, who agreed to let me leave.

Within a few weeks Queens Park Rangers' manager Alec Stock had called to ask me to drop down two divisions and join him at Loftus Road. I had no hesitation in agreeing to the move and was pleased to discover that, at thirty-seven, I was to be paid the highest salary of my career, despite being in the Third Division. Good old Jimmy Hill.

A fellow West Country man, Alec had followed my career for many years and told me he felt that I had the necessary ingredients to become a manager myself. Alec said he could help me to achieve that ambition and offered me the club captaincy, which I gratefully accepted. During my eighteen-month spell with the club Alec promoted me to the position of his unofficial assistant manager, allowing me a say in team affairs and tactics.

In many ways Alec reminded me of my late father. They both disapproved of swearing and Alec would often tell his players that if they couldn't express themselves without swearing then they shouldn't say anything at all. This was the same phrase as Dad had used when I was growing up. The pair of them also disapproved of Bristolian slang. Occasionally, when no-one was around, Alec would say to me, "'Ow bist, Bent?' which roughly translated as, 'How are you, Roy?' If I'd been twenty years younger he would never have joked like that with me. I remember him once refusing to sign a young lad who had been receiving rave reviews from the club scouts because he had been told that the boy was a prodigious liar. 'I don't care how good he is,' said Alec. 'I won't have liars in my team.'

Alec was an old-school manager, a strict disciplinarian rather than one of the lads, but he was a kind man, with great tactical awareness and excellent man-management skills. His first words to me on the training field were, 'I can't tell a player of your experience how to play the game, Roy. All I can tell you is what not to do.' That seemed like sound advice. After all, I was hardly going to change the way I played after twenty years as a professional. I learnt an enormous amount from Alec. He could get a player to respond at half-time if he was having a bad game, and lift him without resorting to shouting, unless it was a player who needed a kick up the backside. Alec knew instinctively which players would respond to a sharp word, and who needed a quiet word or two of encouragement. He rarely got it wrong.

Alec knew that, as a player in my late thirties having made almost 700 appearances, my fitness needed to be managed carefully. He understood that it would be counter-productive to send me out with the younger players on their cross-country runs and allowed me to have a separate, less vigorous training schedule. I was also being troubled by a persistent stomach muscle problem and Alec allowed me to wear special supportive underpants made of elastic to help protect my stomach. Of course, such prevention measures seem obvious nowadays, but back then many managers would simply expect you to play through the pain, which would, more often than not, lead to a worsening of the injury.

In my early career I had often stated in interviews that I had no desire to go into management when I retired but, as my career drew to a close, it appeared to be the obvious career progression.

I enjoyed the tactical side of the game, something that was finally burgeoning in English football after the Hungarians' Magic Magyars revolution, and felt that my experience of being the 'elder statesman' at both Fulham and Queens Park Rangers had helped me acquire the communication skills necessary for the job.

Alec actively encouraged me to apply for management jobs from the summer of 1962 onwards and increasingly took me into his confidence. He would hold meetings with me about our games from the previous Saturday, much as Ted Drake had done many years earlier, and was not afraid to take note of my suggestions and use them himself. Many managers feel threatened by senior professionals on the payroll who are at the end of their career, and worry that they are waiting to take their jobs from them, but Alec knew he had nothing to fear from me and was confident enough in his ability to take my suggestions onboard.

In January 1963 Harry Johnston resigned as manager of Third Division Reading and Alec advised me to apply for the job. The club was struggling at the bottom end of the league and I knew that whoever got the job would face an uphill task, but I felt it was worth the risk, even if the club was relegated, and put my name in the hat. When I was offered the position after an interview I accepted straight away, having received Vi's blessing, and went to Loftus Road for the last time to pick up my belongings. Alec congratulated me and told me that I would be a good manager. I appreciated his kind words, much as I was grateful for the eighteen-month managerial apprenticeship he had given me.

I had seen many changes in football since I had first turned out for Bristol City as a fifteen-year-old. The final two or three years of my career had seen the abolition of the maximum wage for players, the wearing of tight shorts that went right up your crotch, and the replacement of the old lace-up brown footballs with a shiny white variety. In my final season as a professional the Football League had ruled that each team must provide a white match ball to referees, something that certain cash-strapped clubs in the Third Division, including QPR, found rather difficult. Alec had devised a perfect strategy to avoid the club shelling out its hard-earned cash on what at the time seemed a rather fanciful gesture. He decided merely to paint all the club's existing brown footballs with whitewash. The painted ball would invariably be scuffed within the first twenty minutes but, by that time, it wouldn't matter. We got away with this tactic for quite a while. One week Alec received a call from an opposition manager in a blind panic.

'What do we do, Alec? These white balls are bloody expensive. We can't afford to have a new one every game.'

'Don't worry,' Alec replied. 'We paint ours every week. Just do the same.'

Alec's opposite number got off the phone pretty relieved to have been given such helpful advice. However, he then proceeded to make the rather basic error of waiting until an hour or so before kick-off to paint the ball, in order to give it as good a sheen as possible. As we lined up in the tunnel I watched the groundsman throw the ball to the referee for him to catch. The paint had not yet dried and, as the poor ref led the teams onto the field, he discovered that the ball was stuck to his hands. After prising the ball from his fingers the official found that both his hands were covered in fresh white paint. It was one of the funniest things I ever saw on a football pitch. Fortunately the referee saw the joke as well and agreed not to report the incident to the League. Instead, the match was played with an old-fashioned brown ball, but I think the club was shamed into shelling out for some white replacements by the time of their next home match.

Within a few weeks of that incident I hung up my boots for the last time. It was more than twenty-three years since I had made my first-team debut for Bristol City and in that time I had played 560 League games, scoring 173 goals in the process, plus a few dozen more in the FA Cup and for England. Had the Second World War not intervened I would probably have made another 200 or so appearances. I was sad that I would never again experience the buzz of playing in front of a crowd, but reasoned that sitting in the dugout would be the next best thing. My only hope was that I would make enough of an impression in the job not to be thrown on the scrapheap at the end of the season, as had happened to so many managers. I knew that football management was a cut-throat business and that there would be no second chances if I messed up in the job. On the other hand, I had always relished a challenge. The task of pulling Reading away from the Third Division relegation zone was to be one of my biggest challenges yet.

TWELVE

Management, Maxwell and Making Ends Meet

I began taking an active interest in coaching in the 1950s, completing a series of FA courses arranged by England manager Walter Winterbottom. In the wake of the national side's two heavy defeats to the Hungarians, the FA began taking the idea of coaching seriously. Walter was keen to encourage England internationals, past and present, to acquire some qualifications in that field and I was accompanied on my first course by fellow players Don Welsh and Eddie Baily. Both men would eventually make a name for themselves in coaching, Don as manager of Liverpool and Eddie as assistant to Tottenham's Bill Nicholson.

Once we had passed the first test, we were entrusted with the job of training recruits from various walks of life who wanted to become qualified FA coaches. The courses would take place over six weeks and those who were successful would qualify for an intensive course at the FA's Bisham Abbey base. Many of those I trained were schoolteachers, some of whom seemed more interested in the theoretical side of coaching as opposed to the physical. They were divided into classes of thirty and I have to admit that I was rather a harsh judge, only deeming perhaps six or seven at a time as worthy of a certificate. I was told in no uncertain terms by the powers that be that I must allow at least fifty per cent of applicants to pass in order to keep up the numbers, which I found a rather odd philosophy. I felt strongly that to allow people to coach when they weren't ready rather defeated the purpose.

In the summer of 1958 I coached the Great Western Rail team. Although the players were amateurs, I found my stint at GWR a very useful experience. I was pleased to discover that I could gain the respect and trust of a group of players and improve their performance by imposing my ideas on both their training sessions and matchday tactics.

I had thought for a while that I might make a decent coach, and had been considering it as a career move ever since Billy Birrell first mentioned the idea to me at Chelsea. I admit that I did have serious doubts about going into management. The job provided no security and, however good a manager you were, it only took a run of bad results before you were out on your ear. I also thought that it must be difficult for former managers to move back into coaching after they had been sacked. This was for two reasons. Firstly, because the idea of having to play second fiddle to somebody else once you were used to being in charge could not be easy on the ego. Secondly, many managers were paranoid about appointing an experienced former boss, knowing that this provided the club with a ready-made replacement if results went badly. Yet, after working with Alec Stock for eighteen months, I was convinced that I could be a manager and decided I would take the opportunity should one arise. I was the only candidate interviewed by Reading chairman Jimmy Carter in January 1963 and when he offered me a salary of £42 a week, plus a £2,000 bonus if we avoided relegation, I eagerly accepted.

Upon my arrival at Reading I stamped my personality on the club from the first day. I believed it was essential to make any radical changes to the team early in my tenure, while retaining the goodwill of both the players and the board. I had decided in advance that I would take the role of a 'tracksuit manager', with full responsibility for training sessions, as opposed to an old-fashioned boss who sat in his office all day long wearing a suit. I liked my players to be fit, but I also wanted them to maximise their individual potential, and introduced a number of techniques that I had seen or read about to improve their awareness and on-field decision-making.

Footballers have always been an odd breed, even before the days of megabucks salaries, and it was vital for me as manager to establish my authority from the beginning. I had played for a total of ten managers and I attempted to combine what I regarded as the best qualities of each man. My two biggest role models were undoubtedly Ted Drake and Alec Stock. As Ted had done when he took the reins at Chelsea, I gathered as much information about my players as I could from various sources. I wanted to know who the potential troublemakers were, which players hung around in cliques and who had not been pulling their weight on the field. As any manager will testify, if you don't get a grip on the dressing room at the start, players can quickly undermine and destroy your authority.

Reading were at the bottom of the table when I arrived, so I knew that things weren't right with the players, and I wanted to find out what, or who, I was up against. Once I established a general view of my players, I then put the information to the back of my mind and allowed each of them to start from scratch, without prejudice. The information I gleaned was purely background knowledge to help me avoid troublesome situations. There was no point in writing off a player purely on the basis of second-hand information, and I like to think that I gave every one of them a decent chance, judging them on their merits. Predictably, a few of the more experienced professionals didn't take kindly to a manager not much older than themselves changing things around, but I soon established a rapport with the players.

I developed a reputation as a disciplinarian, which was probably fair, although I would sometimes turn a blind eye to minor things that I didn't think needed my involvement. Occasionally fights between players would flare up in training, and whenever that happened I would get in between them and make it clear that if they did it again I would give them a whack. I'm sure that attitude wouldn't be seen as acceptable today because the players would get their agents on to me. I suppose that this is the way society has gone in general.

I tried to avoid dressing-room inquests after a defeat. I well remembered how I would feel, as a player, straight after losing a match and reckoned that this was the worst time to start bawling people out. There was no point in getting into a slanging match in front of the players. If something needed to be said to a player about his performance, then it was better done on the following Monday, man to man. Otherwise there was a danger of my losing both my temper and the players' respect. Management was always a delicate balancing act and I was grateful at having had such good role models as Ted and Alec. They knew how to handle every player as an individual and, although I got my man-management wrong at times, I believe I learnt a lot from the pair of them.

One of the worst mistakes I made was when I put a young local lad in the first team before he was ready. The boy was only seventeen years old and I gave him his debut away at Millwall, which was one of the most difficult grounds for a youngster to play at. The lad in question had a very unusual gait, and the Millwall fans crucified him. He was playing at outside left, positioned very close to the crowd, and they gave him no respite throughout the ninety minutes. The lad came off the field shell-shocked. In hindsight I should have given him his first game at home, not away to Millwall, but we had injury problems and he seemed the obvious choice in that position. Unfortunately, the experience left its mark on him and he never performed as well for Reading as he should have done.

Confidence is always an issue with footballers, even for those who have been playing for years. There can be any number of reasons for a loss of self-belief and, when I arrived at our Elm Park ground, I could see that confidence among the players was low. Whenever we played against a club from the top end of the table I would choose not to dwell on how good our opponents were in my team talks, focusing instead on my players' strengths. I often passed on some excellent advice that my dad had given me many years beforehand. He would say, 'When you get out on the field tell yourself you are the best player out there. Never tell anyone else because you'll be heading for a fall. But always think to yourself that you are the best.'

The first few weeks at Reading were incredibly frustrating. Britain was enduring one of its worst winters in decades and, with most of the country engulfed in snow, the first nine matches of my tenure were postponed. It was six weeks before I finally got to see my new team in action, away at Brighton & Hove Albion. The game was a cracker but, despite our taking the lead four times in the match, we went down 5-4. Although we had lost to one of our relegation rivals, I felt I had seen enough signs that afternoon to believe the team was good enough to avoid relegation, and I told the players how pleased I was with their performance.

Results gradually picked up but, by the beginning of May, we remained rock bottom. Although the season had been extended because of the heavy winter, Reading were faced with the herculean task of playing our last eight games in a mere eighteen days. Our cause was not helped by the disappointing decision of record-signing Ron Tindall to play county cricket for Surrey, who he was under contract to represent during the summer. I had made it clear to him when he signed that if we were at either end of the table, football must come first. Despite the loss of such a key player, the team stuck together and won three of the next five matches. Although we proceeded to lose our final two games, we avoided relegation by virtue of goal difference. It was a great relief to everyone to have preserved Third Division status and the board passed on their congratulations to me and to the team. Tragically, within a week of the last game, Jimmy Carter – a popular local businessman who had been instrumental in appointing me as manager – dropped dead. I was deeply saddened by the loss of such a good man.

After putting the players through a rigorous pre-season training programme, the 1963/64 campaign saw the lads' increased efforts pay dividends with a sixth-placed finish. This earned me a salary increase to £3,000 a year, plus the offer of £5,000 if we were promoted, although, with no money in the kitty for players, that bonus never looked very likely.

We remained mid-table for most of the 1964/65 season, finishing thirteenth, but enjoyed a fine run in the fledgling League Cup tournament, which included victories over two of my former clubs. In the first round of the tournament we beat Queens Park Rangers 4-0, which was a fine way to repay Alec Stock for all his help and advice. Alec was as gracious as ever about my putting one over on him and I was delighted when two seasons later QPR won the trophy by beating West Bromwich Albion at Wembley. In the next round we drew 1-1 against First Division Fulham at Elm Park. In the replay the lads did me proud and my return to Craven Cottage provided the shock of the round by pulling off a stunning 3-1 victory. Unfortunately, our interest in the competition ended in the next round at Aston Villa, but the lads had provided some happy memories for our fans and added a few well-needed pounds to the club's bank balance.

In the summer of 1964 I appointed Jimmy Wheeler as my assistant manager. Jimmy was a popular centre forward at Elm Park for many years before a broken leg ended his career. Having spotted his natural coaching ability on the training field I felt he was a good choice as my number two, and I look back on his appointment as having been crucial. Part of Jimmy's duties involved running the reserve side, a task to which he took superbly, winning the Football Combination Second Division title in his first season. The first team ended the campaign in eighth position and I felt that, with some new signings, we had a good chance to secure promotion the following year.

During the summer I signed George Harris, an old-fashioned outside left, from Watford for the bargain price of £1,500. George turned out to be one of my best signings. He was brilliant in the air, with a good left foot, and he immediately made a difference to the team. I also tried to sign two players from Aston Villa, a midfielder and forward, who had been offered to me by Villa manager Tommy Docherty. The pair of them, who were stuck in the Villa reserves, would have cost me a total of £15,000, which wasn't a great deal of money at the time. Unfortunately the board pulled the plug on the deal. It seemed to be more important for the club to make a profit than get promoted although, as the players in question were sold by Villa some months later for a total of £30,000, this rather challenged our board's conservative logic.

Reading still had a number of good players at the time, though, and I remained quietly confident about our prospects. I had Pat Terry up front, a superb header of a ball, while Colin Meldrum, who I signed from Arsenal, was a really classy left-back. I liked players at the back who were comfortable on the ball, and Colin was a great servant to Reading despite some difficult personal problems. Throughout my management career I wanted my teams to play attacking football, believing, perhaps naively, that football was about entertainment as well as results. Even in the Third Division I believed that fans liked to watch attacking football, and I'd like to think that, regardless of our results each week, we succeeded in providing some excitement most of the time.

Although we started the 1966/67 season poorly, the team gelled in the second half of the campaign, and came within a whisker of gaining promotion to the Second Division. Having won seven games in a row we needed to beat Workington away on the last Saturday of the season while hoping that other results went our way. Having won the match 2-1 we rushed back to the changing room to listen to the other results on the radio. We needed Watford to lose their match for us to stay in second place and, when we heard that they were a goal down with fifteen minutes to play, it looked as if luck was on our side.

Watford's match had begun late and, as I listened to the transistor, my thoughts turned to the day when I had sat in the Stamford Bridge dressing room waiting for confirmation that Chelsea were champions. Sadly there was to be no happy ending this time, a late Watford penalty condemning us to another season in the Third Division. Middlesbrough pipped Watford for promotion by winning their final game in hand a few days later, and we moved into fourth spot. We consoled ourselves with the thought that it would have been a more bitter pill to swallow had Watford not scored that equaliser a few days earlier. I believe to this day that if I had had been given permission to sign those two lads from Villa we would have been promoted. There was no point crying over spilt milk, though. I'm not the only manager to have made such a complaint when he has come so close to success.

The 1967/68 season began well and three straight wins extended our winning run from the previous campaign to eleven matches. However, we lost a number of crucial matches to the teams in the top third of the table and ended the season fifth, missing promotion by five points. Three thrilling cup ties against First Division opponents gave our fans some extra excitement. In the first of these we faced West Bromwich Albion in the second round of the League Cup. West Brom had been finalists in the previous two seasons and were hot favourites to beat us at Elm Park but, with a 19,000 crowd behind us, we triumphed 3-1, George Harris scoring twice.

In the next round we were drawn away to a star-studded Arsenal. We took about fifty coaches of supporters to north London and kick-off was held up for half an hour because many of them were stuck in traffic. The boys put on a magnificent display that night and George again got the ball in the net, only for the goal to be disallowed. Ron Bayliss then struck a shot against the crossbar with such force that the groundsman was forced to realign the goal frame after the match. Although we gave them a real run for their money, the Gunners scored the only goal during the first half, but I told my players afterwards they could be proud of their efforts that night.

Having stumbled past non-League Dagenham in the FA Cup with the aid of a replay, we received another plum draw, away to Manchester City. The City forward line contained Francis Lee, Mike Summerbee, Neil Young and Colin Bell, and the away supporters set out that morning more in hope than in expectation, but we held them to a gritty 0-0 draw. We almost snatched a famous victory when a shot from one of our forwards appeared to go over the goal line by a yard or so, but the linesman kept his flag down. I felt that, with home advantage, we would have an even better chance in the replay, but City staged what many of our fans claimed was the best attacking display ever seen at Elm Park as they thrashed us 7-0. City went on to win the League title that year, a feat they have never managed since.

The following summer was a difficult period for me. While I was on holiday Jimmy Wheeler was offered the manager's job at

Bradford. It was a good opportunity for him and I wished him all the best, but it was a huge blow nonetheless. I was also under increased pressure from an ambitious new chairman, Frank Waller, to get the club promoted. In an effort to give us a more experienced edge, I attempted to sign a couple of big-name players at the end of their career, making bids for Tottenham's Dave Mackay and my old Fulham teammate Johnny Haynes. I wanted Johnny to be my assistant manager, in addition to adding his touch of class to our attack. Neither transfer came off, and Dave Mackay in fact ended up at First Division Derby County when Brian Clough nipped in and signed him. Dave then went on to succeed Cloughie at the Baseball Ground and take Derby to a famous League Championship win, so I'm sure he never regretted turning down Reading.

Another blow came when two of Reading's most experienced players, Douggie Webb and Maurice Evans, retired during the summer, leaving our prospects for promotion looking bleak. An indifferent first half of the 1968/69 season saw us bobbing around in mid-table, although the club's spirits were brightened briefly by the prospect of another money-spinning FA Cup tie, this time away to Newcastle United. It was a nice moment for me, going back to my old stomping ground twenty years after being part of 'the Bank of England Five', but our 4-0 defeat rather took the shine off my return.

I knew by now that my job prospects were not looking good. Despite two close encounters, promotion had not yet been achieved but I was still surprised when, on 10 February 1969, I was called into Frank's office and sacked. I knew that I had made mistakes during my time in charge but I felt that my managerial record stood up well, particularly when the club's lack of transfer funds throughout my time in charge was taken into account. My biggest failing as a manager came as a result of playing the majority of my career in the top flight. I had expectations of Third Division players that were unrealistic. Players were giving all they had but many did not have the ability to perform the tasks that I expected of them. I was determined not to make the same mistake if I got another chance in management.

I felt confident that I would get another crack at a job, having attracted the interest of both Charlton Athletic and Manchester City in recent years. However, I also knew that managers were far more sought after by club chairmen while already in a job than when they were sitting at home unemployed. I wanted an opportunity to recharge my batteries before I applied for jobs, though, and immediately took my family on holiday. Management inevitably takes its toll on family life and I was pleased to be able to spend a long period of time with Vi, Loraine and Jane.

I was helped by the fact that I had received a pay-off of about £2,000 from Reading, although I knew that this wouldn't last forever. Every time a managerial job came up I would send in an application, while watching as much football as I could to keep my eye in and run the rule over potential future signings. I have read in a number of newspaper articles that I spent some of this time working as a scout for Bradford City, but I don't know where that story came from. I was never even approached by anybody at Bradford.

In August 1969, after almost six months without a job, I was appointed manager of Swansea City, much to the relief of my family. The club, who a few weeks earlier had changed their name from Swansea Town, were languishing in the Fourth Division, but they had a very ambitious board.

Swansea had been relegated from the Second Division in 1965 before falling out of the Third Division two years later and, when I was first introduced to the players, I was shocked at their lack of professionalism. The club's previous manager, Bill Lucas, had resigned a full six months earlier and I was immediately struck by the absence of basic discipline surrounding the players. On the first day of pre-season training I informed them that I was a hard-line disciplinarian who would come down on anyone that stepped out of line like a ton of bricks. I recall one incident when I tripped over a pair of boots left lying on the dressing room floor. I yelled at the players at the top of my voice, telling them I would not accept untidiness. My reaction was probably a little excessive, but I felt that, if I was going to succeed in ending the apathetic culture at the club, I should not tolerate even the slightest breach of discipline.

One momentous decision I made early in my tenure at Swansea was to drop goalkeeper Tony Millington four games into the 1969/70 season. Tony was a Welsh international and had played for West Bromwich Albion and Crystal Palace, but had never settled down anywhere. He was one of the game's natural clowns, never taking anything seriously, and he looked a couple of stone overweight, with a big fat stomach. I couldn't believe that a professional footballer had allowed himself to get into that condition. After a 3-0 defeat at Hartlepool United I let rip at Tony, accusing him of at being at fault for nine of the twelve goals we had conceded that season, and ordering him to lose his excess weight. Until that time I told him he would not be considered for a first-team place.

Everyone at the club was shocked, not least Tony's teammates, but my drastic action seemed to do the trick. Within a short while we were on a winning roll and Tony had worked his socks off, shedding two stone in six weeks. When I put him back in the team it was like buying a new player. He was coming off his line again, collecting crosses, and his newly discovered agility allowed him to react faster to shots. Tony could easily have sulked and asked for a transfer, but it said a lot for his character that he agreed to knuckle down and address his problems.

I had inherited some classy players like Brian Wright, Herbie Williams and Dai Gwyther and, after bringing the experienced Len Allchurch back to the club, Swansea gained promotion in my first season in charge. It was my first ever managerial involvement with a promotion team, clinched with a 2-1 win away to Welsh rivals Newport County. We were in strong contention to win the championship, which would have been the icing on the cake, but two defeats and a draw in our final three games meant that we had to settle for third place behind Chesterfield and Wrexham. The promotion season also included a memorable FA Cup third-round trip to Leeds United, who beat us 2-1 in a hard-fought match at Elland Road after one of our players, Mel Nurse, was sent off.

Swansea consolidated our place in the Third Division, finishing eleventh in 1970/71. Despite a League Cup trip to Tottenham and an FA Cup date at Anfield with Liverpool, both of which we lost, money remained at a premium and my forays into the transfer market were few and far between. One of the first changes I had made was to introduce an apprentice scheme at the club and, during the 1971/72 season, I gave a few young lads some first-team experience. We ended the campaign in fourteenth place, but the retirement that summer of two of my most experienced players, Mel Nurse and Len Allchurch, spelled a problem. I was obliged to give regular berths in the team to too many youngsters, lads who understandably took a while to adjust to the physical demands of the Third Division. We were in the relegation zone within weeks and, on 16 October 1972, two days after a 3-1 defeat at Plymouth Argyle, I was dismissed. The club were eventually relegated, finishing twenty-third in a twenty-four-team division.

I felt very sad to leave Swansea, even though it wasn't a complete surprise. I had great affection for the club's fans, who had backed me all the way, and found the Welsh people an incredibly welcoming and friendly bunch. I was also fond of my players. As a manager I had developed something of a smoking habit and some of the players clubbed together to buy me an engraved cigarette lighter as a farewell gift. I was very touched by the gesture.

My family was also settled in the area, and both my daughters had found jobs in Swansea and were happy. In fact, my youngest daughter Jane had met the man who was to become her husband while living in the city. There was certainly no great desire in the Bentley clan to leave Wales. Another difficulty was that my contract was close to expiry, so there was no healthy pay cheque to soften the blow of unemployment. Although I had worked hard in the game for almost thirty-five years and had saved money whenever I could, my family were by no means comfortably off, and it was essential that I found another job quickly. I couldn't wait around for another management job, so I took a job for a few months working for a firm of painters and decorators. It was a far cry from managing a football club and at times I found the experience demoralising, but I had responsibilities to my wife and children and forced myself to swallow my pride.

I continued to apply for management jobs but, having been sacked twice, it was never going to be easy to get another job, particularly as I had not yet coached at the top level. After some months I was offered the manager's job at non-League Thatcham Town in Berkshire. It was the only job on offer and I hoped that, if I made a success of it, I could climb back up the managerial ladder. Vi and myself packed up our belongings in Swansea and moved back to Reading, which was a few miles down the road from Thatcham. The job was part-time, with a fairly unimpressive salary, so it was necessary to find some extra income. After some lengthy discussions, Vi and I decided to invest our savings in a newsagents, which we ran for four years. We enjoyed running the shop and made some good friends, but when the offer came to return to Elm Park as Reading's club secretary I jumped at the chance.

The opportunity came about quite by chance. We delivered a daily newspaper to a local builder who had connections with the club and, when he came in the shop to pay his bill one day, he told Vi that the job of club secretary was vacant. He strongly advised her to encourage me to apply and when Vi passed on the message I decided right away to go for the job. Although I wouldn't have any involvement with coaching the side, I had missed being involved with professional football and had found the occupation of part-time non-League manager difficult. I had wanted desperately to be successful at Thatcham and subsequently found it difficult to switch off from football while running the shop. It was also pretty clear that being at Thatcham hadn't made my return to League management any more likely. Being manager of a non-League club, I simply didn't appear on the radar of professional chairmen. It was tough to acknowledge, but I was regarded as 'yesterday's man' in the world of professional management, so the occupation of club secretary seemed to me the next best thing.

The job at Reading was also a steady one. The club was pretty stable in those days and I felt that, at the age of fifty-three, this was a job I might be able to continue until my retirement. Fortunately I was offered it, so Vi and I decided to sell the shop, and I started work back at Reading in August 1977. My responsibilities included various administrative functions, including organising the club's travel arrangements and wage bill, and taking the minutes at board meetings. At around the same time Maurice Evans, one of my players at Reading a few years earlier, stepped into my old shoes as manager after the sacking of Jack Mansell, who had presided over the club's recent relegation to the Fourth Division.

I developed a terrific working relationship with Maurice, who was one of the most honest people in the game and a man who had already had a two-year stint in management at Shrewsbury Town. One of Maurice's first signings at Reading was Lawrie Sanchez, whom I had recommended. Lawrie was then eighteen and had played for me at Thatcham Town, standing head and shoulders above his teammates, despite his tender age. His father was unsure about letting him sign for Reading because Lawrie was undertaking a degree in Management Sciences at Loughborough University, but Maurice agreed to take him on part-time. I recall arranging many an away trip that required a detour to the Loughborough campus to pick up the fresh-faced young Lawrie, who of course went on to score the winning goal for Wimbledon in the 1988 FA Cup final. As one of the game's most intelligent thinkers it was no surprise when Lawrie became a successful manager, first at Wycombe Wanderers and later at international level with Northern Ireland.

I enjoyed the job of secretary immensely, despite Reading's precarious financial position, and it always seemed a happy ship until the infamous Robert Maxwell affair erupted, splitting the club down the middle. Robert was one of the richest businessmen in the world at the time and already owned a controlling share in Oxford United, where he was chairman, but in April 1983 he launched a takeover bid for Reading. Robert stunned the football world by announcing his intention to merge the club with Oxford United and create a new team called the Thames Valley Royals.

Having offered the Reading shareholders £3 a share, Robert announced that the team would play its League matches alternately at Reading and Oxford and that the team would wear royal blue and gold shirts to reflect the identity of both clubs. All the current directors were to be invited onto the new board and Robert pledged to honour the contracts of all players and staff. When he announced that the Football League had given its blessing to the scheme the deal looked done and dusted.

As you can imagine there was a lot of opposition from fans of both teams. Protests took place at both grounds, including the carrying of a mock coffin at Reading's home match against Millwall. However, a rival bid for Reading was successfully made by some of the club's existing directors, involving former player Roger Smee. After the battle for the future of the club grew increasingly ugly, Robert ended his interest in the club and Roger, whom I had signed as a player from Chelsea more than fifteen years earlier, was installed as the new chairman.

Despite everything that has been said about Robert since his mysterious death in 1991, I rather liked him. Prior to his takeover bid I had met him on a number of occasions and found him a pleasant man with always a joke at the ready, and he was respected by all his staff. There was a tradition at the time whereby all the football clubs in the Thames Valley region, including Reading, Oxford and Aldershot, took it in turns to organise a dinner. Whenever it was the turn of Oxford, Robert would pull out all the stops, putting on an amazing evening of dinner and entertainment at his palatial home and generally being a charming host. I was amazed when all the details about his misdemeanours were made public after his death.

When the new board got their feet under the table it became clear that neither myself nor Maurice Evans would be retained for long. Neither of us had taken sides in the Maxwell affair, even though I could see the sense in what Robert Maxwell had tried to achieve. Neither Oxford nor Reading had the financial clout to be a threat to the big clubs and it seemed a radical way of combining the strength of both teams. However, despite keeping any individual opinions we held to ourselves, it was clear that, in the cases of both Maurice and myself, neither of our faces fitted in the new regime.

I believed that the sale of our star striker Kerry Dixon was the sign of things to come. Reading had been relegated in the summer of 1983, but the club had unearthed one bright new talent in the shape of Kerry, who I'd seen play for Dunstable three years earlier and recommended to Maurice. Kerry was a big strong lad, very physical in the air but with good control and a hard, accurate shot. At Reading he was almost unstoppable and it was rare for him to end a game without a goal to his name.

In 1983 Kerry had been the division's top scorer despite playing in a relegated side and missing a number of games through injury. Although a few clubs were sniffing around after him I was hoping that we might be able to get Kerry to stay for one more year to help us get promoted at the first attempt. Yet, when I was on holiday, Kerry was sold to Chelsea, even though it was usually the secretary's job to sign the contract. I was disappointed when I heard the news, but was grateful to still be in a job and when the team started the season well, things began looking up.

However, in January 1984 Maurice Evans was sacked, even though the team were third in the league, and a month later I was also dismissed, leaving a sour taste in my mouth. Interestingly, one of the first people to phone me and say how sorry he was to hear that I had been sacked was Robert Maxwell, who more or less said that if a similar vacancy at Oxford was ever to come up he would take me on. That was a kind gesture and one completely out of keeping with the public perception of the man. At around the same time, Robert employed Maurice as youth development officer, and later as chief scout. Within a year he had made Maurice manager, which was a masterstroke because, twelve months later, Oxford won the League Cup at Wembley.

I can remember Robert warning about the dangers of clubs giving in to television companies' demands. He said that the moment football clubs began backing down on things like kick-off times, then television would control the game. A lot of people didn't take it seriously, but he has certainly been proved right in that regard, if nothing else.

A few months after leaving Reading I was asked to become club secretary at Aldershot. Chelsea legend Ron 'Chopper' Harris had been appointed manager and wanted a trusted friend to help him. Ron had captained the side for several years, lifting the FA Cup in 1970 and European Cup-Winners' Cup a year later, and I became friendly with him four or five years later. It was ironic that I should finish my working career employed by the only other Chelsea captain at the time to have won a trophy although, unlike me, Ron had actually been allowed to lift the silverware. When you think of how big a club Chelsea is now, it is rather strange to recall that, until 1997, when Chelsea skipper Dennis Wise lifted the FA Cup, Ron was the only Chelsea captain ever to be presented with a major trophy.

Aldershot was close to Reading, where Vi and I still lived, and I enjoyed my time getting my hands dirty there. However, within eighteen months Ron had parted company with Aldershot and decided to concentrate on his golf club near Warminster. He asked me to follow him as club secretary and bookkeeper, and I took up his offer, having realised just what an unhappy club Aldershot had become. The club seemed to be permanently in financial trouble and by 1992 they had gone out of existence altogether. Ron made a great success of the golf club, adding two fishing lakes to his portfolio, before eventually selling his interests for a large profit. He was also a very generous employer and, after selling the business, he took some of his staff, myself included, on a twenty-one-day cruise to the Caribbean as a thank you.

By the time Ron sold up I was sixty-five years old and just about ready for retirement. Vi and I were settled in the Reading area, following our move back to the area in 1973, and decided that we would see out our retirement there. With Loraine and Jane having grown up and started their own families, we decided to stay in our home in Reading, and we have lived in the same house ever since.

Although it has been nearly two decades since I worked in football, I have followed developments in the game eagerly. Having spent the happiest and most successful days of my life as a Chelsea player it is perhaps only natural that I have continued to support them since my retirement. I was naturally delighted by the club's upturn in fortunes in the Ken Bates era, when Chelsea won the

FA Cup in 1997 and 2000, and the European Cup-Winners' Cup in 1998. But until the club's finances were transformed two summers ago by Russian billionaire Roman Abramovich, I had feared that I would never live to see Chelsea crowned champions again.

THIRTEEN

Champions Again

On 23 April 2005 I found myself back on the pitch at Stamford Bridge being cheered by a full house of 42,000 supporters. It was fifty years to the day since I'd addressed the Stamford Bridge faithful from the directors' box, alongside Ted Drake, as we basked in the glory of the club's first League Championship win. Half a century later, the parallels were strong. Chelsea were within striking distance of clinching their first championship, or Premiership as it is now known, since that 1955 success, while the Blues' matchday opponents were Fulham, the club I had moved to eighteen months after our triumph.

It was half-time as I strode around the immaculate Stamford Bridge turf and looked around what was by now a very different stadium. Gone were the wooden terraces, the cloth caps and pipes, to be replaced by a sea of blue-and-white scarves, replica shirts and people taking photographs with mobile phones. It was a far cry from 1955, although the atmosphere was electric. For the eight-year period in which I donned the blue number nine shirt, the fans behind both goals were separated from the pitch by an arc of between ten and thirty feet, created by the old dog track, long since abandoned. Both ends of the ground had been uncovered, with much of the noise generated from the terraces disappearing into the air. The new stadium, with its four towering stands in close proximity to the pitch, looked stunning from ground level.

I was generously cheered by both sets of fans, only a small minority of whom could have been old enough to have seen me play. I had been back on the pitch at half-time during other Chelsea home matches over the previous couple of years, but this time it felt different. The club was on the verge of ending half a century of underachievement, so when I was introduced as the first Chelsea title-winning captain the crowd's excitement was palpable. It might sound clichéd but, as I crossed the white line onto the pitch, I was instantly taken back to 1955. Although I was by now a few weeks shy of my eighty-first birthday, as I stood on the Stamford Bridge pitch I felt thirty-one years old again. For a few golden minutes I forgot my status as a senior citizen and, as five decades rolled away, I found myself kicking a ball into the net and jumping for a header in front of the old Shed end. The fans must have thought I'd lost my mind. I'm sure Vi must have been worried that I'd do myself an injury as she watched from her usual vantage point in the stand.

After a strong second-half performance Chelsea won the match 3-1 and the once-elusive title was almost in the bag. Two days later our closest rivals, Arsenal, were playing at home to Tottenham. If Arsenal failed to win, Chelsea would be crowned champions with four matches to play. In the event, the Gunners ran out 1-0 winners, which merely delayed the inevitable by a further five days. The stage was set for Chelsea's next match the following Saturday evening, away to Bolton Wanderers. The game was screened live on Sky Sports and, as an avid football watcher, I was fortunate to be able to watch the match from the comfort of the armchair in my Reading home.

When Frank Lampard opened the scoring after an hour I was out of my chair and punching the air like thousands of Chelsea supporters across the country. It was fitting that Frank would also score our second goal, the one that would clinch the title. After all, alongside captain John Terry, Frank had been the driving force behind Jose Mourinho's team, a natural leader who could grab the game by the scruff of the neck and someone who had been remarkably consistent throughout the season. At the final whistle, the Chelsea players celebrated wildly. I sat with a huge grin on my face, grateful to have seen my team win a second title in my lifetime. I had sometimes doubted that I would ever live to see such a day.

Within minutes, journalists from all the national newspapers were on the phone, asking for my comments on the club's title success. Some reporters clearly expected me to feel a sense of disappointment that I was no longer the only captain of Chelsea to win a League title. My answer to all of them was the same: 'I might not be the only Chelsea captain to have won the title. But I'll always be the first.'

I was absolutely delighted that Chelsea had won the League. Although it had been forty-nine years since I had last played for the club, Chelsea had remained in my blood for the rest of my working career, throughout my time at Fulham, QPR, Reading, Swansea and Aldershot, and throughout my retirement. Their result was always the first result I looked for on a Saturday and over the past few seasons I have become a regular guest at home matches with Vi, who is almost as passionate a Chelsea fan as I am.

The following Saturday was Chelsea's final home match of the season, against London rivals Charlton Athletic. A carnival atmosphere prevailed as John Terry lifted the gleaming Premiership silverware. I was proud to be invited onto the Stamford Bridge pitch again, this time accompanied by my surviving teammates from the 1954/55 campaign, for a lap of honour. I had a lump in my throat as the home fans cheered the boys of '55. As we left the field, buzzing with excitement, I recalled the glory days with my old mates Stan Willemse, Eric Parsons and Frank Blunstone. It was a very emotional day and I'm sure that, if those of our teammates who have passed away had been looking down on us from above, along with Ted, they would have shed a tear. It was smashing that the club saw fit to recognise our achievements and invited us along to the Premiership party.

I'm often asked to compare the teams of 1955 and 2005, but I find it an impossible task. Football has changed so much: the formations and tactics, the fitness, the rules and even the equipment are all so different that it is pointless to speculate on which is the better team. I do wonder, though, how far someone like Peter Sillett would have been able to strike a modern lightweight ball. After all, Peter could hit a forty-yard piledriver past a goalkeeper with the old lace-up ball. He'd have probably broken the net if he'd been playing nowadays. Some of the tricks that players perform with a ball simply wouldn't have worked fifty years ago. You couldn't swerve a free-kick like David Beckham using the old ball. It would have gone no more than six feet, particularly if there had been a lot of rain and it had absorbed a lot of water.

What I can say with some certainty is that winning the League back in 1955 was a more difficult proposition than it was for the current Chelsea team. In our day there were between ten and twelve clubs at the start of each season with a realistic chance of winning a title. Today there are only three teams, Chelsea, Arsenal and Manchester United, who are realistically in the running, with the possible addition of Liverpool. Money has created a divide in the Premiership that didn't exist when I was a player and there were many more difficult matches back then because the league was so much tighter. Take last season, for example. Fifth-placed Liverpool gathered a points total that was closer to bottom club Southampton than to Chelsea. It's a mind-boggling statistic. In 1955 we won the League despite losing ten matches. That would be unthinkable now.

That's not to take anything away from Chelsea's achievement in 2005. They blew away most of the previous British records and the team's final haul of ninety-five points, with a solitary defeat, was a magnificent achievement. Yet there is no doubt that the team was helped immensely by the enormous sums of money spent by owner Roman Abramovich. Remember, if you will, that many of the 1954/55 side were either amateur players or had been recruited from the Third Division. By contrast, virtually every member of Chelsea's twenty-five-man squad was a full international.

With Abramovich's money behind the team, it was obvious that Chelsea would be in with a very good chance of winning the Premiership, if not in his first season as owner then in the following two or three years. But, despite his seemingly endless supply of money, I'm sure the Russian businessman knows that, in sport, hard currency can only take you so far. English football has been littered with teams who have gone on massive spending sprees only to end up with a team of players with huge egos, all at odds with each other, with little understanding on the pitch and no trophies in the cabinet. You can't buy team spirit, and cash can only get you so far in making eleven players sing from the same hymn sheet. The Leeds United team of recent years is one example of how reckless spending can destroy a football club. You can go back as far as the 1950s for another example. Sunderland were known as the 'Bank of England' club, spending money willy-nilly, yet they found themselves in the League's second tier by the end of that decade. It's not a new phenomenon.

Abramovich has his head screwed on and has some good advisors around him, something that was made clear by his appointment of Jose Mourinho. Handing the management reigns to the colourful Portuguese manager could have backfired spectacularly. Mourinho's predecessor, Claudio Ranieri, was a cult figure both among the Chelsea supporters and the English media, who were won over by his immense charm and genuine warmth. If Mourinho hadn't succeeded at Stamford Bridge the Russian could have been left with egg on his face.

I talked to Ranieri on a few occasions at the Chelsea training ground and thought he was a lovely man. I thought the constant media speculation surrounding his job in his final year at the club was most unfair and, at the time, I would have liked to see him stay as manager. After Chelsea finished as runners-up to Arsenal and reached the Champions League semi-final in 2003/04, Abramovich's first season holding the pay strings, it was a brave decision to dispense with Ranieri's services. I have to admit, with hindsight, that it was the right move for the club. Mourinho has taken Chelsea onto another level and has brought out the best in his talented squad.

At the beginning of the championship season Chelsea were winning a lot of games 1-0 and Mourinho faced criticism that Chelsea were becoming a boring team to watch. I always thought that this accusation was daft. I could see that Mourinho was trying to build his team from the back, which is how all great sides are constructed. Making your team hard to beat is the single most important element to building a championship side. A team that can win by five or six goals one week and then lose the next might be entertaining to watch and could even win the odd cup for their troubles, but they will never win a League title.

When Mourinho bought in twenty-three-year-old goalkeeper Petr Cech from French club Rennes for £7 million there were a few eyebrows raised. After all, Chelsea already possessed Carlo Cudicini, widely regarded as the best goalkeeper in the Premiership. Yet the signing of Cech was a masterstroke. He proved himself a phenomenal shot-stopper and his ability to deal with crosses gave him an aura of invincibility. The recruitment of £13.5 million right-back Paulo Ferreira, a position that few believed needed strengthening, was another shrewd move. The fact that Chelsea broke the record for the least number of goals conceded in a League season – a paltry fifteen – gives the lie to any idea that Mourinho had his priorities wrong.

By building from the back Mourinho created a confidence throughout the team and gave his players a stubbornness on the field to match his own hard-nosed professionalism in the dugout. Seven or eight matches into the season, once the players had become accustomed to their new manager's methods, he slowly began to encourage the free-flowing football that they would become known for. It wasn't long before three and four-goal scores from the boys in blue became a regular occurrence. Although arguably not as exciting to watch as Arsene Wenger's Arsenal charges, it is hard to argue that a team containing any two players from the attacking midfield trio of Arjen Robben, Damien Duff and Joe Cole could ever be boring to watch. I find all three tremendously exciting players, each of whom enjoy running at players with the ball at their feet and terrifying the opposition, while thrilling their own supporters. Their style of play reminds me of the kind of players who starred in my day, when the likes of Tom Finney, Stanley Matthews and Eric Parsons were always running at defenders. Robben Red Breast, as I call him, runs with the ball as if it is glued to his feet and was an inspired final signing by Claudio Ranieri, even if the Italian never got the chance to see the Dutch wizard play in a Chelsea shirt. Damien Duff is a similar player and when he and Robben are together in the side I almost feel sorry for opposing defenders. It must be an absolute nightmare to mark them. In the old days a full-back could kick a winger up in the air almost with impunity, providing he could get within a yard of him. Nowadays things are very different. The laws of the game are so much more strict these days that one mistimed tackle could result in an instant red card for the miscreant. Damien can play on either side of the field, although he favours his left foot, and he is about as complete an attacking midfielder as it is possible to find.

Joe Cole found his opportunities limited when he first came to Chelsea but, like Frank Lampard before him, he has improved immeasurably since he left West Ham. This is perhaps because he is playing with better players around him. Joe played so well in the second half of the season that he is rapidly becoming an automatic first-choice selection for both his club and his country, where the problematic left side of midfield is still very much up for grabs. Joe may not have quite the guile or shooting ability of Robben but he can run through congested areas with the ball and open up defences for his teammates.

The one player who possessed the combination of all three lads' abilities was undoubtedly Gianfranco Zola, Chelsea's best player of recent years. It's just a pity that Zola isn't three or four years younger. I can't begin to imagine what he could have achieved had he been part of the Chelsea side of today.

As I've said, John Terry and Frank Lampard are the two rocks of the side. Take either of them out of the line-up and Chelsea are simply not the same team. John and Frank are utterly dependable, the English heartbeat of the side, and the two men capable of lifting their teammates during the most difficult of times. Frank Lampard has been outstanding for the past two seasons. He covers so much ground and seldom gives the ball away. When I hear footballers today complaining about how many games they have to play in England I always think they should take a look at Frank, who runs twice as far as anybody else each week yet hardly ever misses a game. He's an example to every professional. It took Frank a while to settle in at Stamford Bridge and a lot of people were questioning his £11 million price tag when he first arrived. No-one would dare question that piece of business today. During Frank's early Chelsea career he played alongside Emmanuel Petit in the middle of the park and I felt they were too similar in style, which resulted in Frank, as the junior partner, having to alter his game. Also, at West Ham, Frank would always have three players to aim for, with the likes of Joe Cole, Paolo di Canio and Freddie Kanoute all looking for a pass, whereas at Chelsea his new teammates didn't play the same way. It took a year or so for him to develop a better understanding with his new colleagues, but since that has happened there's been no stopping him. I don't know Frank well personally, but whenever I've met him I've always thought he comes across as a fine young man.

I've become quite close to John Terry over the past year or so. I was a little worried about him a few years ago, at around the time he got into trouble at a nightclub and was questioned by the police. I told John that with his talent he could reach the very top and, to his credit, he has done just that. He learnt from his mistakes, distanced himself from those friends who were no good for him, and buckled down to playing football. Being given the captaincy by Claudio Ranieri definitely helped John develop. He has thrived on the responsibility, leads by example and is a great role model for youngsters.

I also think, at the risk of sounding biased, that John is the best English centre half and should be one of the first names on Sven-Goran Ericsson's team sheet. Although Rio Ferdinand is a world-class talent, he still makes the odd mistake through a lack of concentration, whereas John has never let his country down. The days of just whacking the ball out of defence have gone and fortunately John can play with both feet and has good distribu-tion. Rio probably has the edge over John in this regard, but I'd still rather have John in the side. I wouldn't be surprised if Rio and John became the bedrock of the England side from now on, although that would of course be tough on Sol Campbell, who is another towering presence at the back.

Now that Chelsea have won the Premiership for the first time they will probably find it easier to do so again. The players have a taste for success now and they go out onto the pitch expecting to win every time they play. That is a great habit to get into. The team know that they are the ones that everyone else wants to beat and each player is also aware that, if he doesn't perform consistently, the boss will have him out on his ear. The likes of Adrian Mutu and Mateja Kezman were shipped out ruthlessly by Mourinho and poor old Scott Parker never really had a look in. Every player, even John and Frank, will have to be on their guard, as their ambitious young manager permanently seeks to improve his side.

I believe that the sky is the limit for Chelsea over the next five years or so. The club is well run, the team has a solid base, the manager seemingly wants to put down roots at Stamford Bridge and the board has virtually unlimited finances to play with. They could dominate the domestic and European game for a long time to come. I certainly hope so.

I am fortunate to have found myself involved with the club again over recent years. I am employed occasionally to conduct tours of the Stamford Bridge stadium, which is something I really enjoy. There are sometimes people on the tour who watched me play for Chelsea and I always get a great thrill from talking to them about games that took place in the 1940s and 1950s.

My involvement with Chelsea resumed after the club got in touch to inform me that they had opened a bar in my name. Whenever I walk past Bentleys on the way to my seat in the stand I feel a sense of pride and nostalgia for the old days. Soon after the bar's opening, the club was also involved in helping me sell some of my memorabilia. I was a little short of money at the time and decided to sell my League Championship medal. As you can imagine this was something of a wrench, but the medal had been gathering dust over the years and I knew that whenever I passed on that it couldn't easily be split between my two daughters, so I reluctantly let it go. I received a decent price for it and was touched that the chap who bought it insisted on having two duplicate medals made, one each for Loraine and Jane. That was a nice touch. I only hope that I never have to resort to selling my other mementos, like my England caps and jerseys.

Another pastime that I enjoy is my involvement in an education project run by Westminster Council Archives and their education officer, Peter Daniel. Peter is a Chelsea fanatic who came up with the idea of using football to interest primary school kids in reading. Under his scheme the kids study how life in Britain has changed since the Second World War, using football as a medium, comparing how living and playing conditions have changed for footballers. The kids come to Stamford Bridge and listen to me talk for half an hour or so about my career, and they ask me questions at the end. They also get to write poems and stories about my career, which is very flattering for me. It's a great project and I love working with the kids. They are so enthusiastic and I often find myself surprised at how knowledgeable these youngsters are about the game.

It's great to be involved with Chelsea again and also with the Chelsea Pitch Owners (CPO), who put on various functions at the ground, having purchased it from Ken Bates when he was chairman. The CPO have set up a lounge for former players like myself, and Vi and I often pop in there after a home match. The fiftieth anniversary of the club's first title win meant that there has been a lot of attention given to the former players, including myself, and the past year has been fantastic for all of us. It's great to see the lads from 1955 again and reminisce about the good old days. Sadly, a few of my teammates have passed away over the years, but those of us still around get on well and have great affection for each other.

All my teammates owe a debt of gratitude to Tony Banks and the CPO for everything they have done for us. Although he was a successful Labour politician and one-time Sports Minister, I know Tony as first and foremost a massive Chelsea fan. He used to watch me play at Stamford Bridge when he was a lad and stood on the terraces throughout the championship season. Now he is in charge of the Chelsea Centenary Committee and looks out for all the lads from '55, putting on a regular lunch for us at the House of Commons.

Football in the twenty-first century is certainly unrecognisable from when I was a player. The biggest change in football is the amount of money swilling around, particularly in relation to players' wages. If you consider that I earned £15 a week during Chelsea's championship season and that, when I retired at QPR, my weekly wage was £40, I might be forgiven for being jealous of players today. I suppose I do have a slight sense of envy, but I also think it's good that footballers can make enough money over their career to never have any financial worries again. You can't blame the players for the wages they receive. What I can't abide is players who would rather stay at a club on a big salary and not kick a ball than take a wage cut and get a regular game elsewhere. Footballers who have no ambition to succeed on the pitch are no use to anyone. The biggest downside of high wages is that many young lads can't cope with them. Clubs can't keep an eye on their players all the time, especially the younger ones, but more needs to be done to educate young footballers on how to keep their feet on the ground. When I read that players are buying bottles of champagne for £400 and getting into scrapes, I shake my head in despair. But, as I said, a lot of them have more money than they can cope with and don't receive enough advice. That's why I'm all in favour of agents, who have something of a poor reputation in the media. Of course there are some agents who act unscrupulously and destabilise players, but overall I think that they help players more than they do harm.

Nor am I one of those who complain that there is too much football on the television. Although there were no live games on TV in my day, except for the FA Cup final, I think it's terrific that you can turn on Sky every weekend and watch four or five top-division matches. I watch virtually every game that's on, and so does Vi, which is lucky. I don't know how other chaps cope when their wives tell them to turn off the television whenever there's a match on.

Marriage is a great stabiliser on a footballer and I was very lucky to have had such a supportive wife throughout my playing career and beyond. I have been married to Vi for almost sixty years and have had a super life with her. She has always been a tower of strength for me and I feel very fortunate to have spent almost six decades by her side. She has always been a bright girl, a fantastic cook, and of course she loves football! What could be better? Our two terrific children, Loraine and Jane, have provided us with a total of six grandchildren, Simon, Louise, Lucy, Jesse, James and Emily, and we see all of them regularly. I've had a blessed life.

Looking back over my career I certainly had my fair share of ups and downs. Having to leave Newcastle because of poor health was a great shame. Going on strike at Chelsea and being pushed out of the club little more than a year after captaining them to a championship win was also no fun. Being sacked as manager of Reading and Swansea were further disappointments. Yet the good days definitely won out overall. I enjoyed a twenty-three-year play-ing career, longer than most footballers manage. I played twelve times for my country, including a memorable World Cup campaign, and scored a hat-trick for England at Wembley. I also won a League Championship medal, which I am as proud of today as I was in 1955. More importantly, I enjoyed almost every minute on the pitch, playing with some smashing players and in front of some of the best supporters you could imagine. I have a head full of happy memories and am proud of what I achieved in the game.

Would I do it all again if I had the chance? Of course I would.

If you are interested in purchasing other books published by Tempus, or in case you have difficulty finding any Tempus books in your local bookshop, you can also place orders directly through our website

www.tempus-publishing.com